This Book Is Presented

TO _____

BY _____

ON_____

"Lord, teach us to pray." (Lk 11:1)

CATHOLIC
HOUSEHOLD
BLESSINGS & PRAYERS

CATHOLIC
HOUSEHOLD
BLESSINGS & PRAYERS

IMAGE

NEW YORK

This revised edition of *Catholic Household Blessings and Prayers* was developed as a resource by the Bishops' Committee on the Liturgy of the United States Conference of Catholic Bishops (USCCB). It was reviewed by the committee chairman, Bishop Donald W. Trautman, and has been authorized for publication by the undersigned.

Msgr. David J. Malloy, STD
General Secretary, USCCB

Library of Congress Cataloging-in-Publication Data is available upon request.

ISBN 978-0-307-98652-8

Printed in the United States of America

Cover art: Restored Traditions

First Image Edition

CONTENTS

CATHOLIC
HOUSEHOLD
BLESSINGS & PRAYERS

INTRODUCTION

> The source from whom every good gift comes is God, who is above all, blessed for ever. He who is all good has made all things good, so that he might fill his creatures with blessings and even after the Fall he has continued his blessings as a sign of his merciful love.
> (*Book of Blessings*, no. 1)

*E*ach day we echo the words of the disciples, "Lord, teach us to pray" (Lk 11:1), as we strive to bring to God our joys and our sorrows, our hope and our fears. This book lends words to these efforts.

As its title suggests, this book consists of Catholic prayers and blessings for you and your family. Some of the blessings and prayers in this book are thousands of years old, while others are newly written to address the needs of Christians in the third millennium. They come from the treasury of the Church, past and present, "like the head of a household who brings from his storeroom both the new and the old" (Mt 13:52).

The family is rightly called the "domestic church." It is in the family that we learn to recognize the love of God and to turn to him in prayer. It is in the family that we first learn the language of prayer and the virtues of Christian living. Families and other Catholic households should use this book as an aid to fulfill the Lord's command to pray always (see Lk 18:1) and to offer their lives to the Lord as a sacrifice of praise. In time, the words of Scripture and of these prayers and blessings will be written on your heart.

Prayers

Prayer is the daily bread that Jesus taught his disciples to seek from his heavenly Father. "One does not live by bread alone," Jesus told the devil who was trying to lead him into temptation, "but by every word that comes forth from the mouth of God" (Mt 4:4).

As you work to keep your family well fed, sheltered from the storms of this world, and safe from danger, the Lord calls each member of the family to pray for each other, for the Church, and for the needs of the world. "Pray without ceasing" (1 Thes 5:17), St. Paul enjoins us. Pope Benedict XVI encourages families, "Even caught up in the sometimes frenetic daily activities, do not neglect to foster prayer, personally and in the family, which is the secret of Christian perseverance" (Homily, January 7, 2007).

Every moment of every day, from the time we get up in the morning until we close our eyes to sleep at night, is sanctified with God's grace, ever-flowing "from the Paschal mystery of the Passion, Death, and Resurrection of Christ" (Catechism of the Catholic Church, no. 1670). God has willed that every moment, every breath, and every thought can be turned into a prayer, so that "there is scarcely any proper use of material things which cannot be thus directed toward the sanctification of men and the praise of God" (Catechism of the Catholic Church, no. 1670).

Blessings

This book also contains blessings for the persons and special times in the life of your family. These blessings are called "sacramentals" because they prepare us to receive the grace of the sacraments and help us to grow to be more like Christ (see Catechism of the Catholic Church, no. 1670).

These blessings are drawn from the Church's liturgy and from the Book of Blessings. They consist of prayer, Scripture, and sometimes a special ritual sign (see Catechism of the Catholic Church, no. 1668).

People are accustomed to seeing bishops, priests, and deacons blessing objects or persons in the name of the Church. Indeed, "the more a blessing concerns ecclesial and sacramental life, the more is its administration reserved to the ordained ministry" (Catechism of the Catholic Church, no. 1669), often with the participation of the local parish community gathered in prayer. Whenever an ordained minister is present, he should be called upon to give the blessing.

However, there are other blessings, like the ones contained in this book, that can be prayed by anyone who has been baptized, "in virtue of the universal priesthood, a dignity they possess because of their baptism and confirmation" (*Book of Blessings*, no. 18). The blessings given by laypersons in this book are exercised because of their special office, such as parents on behalf of their children.

Right after telling his disciples to "love your enemies, do good to those who hate you," Jesus instructs them to "bless those who curse you, pray for those who mistreat you" (Lk 6:28). St. Paul echoes the Lord's command when he exhorts the Romans to "bless those who persecute [you], bless and do not curse them" (Rom 12:14). St. Peter urges that each time we are on the receiving end of evil, we should return "a blessing, because to this you were called, that you might inherit a blessing" (1 Pt 3:9).

This is why the *Catechism of the Catholic Church* tells us that "every baptized person is called to be a 'blessing,' and to bless" (no. 1669; see Gn 12:2; Lk 6:28; Rom 12:14; 1 Pt 3:9).

Like the Lord into whom they have been baptized, parents should bless and pray for their children. Each one of us should remember the sick and those who suffer. Each time we gather around the family table, we should bless God and the food he has given us. On special occasions, we will observe the traditions of the season, sanctifying by prayer and blessing all the seasons of grace that God has given to us.

Conclusion

This book is not intended to sit on a shelf unused. Every member of the household should know where to find it and should be encouraged to use it. Make it a part of family dinners and holiday celebrations, of bedtime routines and special occasions. Keep it in a central part of the house, along with the family Bible. You may wish to create a special prayer space with candles and a crucifix. Such a prayer space will serve as a physical reminder of our need to make space for God and prayer in lives that too often seem overwhelming. The space we create for prayer becomes a harbor of stillness and God's presence in a world crowded with noise.

All of the blessings and prayers in this book draw their power from the Church's sacred liturgy and her sacraments (see *Catechism of the Catholic Church*, no. 1675). Therefore, when we live a life of prayer and blessing, we will be drawn to participate more fully, with our whole heart and soul, in the Mass, the Sacrament of Penance, and the whole sacramental life of the Church. "Prayer," according to Pope Benedict XVI, "is contemplation of the mystery of God and the wonders that he works in the history of salvation" (General Audience, June 8, 2005).

Bishop Donald W. Trautman
Bishop of Erie
Chairman, Committee on Divine Worship
United States Conference of Catholic Bishops (USCCB)

PART I
BASIC PRAYERS

BASIC PRAYERS

*T*his section includes some of the most familiar prayers of the Catholic tradition. These prayers have nurtured the faithful for generations, yet they still speak to us. Some of these prayers you may wish to learn "by heart" so that they become part of your daily living. Other prayers may be less familiar. These open for new generations the treasures of the Church's rich tradition of prayer.

Essential Prayers

The Sign of the Cross
In the name of the Father,
and of the Son,
and of the Holy Spirit. Amen.

Our Father
Our Father, who art in heaven,
hallowed be thy name;
thy kingdom come,
thy will be done
on earth as it is in heaven.
Give us this day our daily bread,
and forgive us our trespasses,
as we forgive those who trespass
    against us;
and lead us not into temptation,
    but deliver us from evil.

Glory Be (Doxology)
Glory be to the Father
and to the Son
and to the Holy Spirit,
as it was in the beginning
is now, and ever shall be
world without end. Amen.

The Hail Mary
Hail, Mary, full of grace,
the Lord is with thee.
Blessed art thou among women
and blessed is the fruit of thy
    womb, Jesus.
Holy Mary, Mother of God,
pray for us sinners,
now and at the hour of our death.
Amen.

Signum Crucis
In nómine Patris,
et Fílii,
et Spíritus Sancti. Amen.

Pater Noster
Pater noster, qui es in cælis:
sanctificétur nomen tuum;
advéniat regnum tuum;
fiat volúntas tua, sicut in cælo,
    et in terra.
Panem nostrum quotidiánum da
    nobis hódie;
et dimítte nobis débita nostra,
sicut et nos dimíttimus
    debitóribus nostris;
et ne nos indúcas in tentatiónem;
sed líbera nos a malo.

Gloria Patri
Glória Patri
et Fílio
et Spirítui Sancto.
Sicut erat in princípio,
et nunc et semper
et in sæcula sæculórum. Amen.

Ave, Maria
Ave, María, grátia plena,
Dóminus tecum.
Benedícta tu in muliéribus,
et benedíctus fructus ventris
    tui, Iesus.
Sancta María, Mater Dei,
ora pro nobis peccatóribus,
nunc et in hora mortis nostræ.
Amen.

Angel of God

Angel of God,
my guardian dear,
to whom God's love commits
    me here,
ever this day be at my side,
to light and guard, to rule
    and guide.
Amen.

Nicene-Constantinopolitan Creed

We believe in one God,
the Father, the Almighty,
maker of heaven and earth,
of all that is seen and unseen.

We believe in one Lord,
    Jesus Christ,
the only Son of God,
eternally begotten of the Father,
God from God, Light from Light,
true God from true God,
begotten, not made, one in Being
    with the Father.
Through him all things were made.
For us men and for our salvation
he came down from heaven:
By the power of the Holy Spirit
he was born of the Virgin Mary,
    and became man.

Angele Dei

Ángele Dei,
qui custos es mei,
me, tibi commíssum
    pietáte supérna,
illúmina, custódi,
rege et gubérna.
Amen.

Symbolum Nicaenum-Constantinopolitanum

Credo in unum Deum,
Patrem omnipoténtem,
    factórem cæli et terræ,
visibílium ómnium et invisibílium.
Et in unum Dóminum
    Iesum Christum,
Fílium Dei Unigénitum,
et ex Patre natum ante
    ómnia saécula.
Deum de Deo, lumen de lúmine,
    Deum verum de Deo vero,
génitum, non factum,
    consubstantiálem Patri:
per quem ómnia facta sunt.
Qui propter nos hómines et
    propter nostram salútem
descéndit de cælis.
Et incarnátus est de Spíritu Sancto
ex María Vírgine, et homo
    factus est.

For our sake he was crucified
under Pontius Pilate;
he suffered, died and was buried.
On the third day he rose again
in fulfillment of the Scriptures;
he ascended into heaven
and is seated at the right hand of
the Father.
He will come again in glory to
judge the living and the dead,
and his kingdom will have no end.
We believe in the Holy Spirit, the
Lord, the giver of life,
who proceeds from the Father and
the Son.
With the Father and the Son he is
worshipped and glorified.
He has spoken through
the Prophets.
We believe in one holy catholic
and apostolic Church.
We acknowledge one baptism for
the forgiveness of sins.
We look for the resurrection
of the dead,
and the life of the world to come.
Amen.

Crucifíxus étiam pro nobis sub
Póntio Piláto;
passus et sepúltus est,
et resurréxit tértia die,
secúndum Scriptúras,
et ascéndit in cælum, sedet ad
déxteram Patris.
Et íterum ventúrus est cum glória,
iudicáre vivos et mórtuos,
cuius regni non erit finis.
Et in Spíritum Sanctum, Dóminum
et vivificántem:
qui ex Patre Filióque procédit.
Qui cum Patre et Fílio simul
adorátur et conglorificátur:
qui locútus est per prophétas.
Et unam, sanctam, cathólicam et
apostólicam Ecclésiam.
Confíteor unum baptísma in
remissiónem peccatórum.
Et exspécto resurrectiónem
mortuórum,
et vitam ventúri saéculi. Amen.

The Apostles' Creed

I believe in God the Father
almighty, Creator of heaven
and earth.
And in Jesus Christ, his only Son,
our Lord, who was conceived
by the Holy Spirit,
born of the Virgin Mary, suffered
under Pontius Pilate,
was crucified, died, and
was buried.
He descended into hell; the third
day he rose again from
the dead;
he ascended into heaven, and
sits at the right hand of God the
Father almighty,
from thence he shall come to judge
the living and the dead.

I believe in the Holy Spirit,
the holy Catholic Church,
the communion of saints,
the forgiveness of sins,
the resurrection of the body
and life everlasting. Amen.

Symbolum Apostolicum

Credo in Deum, Patrem
omnipoténtem,
Creatórem caeli et terrae,
et in Iesum Christum, Filium
eius únicum,
Dóminum nostrum,
qui conceptus est de
Spiritu Sancto,
natus ex María Virgine,
passus sub Póntio Piláto,
crucifixus, mórtuus, et sepúltus,
descendit ad ínferos,
tértia die resurréxit a mórtuis,
ascéndit ad caelos, sedet ad
déxteram Dei
Patris omnipoténtis, inde ventúrus
est iudicáre vivos et mórtuos.

Et in Spíritum Sanctum,
sanctam Ecclésiam cathólicam,
sanctórum communiónem,
remissiónem peccatórum,
carnis resurrectiónem,
vitam aetérnam.
Amen.

Confiteor

I confess to almighty God,
and to you, my brothers and sisters,
that I have sinned through my own fault
in my thoughts and in my words,
in what I have done,
and in what I have failed to do;
and I ask blessed Mary, ever virgin,
all the angels and saints,
and you, my brothers and sisters,
to pray for me to the Lord our God.

Act of Contrition (Traditional)

(Other prayers of contrition may be found in "Penance and
Reconciliation," later in this Part.)

O my God, I am heartily sorry for having offended you,
and I detest all my sins because of your just punishments,
but most of all because they offend you, my God, who are
all good and deserving of all my love. I firmly resolve with
the help of your grace to sin no more and to avoid the near
occasion of sin. Amen.

Te Deum

You are God: we praise you;
you are God: we acclaim you;
you are the eternal Father:
all creation worships you.

To you all angels, all the powers of heaven,
cherubim and seraphim, sing in endless praise:
holy, holy, holy, Lord, God of power and might,
heaven and earth are full of your glory.
The glorious company of apostles praise you.
The noble fellowship of prophets praise you.
The white-robed army of martyrs praise you.
Throughout the world the holy Church acclaims you:
Father, of majesty unbounded,
your true and only Son, worthy of all worship,
and the Holy Spirit, advocate and guide.
You, Christ, are the king of glory,
the eternal Son of the Father.
When you became man to set us free
you did not spurn the Virgin's womb.
You overcame the sting of death,
and opened the Kingdom of Heaven to all believers.
You are seated at God's right hand in glory.
We believe that you will come, and be our judge.
Come then, Lord, and help your people,
bought with the price of your own Blood,
and bring us with your saints
to glory everlasting.
Save your people, Lord, and bless your inheritance.
Govern and uphold them now and always.
Day by day we bless you.
We praise your name forever.
Keep us today, Lord, from all sin.
Have mercy on us, Lord, have mercy.
Lord, show us your love and mercy;
for we put our trust in you.
In you, Lord, is our hope:
and we shall never hope in vain.

Prayers Before the Holy Eucharist

Anima Christi

Soul of Christ, sanctify me.
Body of Christ, save me.
Blood of Christ, inebriate me.
Water from the side of Christ, wash me.
Passion of Christ, strengthen me.
O good Jesus, hear me.
Within your wounds hide me.
Permit me not to be separated from you.
From the malicious enemy defend me.
In the hour of my death call me.
And bid me come to you,
that with your saints I may praise you
forever and ever. Amen.

Tantum Ergo

Down in adoration falling,
Lo! the sacred Host we hail;
Lo! o'er ancient forms departing,
newer rites of grace prevail;
faith for all defects supplying,
where the feeble senses fail.
To the everlasting Father,
and the Son who reigns on high,
with the Holy Spirit proceeding
forth from each eternally,

be salvation, honor, blessing,
might and endless majesty. Amen.

V/. You have given them bread from heaven,
R/. Having all delight within it.

Let us pray. O God, who in this wonderful Sacrament left
us a memorial of your Passion: grant, we implore you,
that we may so venerate the sacred mysteries of your Body
and Blood, as always to be conscious of the fruit of your
redemption. You who live and reign forever and ever. Amen.

Adoro Te Devote

I adore you devoutly, Godhead unseen,
who truly lies hidden under these sacramental forms.
My soul surrenders itself to you without reserve,
for in contemplating you it is completely overwhelmed.

Sight, touch, and taste are no guide in finding you,
and only hearing is a sure guide for our faith.
I believe everything that the Son of God has said,
and nothing can be truer than this Word of the truth.

Only the Godhead was hidden on the Cross,
but here the humanity is hidden as well.
Yet I believe and acknowledge them both
and make the same request as did the repentant thief.

I do not see the marks of the wounds, as Thomas did,
and yet I, too, own you as "My God."
Grant that I believe in you more and more,
that I put my hope in you and that I love you.

(continued)

Living Bread, that ever recalls
the Lord's death and gives life to his servants,
grant to my soul to live by you
and always to taste your sweetness.

Lord Jesus, loving Pelican of heaven,[1]
cleanse me, a sinner, with your Blood;
for a single drop can save
the whole world from all its sin.

Jesus, as I look on your veiled presence,
I pray that what I long for so ardently may come about,
and that I may see your face unveiled
and be happy in the vision of your glory.

—Attributed to St. Thomas Aquinas (1225–1274)

The Divine Praises

Blessed be God.
Blessed be his holy name.
Blessed be Jesus Christ, true God and true man.
Blessed be the name of Jesus.
Blessed be his most Sacred Heart.
Blessed be his most precious Blood.
Blessed be Jesus in the most holy Sacrament of the altar.
Blessed be the Holy Spirit, the Paraclete.
Blessed be the great Mother of God, Mary most holy.
Blessed be her holy and Immaculate Conception.
Blessed be her glorious Assumption.
Blessed be the name of Mary, Virgin and Mother.
Blessed be St. Joseph, her most chaste spouse.
Blessed be God in his angels and in his saints.

---

1 The pelican is an ancient symbol of the eucharistic Lord. It was believed that in times of want, a mother pelican would feed her children with her own blood.

ACTS OF THE THEOLOGICAL VIRTUES

Act of Faith

O my God, I firmly believe that you are one God in three divine Persons, Father, Son, and Holy Spirit. I believe that your divine Son became man and died for our sins and that he will come to judge the living and the dead. I believe these and all the truths which the Holy Catholic Church teaches because you have revealed them, who are eternal truth and wisdom, who can neither deceive nor be deceived. In this faith I intend to live and die. Amen.

Act of Hope

O Lord God, I hope by your grace for the pardon of all my sins and after life here to gain eternal happiness because you have promised it, who are infinitely powerful, faithful, kind, and merciful. In this hope I intend to live and die. Amen.

Act of Love

O Lord God, I love you above all things and I love my neighbor for your sake because you are the highest, infinite and perfect good, worthy of all my love. In this love I intend to live and die. Amen.

PRAYERS TO
MARY, MOTHER OF GOD

The *Magnificat* (Canticle of Mary), a traditional Marian prayer, may be found in Evening Prayer of the Liturgy of the Hours, in Part II: Daily Prayers. See also the prayer for the Feast of Our Lady of Guadalupe, in Part III: Days and Seasons.

Prayer on the Solemnity of the Immaculate Conception

Father,
the image of the Virgin is found in the Church.
Mary had a faith that your Spirit prepared and a love that
    never knew sin,
for you kept her sinless from the first moment of her
    conception.
Trace in our actions the lines of her love,
in our hearts her readiness of faith.
Prepare once again a world for your Son
who lives and reigns with you and the Holy Spirit,
one God, forever and ever.

Angelus

V/. The Angel of the Lord declared unto Mary,
R/. And she conceived of the Holy Spirit.
Hail Mary . . .

V/. Behold the handmaid of the Lord,
R/. Be it done unto me according to your Word.
Hail Mary . . .

V/. And the Word was made flesh,
R/. And dwelt among us.
Hail Mary . . .

V/. Pray for us, O holy Mother of God,
R/. That we may be made worthy of the promises of Christ.

Let us pray. Pour forth, we beseech you, O Lord, your grace
into our hearts: that we, to whom the Incarnation of Christ
your Son was made known by the message of an Angel,
may by his Passion and Cross be brought to the glory of his
Resurrection. Through the same Christ our Lord. Amen.

The Memorare

Remember, O most gracious Virgin Mary, that never was it
known that anyone who fled to your protection, implored
your help, or sought your intercession was left unaided.
Inspired by this confidence, I fly unto you, O Virgin of
virgins, my mother; to you do I come, before you I stand,
sinful and sorrowful. O Mother of the Word Incarnate,
despise not my petitions, but in your mercy hear and answer
me. Amen.

Regina Caeli (Queen of Heaven)

Queen of Heaven, rejoice, alleluia:
for the Son you were privileged to bear, alleluia,
is risen as he said, alleluia.
Pray for us to God, alleluia.

V/. Rejoice and be glad, O Virgin Mary, Alleluia!
R/. For the Lord is truly risen, Alleluia.

Let us pray. O God, who gave joy to the world through the
Resurrection of your Son, our Lord Jesus Christ, grant, we
beseech you, that through the intercession of the Virgin
Mary, his Mother, we may obtain the joys of everlasting life.
Through the same Christ our Lord. Amen.

Salve, Regina (Hail, Holy Queen)

Hail, holy Queen, Mother of mercy: Hail, our life, our
sweetness and our hope. To you do we cry, poor banished
children of Eve. To you do we send up our sighs, mourning
and weeping in this valley of tears. Turn then, most gracious
advocate, your eyes of mercy toward us; and after this our
exile show unto us the blessed fruit of your womb, Jesus. O
clement, O loving, O sweet Virgin Mary.

Sub Tuum Praesidium (We Turn to You for Protection)

We fly to your patronage, O holy Mother of God; despise not
our petitions in our necessities, but deliver us always from
all dangers, O glorious and blessed Virgin.

Akathist Hymn

Hail, Mary! Hail, the restoration of the fallen Adam!
    Hail, the redemption of the tears of Eve.
Intercede for us with the Lord.

Hail, Mary! Height, hard to climb, for human minds;
    hail, depth, hard to explore, even for the eyes of angels.
Intercede for us with the Lord.

Hail, Mary! Throne of wisdom;
    hail, security and hope for all who call upon you.
Intercede for us with the Lord.

Hail, Mary! Heavenly ladder by which God came down to earth;
    hail, bridge leading from earth to heaven.
Intercede for us with the Lord.

Hail, Mary! Favor of God to mortals;
    hail, Mary, access of mortals to God.
Intercede for us with the Lord.

Hail, Mary! Mother of the Lamb and of the Good Shepherd;
    hail, gold for the sheep of his pasture.
Intercede for us with the Lord.

Hail, Mary! Never silent voice of the Apostles;
    hail, never conquered courage of champions.
Intercede for us with the Lord.

Hail, Mary! Mother Star which never sets;
    hail, dawn of the mystic day.
Intercede for us with the Lord.

THE ROSARY

How to Pray the Rosary

Make the sign of the cross. Holding the crucifix, say the Apostles' Creed.

On the first bead, say an Our Father.

Say three Hail Marys on each of the next three beads.

Say the Glory Be.

Go to the main part of the rosary. For each of the five decades, announce the Mystery, then say the Our Father. While fingering each of the ten beads of the decade, next say ten Hail Marys while meditating on the Mystery. Then say a Glory Be.

(After finishing each decade, some say the following prayer requested by the Blessed Virgin Mary at Fatima: "O my Jesus, forgive us our sins, save us from the fires of hell, lead all souls to heaven, especially those who have most need of your mercy.")

After saying the five decades, say the *Salve Regina* (Hail, Holy Queen), followed by this dialogue and prayer:

V/. Pray for us, O holy Mother of God.
R/. That we may be made worthy of the promises of Christ.

Let us pray. O God, whose only-begotten Son, by his life, death, and Resurrection, has purchased for us the rewards of eternal life, grant, we beseech you, that meditating on these mysteries of the most holy rosary of the Blessed Virgin Mary, we may imitate what they contain and obtain what they promise, through the same Christ our Lord. Amen.

The four sets of Mysteries of the Rosary (see the next page) are traditionally said on the following days:

a. *Joyful Mysteries*: Mondays and Saturdays; Sundays of the Christmas Season
b. *Luminous Mysteries*: Thursdays

c. *Sorrowful Mysteries*: Tuesdays and Fridays; Sundays of Lent
d. *Glorious Mysteries*: Wednesdays and Sundays (except as noted above)

Mysteries of the Rosary

JOYFUL MYSTERIES

1. The Annunciation
2. The Visitation
3. The Nativity
4. The Presentation in the Temple
5. The Finding of the Child Jesus After Three Days
   in the Temple

LUMINOUS MYSTERIES

1. The Baptism at the Jordan
2. The Miracle at Cana
3. The Proclamation of the Kingdom and the
   Call to Conversion
4. The Transfiguration
5. The Institution of the Eucharist

SORROWFUL MYSTERIES

1. The Agony in the Garden
2. The Scourging at the Pillar
3. The Crowning with Thorns
4. The Carrying of the Cross
5. The Crucifixion and Death

GLORIOUS MYSTERIES

1. The Resurrection
2. The Ascension
3. The Descent of the Holy Spirit at Pentecost
4. The Assumption of Mary
5. The Crowning of the Blessed Virgin as Queen of Heaven
   and Earth

PENANCE AND
RECONCILIATION

The evil we do to one another and the ways we fail to do good are ever present in our lives and prayer. Daily in the Lord's Prayer, the Christian asks for forgiveness and prays for deliverance from evil. Each night, we ask forgiveness for our faults and express contrition. We ask Mary to "pray for us sinners." We begin the Sunday Eucharist by praising God for a mercy that is greater than our sins. Friday has been a day traditionally set aside for fasting and deeds of charity so that we might turn our lives to the way of the Gospel. Each year, Christians keep the season of Lent: Forty Days for finding anew the strength to renounce evil, to profess Christ as our Lord, and so to live again in the grace of Baptism.

Repentance and reconciliation are thus constant and lifelong. Some moments in each person's life are marked with the sacrament that bears this name of Penance and Reconciliation. Even things as personal as sin, sorrow, and confession are brought to the community, to the Church, and to the Church's ministers. The Church comes together—even if only the penitent and the priest—so that God's pardon may be sought in the confession of sin, sorrow, deeds of penance, and the expression of God's forgiveness in words of absolution. The sacrament embraces all these moments. It springs from the Church's faith that, though sin is personal, it is not private: "Penance always entails reconciliation with our brothers and sisters who are always harmed by our sins" (*Rite of Penance*, no. 5). When the Sacrament of Penance is celebrated with a number of persons present, the rite begins with the reading of Scripture and includes a homily, examination of conscience, individual confession and absolution, praise of God's mercy, and prayers of thanksgiving. When an individual comes alone for the Sacrament of Penance, the order in the following pages is observed.

Prayers for times of penance and reconciliation in the household are on page 342. These prayers, along with the prayers for Fridays and the prayers for Lent (both found in Part III: Days and Seasons) may stir in us a spirit of contrition and conversion that leads to the regular celebration of the Sacrament of Penance.

After a greeting, the priest and penitent make the sign of the cross together:

In the name of the Father, and of the Son, and of the Holy Spirit. Amen.

In these or similar words, the priest invites the penitent to have trust in God.

May God, who has enlightened every heart, help you to know your sins and trust in his mercy.
R/. Amen.

Then the priest reads from the Scripture a text that proclaims God's mercy and calls us to repentance. The penitent then makes a confession of sins. The priest gives suitable counsel and proposes an act of penance.

The penitent then expresses sorrow through one of the following prayers or in similar words. (A traditional form of the Act of Contrition may be found earlier in this Part, on page 8.)

A
My God,
I am sorry for my sins with all my heart.
In choosing to do wrong
and failing to do good,
I have sinned against you
whom I should love above all things.
I firmly intend, with your help,
to do penance,
to sin no more,
and to avoid whatever leads me to sin.

(continued)

Our Savior Jesus Christ
suffered and died for us.
In his name, my God, have mercy.

B

Lord Jesus, Son of God,
have mercy on me, a sinner.

C

Lord Jesus,
you chose to be called the friend of sinners.
By your saving death and Resurrection
free me from my sins.
May your peace take root in my heart
and bring forth a harvest
of love, holiness, and truth.

> The priest extends his hands over the penitent and speaks
> the words of absolution. In conclusion, the priest may say:

Give thanks to the Lord, for he is good.
R/. His mercy endures forever.

> Then the priest dismisses the penitent with these or
> similar words:

The Lord has freed you from your sins. Go in peace.

Pious Invocations

A pious invocation is a short prayer that may be repeated aloud or silently. These prayers elevate the mind to God and remind us that we are always in his loving presence.

Examples of Invocations Currently in Use

Allow me to praise you, Virgin most holy; give me strength against your enemies.

All holy men and women of God, pray for us.

Blessed be the Holy Trinity.

Christ conquers! Christ reigns! Christ rules!

Father, into your hands I commend my spirit. (Lk 23:46; see Ps 31:6)

Glory be to the Father and to the Son and to the Holy Spirit.

Hail, O Cross, our only hope.

Heart of Jesus, all for you.

Heart of Jesus, burning with love for us, inflame our hearts with love for you.

Heart of Jesus, in you I trust.

Holy Mary, Mother of God, pray for me.

Holy Mother of God, ever Virgin Mary, intercede for us.

Jesus, gentle and humble of heart, make my heart like unto yours.

Jesus, Mary, and Joseph.

Jesus, Mary, and Joseph, I give you my heart and my soul.

Jesus, Mary, and Joseph, assist me in my last agony.

Jesus, Mary, and Joseph, may I breathe forth my soul in peace with you.

Lord, increase our faith. (Lk 17:5)

Lord, let our minds be united in truth, and our hearts
in love.

Lord, save us, we are perishing. (Mt 8:25)

Lord, send laborers into your harvest. (See Mt 9:38)

May the Virgin Mary bless us with her holy child.

May the most Blessed Sacrament be praised now
and forevermore.

Merciful Lord Jesus, grant them rest.

Most Sacred Heart of Jesus, have mercy on us.

Mother of Sorrows, pray for us.

My God and my all.

My Lord and my God! (Jn 20:28)

My Mother, my trust.

O God, be merciful to me, a sinner. (Lk 18:13)

O Queen conceived without original sin, pray for us.

Pray for us, O holy Mother of God, that we may be made
worthy of the promises of Christ.

Remain with us, O Lord. (See Lk 24:29)

Teach me to do your will, for you are my God. (Ps 143:10)

Tender heart of Mary, be my safety!

You are the Christ, the Son of the living God. (Mt 16:16)

We adore you, O Christ, and we bless you, because by your
holy Cross you have redeemed the world.

PART II
DAILY PRAYERS

DAILY PRAYERS

For from the rising of the sun, even to its setting,
my name is great among the nations. (Mal 1:11)

*W*hether we are awake or asleep,
we are in God's providential care.
This section includes prayers we can use
throughout the day so that we remain always
aware of God's loving presence. Some are
very brief so that they can become part of
even the most hectic life. Others are longer
and invite us to dedicate time each day to
God, the source of all life.

LITURGY OF THE HOURS

Morning Prayer

(In Lent, omit all Alleluias.)

All make the sign of the cross, saying:

God, come to my assistance.
Lord, make haste to help me.

Glory to the Father, and to the Son, and to the Holy Spirit:
as it was in the beginning, is now, and will be forever.
   Amen. Alleluia.

HYMN

On this day, the first of days,
God the Father's name we praise;
who, creation's Lord and spring,
did the world from darkness bring.

Text: Le Mans Breviary, 1748
Translator: Henry W. Baker, 1821–1877

PSALMODY

Antiphon 1: As morning breaks I look to you, O God, to be
               my strength this day, alleluia.

Psalm 63:2–9

O God, you are my God, for you I long;
for you my soul is thirsting.
My body pines for you
like a dry, weary land without water.
So I gaze on you in the sanctuary
to see your strength and your glory.

For your love is better than life,
my lips will speak your praise.
So I will bless you all my life,
in your name I will lift up my hands.
My soul shall be filled as with a banquet,
my mouth shall praise you with joy.

On my bed I remember you.
On you I muse through the night
for you have been my help;
in the shadow of your wings I rejoice.
My soul clings to you;
your right hand holds me fast.

Glory to the Father, and to the Son, and to the Holy Spirit:
As it was in the beginning, is now, and will be forever.

Psalm-Prayer

Father, Creator of unfailing light, give that same light to
those who call to you. May our lips praise you; our lives
proclaim your goodness; our work give you honor, and our
voices celebrate you forever.

Antiphon 1: As morning breaks I look to you, O God, to be
my strength this day, alleluia.

Antiphon 2: From the midst of the flames the three young
men cried out with one voice: Blessed
be God, alleluia.

CANTICLE

Daniel 3:57–88, 56
Bless the Lord, all you works of the Lord.
Praise and exalt him above all forever.
Angels of the Lord, bless the Lord.
You heavens, bless the Lord.
All you waters above the heavens, bless the Lord.
All you hosts of the Lord, bless the Lord.
Sun and moon, bless the Lord.
Stars of heaven, bless the Lord.

Every shower and dew, bless the Lord.
All you winds, bless the Lord.
Fire and heat, bless the Lord.
Cold and chill, bless the Lord.
Dew and rain, bless the Lord.
Frost and chill, bless the Lord.
Ice and snow, bless the Lord.
Nights and days, bless the Lord.
Light and darkness, bless the Lord.
Lightnings and clouds, bless the Lord.

Let the earth bless the Lord.
Praise and exalt him above all forever.
Mountains and hills, bless the Lord.
Everything growing from the earth, bless the Lord.
You springs, bless the Lord.
Seas and rivers, bless the Lord.
You dolphins and all water creatures, bless the Lord.
All you birds of the air, bless the Lord.
All you beasts, wild and tame, bless the Lord.
You sons of men, bless the Lord.

O Israel, bless the Lord.
Praise and exalt him above all forever.
Priests of the Lord, bless the Lord.
Servants of the Lord, bless the Lord.
Spirits and souls of the just, bless the Lord.
Holy men of humble heart, bless the Lord.
Hananiah, Azariah, Mishael, bless the Lord.
Praise and exalt him above all forever.

Let us bless the Father, and the Son, and the Holy Spirit.
Let us praise and exalt him above all forever.
Blessed are you, Lord, in the firmament of heaven.
Praiseworthy and glorious and exalted above all forever.

Antiphon 2:   From the midst of the flames the three young
men cried out with one voice: Blessed be
God, alleluia.

Antiphon 3:   Let the people of Zion rejoice in their
King, alleluia.

Psalm 149

Sing a new song to the Lord,
his praise in the assembly of the faithful.
Let Israel rejoice in its maker,
let Zion's sons exult in their king.
Let them praise his name with dancing
and make music with timbrel and harp.

For the Lord takes delight in his people.
He crowns the poor with salvation.
Let the faithful rejoice in their glory,
shout for joy and take their rest.
Let the praise of God be on their lips
and a two-edged sword in their hand,

to deal out vengeance to the nations
and punishment on all the peoples;
to bind their kings in chains
and their nobles in fetters of iron;
to carry out the sentence pre-ordained;
this honor is for all his faithful.

Glory to the Father, and to the Son, and to the Holy Spirit:
As it was in the beginning, is now, and will be forever.

Psalm-Prayer

Let Israel rejoice in you, Lord, and acknowledge you as
Creator and Redeemer. We put our trust in your faithfulness
and proclaim the wonderful truths of salvation. May your
loving kindness embrace us now and forever.

Antiphon 3:   Let the people of Zion rejoice in their
              King, alleluia.

READING

Revelation 7:10, 12

Salvation is from our God, who is seated on the throne, and from the Lamb! Praise and glory, wisdom and thanksgiving and honor, power and might, to our God forever and ever. Amen!

RESPONSORY

Christ, Son of the living God, have mercy on us.
R/. Christ, Son of the living God, have mercy on us.

You are seated at the right hand of the Father,
R/. have mercy on us.

Glory to the Father, and to the Son, and to the Holy Spirit:
R/. Christ, Son of the living God, have mercy on us.

CANTICLE OF ZECHARIAH (THE BENEDICTUS)

Blessed be the Lord, the God of Israel;
for he has come to his people and set them free.

He has raised up for us a mighty Savior,
born of the House of his servant David.

Through his prophets he promised of old
    that he would save us from our enemies,
    from the hands of all who hate us.

(continued)

He promised to show mercy to our fathers
and to remember his holy covenant.

This was the oath he swore to our father Abraham:
to set us free from the hand of our enemies,
free to worship him without fear,
holy and righteous in his sight
    all the days of our life.

You, my child, shall be called the prophet of the Most High,
for you will go before the Lord to prepare his way,
to give his people knowledge of salvation
by the forgiveness of their sins.

In the tender compassion of our God
the dawn from on high shall break upon us,
to shine on those who dwell in darkness and the
    shadow of death,
and to guide our feet into the way of peace.

Glory to the Father, and to the Son, and to the Holy Spirit:
As it was in the beginning, is now, and will be forever.

INTERCESSIONS

Christ is the sun that never sets, the true light that shines on
every man. Let us call out to him in praise:

Lord, you are our life and our salvation.

Creator of the stars, we thank you for your gift, the
    first rays of the dawn,
R/. and we commemorate your Resurrection.

May your Holy Spirit teach us to do your will today,
R/. and may your Wisdom guide us always.

Each Sunday give us the joy of gathering as your people,
R/. around the table of your Word and your Body.

From our hearts we thank you,
R/. for your countless blessings.

Our Father . . .

PRAYER
Father,
keep before us the wisdom and love
you have revealed in your Son.
Help us to be like him
in word and deed,
for he lives and reigns with you and the Holy Spirit,
one God, forever and ever.
Amen.

Go in peace.
Thanks be to God.

May the Lord bless us,
protect us from all evil
and bring us to everlasting life.
Amen.

Evening Prayer

(In Lent, omit all Alleluias.)

All make the sign of the cross, saying:

God, come to my assistance.
Lord, make haste to help me.

Glory to the Father, and to the Son, and to the Holy Spirit:
as it was in the beginning, is now, and will be forever.
   Amen. Alleluia.

HYMN

Now thank we all our God
with heart and hands and voices,
who wondrous things has done,
in whom his world rejoices;
who from our mothers' arms,
has blessed us on our way
with countless gifts of love,
and still is ours today.

Text: Martin Rinkart, 1586–1649
Translator: Catherine Winkworth, 1829–1878

PSALMODY

Antiphon 1: Like burning incense, Lord, let my prayer rise
             up to you.

Psalm 141:1–9

I have called to you, Lord; hasten to help me!
Hear my voice when I cry to you.
Let my prayer arise before you like incense,
the raising of my hands like an evening oblation.

Set, O Lord, a guard over my mouth;
keep watch at the door of my lips!
Do not turn my heart to things that are wrong,
to evil deeds with men who are sinners.

Never allow me to share in their feasting.
If a good man strikes or reproves me it is kindness;
but let the oil of the wicked not anoint my head.
Let my prayer be ever against their malice.

Their princes were thrown down by the side of the rock:
then they understood that my words were kind.
As a millstone is shattered to pieces on the ground,
so their bones were strewn at the mouth of the grave.

To you, Lord God, my eyes are turned:
in you I take refuge; spare my soul!
From the trap they have laid for me keep me safe:
keep me from the snares of those who do evil.

Glory to the Father, and to the Son, and to the Holy Spirit:
As it was in the beginning, is now, and will be forever.

Psalm-Prayer

Lord, from the rising of the sun to its setting your name
is worthy of all praise. Let our prayer come like incense
before you. May the lifting up of our hands be as an evening
sacrifice acceptable to you, Lord our God.

Antiphon 1: Like burning incense, Lord, let my prayer rise
up to you.

Antiphon 2: You are my refuge, Lord; you are all that I
desire in life.

Psalm 142

With all my voice I cry to the Lord,
with all my voice I entreat the Lord.
I pour out my trouble before him;
I tell him all my distress
while my spirit faints within me.
But you, O Lord, know my path.

On the way where I shall walk
they have hidden a snare to entrap me.
Look on my right and see:
there is not one who takes my part.
I have no means of escape,
not one who cares for my soul.

I cry to you, O Lord.
I have said: "You are my refuge,
all I have left in the land of the living."
Listen then to my cry
for I am in the depths of distress.

Rescue me from those who pursue me
for they are stronger than I.
Bring my soul out of this prison
and then I shall praise your name.
Around me the just will assemble
because of your goodness to me.

Glory to the Father, and to the Son, and to the Holy Spirit:
As it was in the beginning, is now, and will be forever.

Psalm-Prayer
Lord, we humbly ask for your goodness. May you help us to
hope in you, and give us a share with your chosen ones in
the land of the living.

Antiphon 2: You are my refuge, Lord; you are all that I
desire in life.

Antiphon 3: The Lord Jesus humbled himself, and God
exalted him forever.

CANTICLE
Philippians 2:6–11
Though he was in the form of God,
Jesus did not deem equality with God
something to be grasped at.

Rather, he emptied himself
and took the form of a slave,
being born in the likeness of men.

He was known to be of human estate,
and it was thus that he humbled himself,
obediently accepting even death,
death on a Cross!

Because of this,
God highly exalted him
and bestowed on him the name
above every other name,

so that at Jesus' name
every knee must bend
in the heavens, on the earth,
and under the earth,
and every tongue proclaim
to the glory of God the Father:
JESUS CHRIST IS LORD!

Glory to the Father, and to the Son, and to the Holy Spirit:
As it was in the beginning, is now, and will be forever.

Antiphon 3: The Lord Jesus humbled himself, and God
exalted him forever.

READING

Romans 11:33–36
How deep are the riches and the wisdom and the knowledge
of God! How inscrutable his judgments, how unsearchable
his ways! For "who has known the mind of the Lord? Or
who has been his counselor? Who has given him anything
so as to deserve return?" For from him and through him and
for him all things are. To him be glory forever. Amen.

RESPONSORY

Our hearts are filled with wonder as we contemplate your
works, O Lord.
R/. Our hearts are filled with wonder as we contemplate
your works, O Lord.

We praise the wisdom which wrought them all,
R/. as we contemplate your works, O Lord.

Glory to the Father, and to the Son, and to the Holy Spirit:
R/. Our hearts are filled with wonder as we contemplate
your works, O Lord.

CANTICLE OF MARY (THE MAGNIFICAT)

My soul proclaims the greatness of the Lord;
my spirit rejoices in God my Savior
for he has looked with favor on his lowly servant.

From this day all generations will call me blessed:
the Almighty has done great things for me
and holy is his Name.

He has mercy on those who fear him
in every generation.

He has shown the strength of his arm,
and has scattered the proud in their conceit.

He has cast down the mighty from their thrones,
and has lifted up the lowly.

He has filled the hungry with good things,
and the rich he has sent away empty.

He has come to the help of his servant Israel
for he has remembered his promise of mercy,
the promise he made to our fathers,
to Abraham and his children forever.

Glory to the Father, and to the Son, and to the Holy Spirit:
As it was in the beginning, is now, and will be forever.

INTERCESSIONS

We give glory to the one God—Father, Son, and Holy
Spirit—and in our weakness we pray:

Lord, be with your people.

Holy Lord, Father all-powerful, let justice spring up on the earth,
R/. then your people will dwell in the beauty of peace.

Let every nation come into your kingdom,
R/. so that all peoples will be saved.

Let married couples live in your peace,
R/. and grow in mutual love.

Reward all who have done good to us, Lord,
R/. and grant them eternal life.

Look with compassion on victims of hatred and war,
R/. grant them heavenly peace.

Our Father . . .

PRAYER

Father, watch over your family
and keep us safe in your care,
for all our hope is in you.

Grant this through our Lord Jesus Christ, your Son,
who lives and reigns with you and the Holy Spirit,
one God, forever and ever.

Let us praise the Lord.
R/. And give him thanks.

Night Prayer

(In Lent, omit all Alleluias.)

All make the sign of the cross, saying:

God, come to my assistance.
Lord, make haste to help me.

Glory to the Father, and to the Son, and to the Holy Spirit:
as it was in the beginning, is now, and will be forever.
   Amen. Alleluia.

A brief examination of conscience may be made.

HYMN

Lord Jesus Christ, abide with us,
now that the sun has run its course;
let hope not be obscured by night,
but may faith's darkness be as light.

Text: St. Joseph's Abbey, 1967, 1968
To the tune of "Old Hundredth"

PSALMODY

Antiphon: Day and night I cry to you, my God.

Psalm 88

Lord my God, I call for help by day;
I cry at night before you.
Let my prayer come into your presence.
O turn your ear to my cry.

(*continued*)

For my soul is filled with evils;
my life is on the brink of the grave.
I am reckoned as one in the tomb:
I have reached the end of my strength,

like one alone among the dead;
like the slain lying in their graves;
like those you remember no more,
cut off, as they are, from your hand.

You have laid me in the depths of the tomb,
in places that are dark, in the depths.
Your anger weighs down upon me:
I am drowned beneath your waves.

You have taken away my friends
and made me hateful in their sight.
Imprisoned, I cannot escape;
my eyes are sunken with grief.

I call to you, Lord, all the day long;
to you I stretch out my hands.
Will you work your wonders for the dead?
Will the shades stand and praise you?

Will your love be told in the grave
or your faithfulness among the dead?
Will your wonders be known in the dark
or your justice in the land of oblivion?

As for me, Lord, I call to you for help:
in the morning my prayer comes before you.
Lord, why do you reject me?
Why do you hide your face?

Wretched, close to death from my youth,
I have borne your trials; I am numb.
Your fury has swept down upon me;
your terrors have utterly destroyed me.

They surround me all the day like a flood,
they assail me all together.
Friend and neighbor you have taken away:
my one companion is darkness.

Glory to the Father, and to the Son, and to the Holy Spirit:
as it was in the beginning, is now, and will be forever.

Antiphon: Day and night I cry to you, my God.

READING

Jeremiah 14:9a
You are in our midst, O Lord,
    your name we bear:
    do not forsake us, O Lord, our God!

RESPONSORY

Into your hands, Lord, I commend my spirit.
R/. Into your hands, Lord, I commend my spirit.

You have redeemed us, Lord God of truth.
R/. I commend my spirit.

Glory to the Father, and to the Son, and to the Holy Spirit.
R/. Into your hands, Lord, I commend my spirit.

CANTICLE OF SIMEON (Nunc Dimittis)

Antiphon: Protect us, Lord, as we stay awake;
                    watch over us as we sleep, that awake,
                    we may keep watch with Christ,
                    and asleep, rest in his peace.

Lord, now you let your servant go in peace;
your Word has been fulfilled:

my own eyes have seen the salvation
which you have prepared in the sight of every people:

a light to reveal you to the nations
and the glory of your people Israel.

Glory to the Father, and to the Son, and to the Holy Spirit:
as it was in the beginning, is now, and will be forever.

Antiphon:	Protect us, Lord, as we stay awake;
	watch over us as we sleep, that awake,
	we may keep watch with Christ,
	and asleep, rest in his peace.

PRAYER

All-powerful God,
keep us united with your Son
in his death and burial
so that we may rise to new life with him,
who lives and reigns forever and ever.

CONCLUSION

May the all-powerful Lord grant us a restful night and a
peaceful death.
R/. Amen.

Hail Mary . . .

WAKING

Psalm 118:24 ("This Is the Day the Lord Has Made")

This is the day the LORD has made;
let us be glad and rejoice in it.

Morning Offering

O Jesus, through the Immaculate Heart of Mary,
I offer you my prayers, works, joys, and sufferings
    of this day
for all the intentions of your Sacred Heart,
in union with the Holy Sacrifice of the Mass throughout
    the world,
for the salvation of souls, the reparation for sins, the reunion
    of all Christians,
and in particular for the intentions of the Holy Father this
    month. Amen.

Sanctus (Holy, Holy, Holy)

Holy, holy, holy Lord, God of power and might.
Heaven and earth are full of your glory.
Hosanna in the highest.
Blessed is he who comes in the name of the Lord.
Hosanna in the highest.

Canticle of St. Francis (Canticle of the Sun)

Most high, all-powerful, good Lord,
    yours are the praises, the glory, and the honor, and
        all blessing,
to you alone, Most High, do they belong,
    and no human is worthy to mention your name.
Praised be you, my Lord, with all your creatures,
    especially Sir Brother Sun,
    who is the day and through whom you give us light.
And he is beautiful and radiant with great splendor;
    and bears a likeness of you, Most High One.
Praised be you, my Lord, through Sister Moon and the stars,
    in heaven you formed them clear and precious
        and beautiful.
Praised be you, my Lord, through Brother Wind,
    and through the air, cloudy and serene, and every
        kind of weather,
    through whom you give sustenance to your creatures.
Praised be you, my Lord, through Sister Water,
    who is very useful and humble and precious and chaste.
Praised be you, my Lord, through Brother Fire,
    through whom you light the night,
    and he is beautiful and playful and robust and strong.
Praised be you, my Lord, through our Sister Mother Earth,
    who sustains and governs us,
    and who produces various fruit with colored flowers
        and herbs.

(continued)

Praised be you, my Lord, through those who give pardon for
   your love,
   and bear infirmity and tribulation.
Blessed are those who endure in peace
   for by you, Most High, shall they be crowned.
Praised be you, my Lord, through our Sister Bodily Death,
   from whom no one living can escape.
Woe to those who die in mortal sin.
   Blessed are those whom death will find in your most
      holy will,
   for the second death shall do them no harm.
Praise and bless my Lord and give him thanks
   and serve him with great humility.

At Mealtimes

Grace Before Meals

Bless us, O Lord, and these thy gifts, which we are about to receive from thy bounty, through Christ our Lord. Amen.

Grace After Meals

We give thee thanks, for all thy benefits, almighty God, who lives and reigns forever. [And may the souls of the faithful departed, through the mercy of God, rest in peace.] Amen.

Extended Blessing at Table

[1030]

Christians, whether alone or with companions at table, say grace before and after meals to thank God for his goodness in providing their daily food.

[1031]

As they gather at table and see in the food they share a sign of God's blessings on them, Christians should be mindful of the poor, who lack even the bare minimum of food that those at table may have in abundance.

(continued)

BEFORE THE MEAL

When the household has gathered around the table, all make the sign of the cross.

Then the Scripture is read:

[1039]

Listen to the words of the Prophet Isaiah: 58:10–11a

If you bestow your bread on the hungry
and satisfy the afflicted;
Then light shall rise for you in the darkness,
and the gloom shall become for you like midday;
Then the LORD will guide you always
and give you plenty even on the parched land.

(The family's Bible may be used for an alternate reading such as Acts 2:42–47a.)

After a short silence, the leader prays:

[1069]

Blessed are you, almighty Father,
who give us our daily bread.
Blessed is your only begotten Son,
who continually feeds us with the Word of life.
Blessed is the Holy Spirit,
who brings us together at this table of love.
Blessed be God now and forever.
R/. Amen.

AFTER THE MEAL

Leader: Blessed be the name of the Lord.
R/. Now and forever.

·   The leader prays:

God our Father,
we thank you for the food your bounty has given us,
your gathered family.
Grant that we also may freely give to others
what you have so generously given to us,
and that we may all share
in the banquet of heaven.
We ask this through Christ our Lord.
R/. Amen.

—*From Book of Blessings*

Beginning Each Day's Work

Blessing Before Going to Work

May God bless the work I will do this day,
that all my actions
may bring Christ to the world.

Blessing Before Going to School

May God bless your day at school
that you may grow in knowledge of the world
and in love for all God's children.

Prayer for the Day's Work at Home

God be in my head, and in my understanding;
God be in my eyes, and in my looking;
God be in my mouth, and in my speaking;
God be in my heart, and in my thinking;
God be at my end, and at my departing.

LABOR, SERVICE, STUDY, AND ALMSGIVING

Prayer of St. Francis (Peace Prayer)

Lord, make me an instrument of your peace:
where there is hatred, let me sow love;
where there is injury, pardon;
where there is doubt, faith;
where there is despair, hope;
where there is darkness, light;
where there is sadness, joy.

O divine Master, grant that I may not so much seek
to be consoled as to console,
to be understood as to understand,
to be loved as to love.

For it is in giving that we receive,
it is in pardoning that we are pardoned,
it is in dying that we are born to eternal life.
Amen.

—St. Francis of Assisi

Prayer for Success at Work

God our Father,
Creator and ruler of the universe,
in every age you call your children
to develop and use their gifts for the good of others.
With St. Joseph as our example and guide,
help us to do the work you have asked
and come to the rewards you have promised.

Hear the prayers of your people
and give us work that enhances our human dignity
and draws us closer to each other
in the service of our brothers and sisters.

We ask this through our Lord Jesus Christ, your Son,
who lives and reigns with you and the Holy Spirit,
one God, forever and ever.
R/. Amen.

WORK AND STUDY

Prayer at Work

Day by day we bless you, Lord.
We praise your name forever.

Jesus, gentle and humble of heart, have mercy on us.
Mary, mirror of justice, pray for us.
Joseph, model of workers, pray for us.

May we know the shortness of our days,
that we may learn wisdom.

From 1 Peter 4:11

May God be glorified in all things
through Jesus Christ.

From 2 Peter 3:18

May we grow in grace and in the knowledge
of our Lord and savior Jesus Christ.
To him be glory now and to the day of eternity.

From Philippians 4:7

May the peace of God that is
beyond all understanding
guard our hearts and our thoughts
in Christ Jesus.

From Colossians 1:12

We give you thanks, our Father!
You call us to share the lot of the
saints in light!

From Psalm 143:10

Teach me to do your will, for you are my God.

SERVICE AND FAITH IN ACTION

From Colossians 3:17

In all our words and actions
let us give thanks to God
in the name of the Lord Jesus.

From 1 Thessalonians 1:3

May God put our faith into action,
to work in love, to persevere in hope,
through our Lord Jesus Christ.

GIVING OR RECEIVING OF ALMS

From Philippians 4:19–20

May God fully supply all our needs
according to his generosity, with magnificence,
in Christ Jesus!
To God be glory forever and ever!

From Exodus 34:6

Blessed are you, Lord, God of tenderness and compassion,
rich in kindness and faithfulness.

From Judith 9:11

God of the humble and help of the oppressed:
Blessed are you, Lord!
Support of the weak and refuge of the forsaken:
Blessed are you, Lord!

From Tobit 4:7

Do not turn your face away from the poor,
and God's face will not be turned away from you.

AT NOON

At midday, it is traditional to pray the *Angelus*, found in the Prayers to
Mary in Part I: Basic Prayers. During the Easter season, the *Regina Caeli*
(also found in Part I: Basic Prayers) replaces the *Angelus*.

Coming Home Each Day

Prayer When Family Comes Home

Hear us, Lord,
and send your angel from heaven
to visit and protect,
to comfort and defend
all who live in this house.

Now Thank We All Our God

Now thank we all our God
with heart and hands and voices,
who wondrous things has done,
in whom his world rejoices;
who from our mothers' arms,
has blessed us on our way
with countless gifts of love,
and still is ours today.

Text: Martin Rinkart, 1586–1649
Translator: Catherine Winkworth, 1829–1878

From 2 Thessalonians 3:16

May the Lord of peace give us peace
all the time and in every way.
The Lord be with us.

"Phos Hilaron":
Ancient Greek Hymn for Evening

O radiant Light, O Sun divine,
of God the Father's deathless face,
O Image of the light sublime
that fills the heav'nly dwelling place:

O Son of God, the source of life,
praise is your due by night and day;
unsullied lips must raise the strain
of your esteemed and splendid name.

Lord Jesus Christ, as daylight fades,
as shine the lights of eventide,
we praise the Father with the Son,
the Spirit blest and with them one.

A Family Evening Prayer

Lord, behold our family here assembled.
We thank you for this place in which we dwell,
for the love that unites us,
for the peace accorded to us this day,
for the hope with which we expect the morrow;
for the health, the work, the food, and the bright skies
that make our lives delightful;
for our friends in all parts of the earth. Amen.

—*Robert Louis Stevenson*

At Bedtime

See Night Prayer in the Liturgy of the Hours, at the beginning of this Part. A suitable bedtime psalm is Psalm 91, "You Who Dwell," located in Part VIII: God's Word in Times of Need. Evening Intercessions may be found at the end of Part V: Prayers for Catholic Living.

Evening Prayer from the Byzantine Tradition

In the evening, in the morning, and at noon
we praise you, we bless you,
we give you thanks, and we beg you,
Master of the universe,
grant that our hearts not yield to evil words
but free us from all who try to enslave our souls,
because our eyes are turned to you, O Lord,
and we have placed our hope in you.
Do not abandon us, O God!
For every glory, honor, and adoration is due to you,
Father, Son, and Holy Spirit,
now and always and forever and ever. Amen.

A Child's Evening Hymn

I hear no voice, I feel no touch,
I see no glory bright;
but yet I know that God is near,
in darkness as in light.

He watches ever by my side,
and hears my whispered prayer:
the Father for his little child
both night and day does care.

PART III
DAYS AND
SEASONS

DAYS AND
SEASONS

Christ yesterday and today
the beginning and the end
Alpha
and Omega
all time belongs to him
and all the ages
to him be glory and power
through every age forever. Amen.

—*Preparation of the Easter Candle*

From the first page of the Bible, we begin to count time. Evening comes; morning follows; the days pass. God, who is beyond time, who dwells in eternity, creates the world and gives shape to human history. Days, weeks, months, and seasons are made holy as we remember the wondrous actions of God and ask him to bless our days.

When Jesus Christ becomes incarnate, God enters human history in a new and intimate way. By his birth, his preaching and ministry, and, most especially, by his suffering, death, and Resurrection, all is changed.

Still today the Church lives by the rhythm of days and seasons, rejoicing and repenting, feast and fasting. The high point for each week is Sunday, on which we recall Christ's glorious Resurrection, dispelling the gloom of Fridays with the hope of eternal life.

On Christmas we celebrate Jesus' birth—God humbling himself to become human so that we might live forever with God. During the Christmas season, we celebrate the Holy Family of Jesus, Mary, and Joseph, as well as Jesus' early manifestations to the Magi from the east and to John at the River Jordan. Through Advent, we prepare for Christ's coming at Christmas and his coming again at the end of time.

The high point of the Church's liturgical year is the Easter Triduum. Beginning on Holy Thursday evening and continuing until evening on Easter Sunday, on these days we recall the Paschal Mystery that brings us salvation: Christ's suffering, death, and Resurrection. The Fifty Days of Easter—from Easter Sunday to Pentecost—are celebrated as one great Sunday, filled with the joy of the Resurrection and the sound of Alleluia. The Forty Days before the Triduum we keep as Lent, a time of penance and preparation, recalling and renewing our Baptism so that we can die with Christ so as to live with him forever.

Through the rest of the year, we count the Sundays of Ordinary Time, recalling Christ's ministry here on earth. In these Sundays, we remember that God has ordered our days to lead us to him.

In the course of the year, we observe other days as well—the feasts of saints, days of prayer and penance, and civil holidays. In all these things, we see the hand of God, drawing us closer to him through Christ, in the power of the Holy Spirit.

> Dear brothers and sisters,
> the glory of the Lord has shone upon us,
> and shall ever be manifest among us,
> until the day of his return.
> Through the rhythms of times and seasons
> let us celebrate the mysteries of salvation.
>
> *—Proclamation of the Date of Easter*

ON SUNDAY

From the days of the Apostles, Christians have gathered on Sunday, the first day of the week, to recall Jesus' Resurrection from the dead. We call it the "Lord's Day," a day to celebrate Christ's victory over sin and death, his fulfillment of the first creation and the dawn of "the new creation."

In Baptism, we become part of the new creation in Christ. For us, Sunday is a day of rest and renewal. As Pope John Paul II taught, "Sunday is the day of joy in a very special way, indeed the day most suitable for learning how to rejoice and to rediscover the true nature and deep roots of joy" (*Dies Domini* [*On Keeping the Lord's Day Holy*], 1998, no. 57). Our deepest expression of joy is found in the Sunday eucharistic liturgy. We gather as one people, united in Christ, to give thanks to God and to join the hopes and struggles of our lives to Jesus' perfect Sacrifice on the Cross.

We prepare for the Sunday liturgy by fasting from other food, by pondering the Scriptures, and by setting aside a part of our own belongings for the poor and the Church. For the rest of the day, we refrain from work, spending our time in fellowship and prayer with our loved ones, so that we may face the new week refreshed and renewed, ready to serve all God's children.

The following prayers may be used to keep holy the Lord's Day.

In the Morning

FROM PSALM 92:2–6

It is good to give thanks to the LORD,
    to sing praise to your name, Most High,
To proclaim your kindness at dawn
    and your faithfulness throughout the night,

(continued)

With ten-stringed instrument and lyre,
   with melody upon the harp.
For you make me glad, O LORD, by your deeds;
   at the works of your hands I rejoice.

How great are your works, O LORD!
   How very deep are your thoughts!

FROM 1 PETER 1:3

Blessed be the God and Father of our Lord Jesus Christ,
who in his great mercy gave us a new birth to a living hope
through the resurrection of Jesus Christ from the dead.

Alleluia!
Jesus Christ is Lord!

Preparing to Join the Liturgical Assembly for Eucharist

For example, these may be said in the car on the way to Mass.

FROM PSALM 122:1

With great joy, let us go up to the house of the Lord!

FROM PSALM 43:4

Then will I go in to the altar of God,
the God of my gladness and joy.

During the Communion Fast

How holy this feast
in which Christ is our food:
his Passion is recalled,
grace fills our hearts,
and we receive a pledge of the glory to come.

—*St. Thomas Aquinas*

Studying the Sunday's Scripture

BEFORE STUDY: FROM PSALM 119:105

Before reading the Scriptures, you may pray:

A lamp to my feet is your word,
a light to my path.

The Sunday's Scriptures may be read by one alone or
by the household.

AFTER STUDY

After reading the Scriptures, you may pray:

May the words of Scripture nourish us
And strengthen us to follow Christ.

When Taking Holy Water

Blessed be God who has given us a new birth
by water and the Holy Spirit.

Prayer for the Catechumens

Lord, look with love on the catechumens
through this time of preparation.
Enfold them within your Church.

On Sunday Evening

Our God, we thank you for the joy and rest of this day.
May we yearn for the coming of your Kingdom!

Lord, by your Cross and Resurrection
you have set us free.
You are the Savior of the world.

ADVENT

Blessing of an Advent Wreath

[1509]
The use of the Advent Wreath is a traditional practice which has found its place in the Church as well as in the home. The blessing of an Advent Wreath takes place on the First Sunday of Advent or on the evening before the First Sunday of Advent.

[1510]
Customarily the Advent Wreath is constructed of a circle of evergreen branches into which are inserted four candles. According to tradition, three candles are violet and the fourth is rose. However, four violet or white candles may be used.

[1511]
The candles represent the four weeks of Advent, and the number of candles lighted each week corresponds to the number of the current week of Advent. The rose candle is lighted on the Third Sunday of Advent, also known as Gaudete Sunday.

[1514]
When the blessing of the Advent Wreath is celebrated in the home, it is appropriate that it be blessed by a parent or another member of the family.

[1537]
All make the sign of the cross as the leader says:

Our help is in the name of the Lord.
R/. Who made heaven and earth.

Then the Scripture is read:

[1538]

Listen to the words of the Prophet Isaiah: 9:1–2, 5–6

> The people who walked in darkness
> have seen a great light;
> Upon those who dwelt in the land of gloom
> a light has shone.
> You have brought them abundant joy
> and great rejoicing.
> As they rejoice before you as at the harvest,
> as people make merry when dividing spoils.
> For a child is born to us, a son is given us;
> upon his shoulder dominion rests.
> They name him Wonder-Counselor, God-Hero,
> Father-Forever, Prince of Peace.
> His dominion is vast
> and forever peaceful,
> from David's throne, and over his kingdom,
> which he confirms and sustains
> by judgment and justice,
> both now and forever.

[1527]

Or Isaiah 63:16–17, 19; 64:2–7—*You, Lord, are our redeemer.*

Reader: The Word of the Lord.
R/. Thanks be to God.

With hands joined, the leader says:

Lord our God,
we praise you for your Son, Jesus Christ:
he is Emmanuel, the hope of the peoples,
he is the wisdom that teaches and guides us,
he is the Savior of every nation.

Lord God,
let your blessing come upon us
as we light the candles of this wreath.
May the wreath and its light
be a sign of Christ's promise to bring us salvation.
May he come quickly and not delay.
We ask this through Christ our Lord.
R/. Amen.

The blessing may conclude with a verse from "O Come,
O Come, Emmanuel":

O come, desire of nations, bind
in one the hearts of humankind;
bid ev'ry sad division cease
and be thyself our Prince of peace.
Rejoice! Rejoice! Emmanuel
shall come to thee, O Israel.

—From Book of Blessings

The "O Antiphons" of Advent

On the last days of Advent, you may wish to add these "O Antiphons" to
your evening prayer, your prayer at table, or your bedtime prayer.

DECEMBER 17

O Wisdom of our God Most High,
guiding creation with power and love:
come to teach us the path of knowledge!

DECEMBER 18

O Leader of the House of Israel,
giver of the Law to Moses on Sinai:
come to rescue us with your mighty power!

DECEMBER 19

O Root of Jesse's stem,
sign of God's love for all his people:
come to save us without delay!

DECEMBER 20

O Key of David,
opening the gates of God's eternal Kingdom:
come and free the prisoners of darkness!

DECEMBER 21

O Radiant Dawn,
splendor of eternal light, sun of justice:
come and shine on those who dwell in darkness and in the
 shadow of death.

DECEMBER 22

O King of all nations and keystone of the Church:
come and save man, whom you formed from the dust!

DECEMBER 23

O Emmanuel, our King and Giver of Law:
come to save us, Lord our God!

CHRISTMAS SEASON

Blessing of a Christmas Tree

[1570]

The use of the Christmas tree is relatively modern. Its origins are found in the medieval mystery plays that depicted the tree of paradise and the Christmas light or candle that symbolized Christ, the Light of the world.

[1571]

According to custom, the Christmas tree is set up just before Christmas and may remain in place until the Solemnity of Epiphany.

[1573]

The lights of the tree are illuminated after the prayer of blessing.

[1574]

In the home the Christmas tree may be blessed by a parent or another family member, in connection with the evening meal on the Vigil of Christmas or at another suitable time on Christmas Day.

[1576]

When all have gathered, a suitable song may be sung. The leader makes the sign of the cross, and all reply "Amen."

[1578]

The leader may greet those present in the following words:

Let us glorify Christ our light, who brings salvation and peace into our midst, now and forever.
R/. Amen.

In the following or similar words, the leader prepares those present for the blessing:

My brothers and sisters, amidst signs and wonders Christ Jesus was born in Bethlehem of Judea: his birth brings joy to our hearts and enlightenment to our minds. With this tree, decorated and adorned, may we welcome Christ among us; may its lights guide us to the perfect light.

One of those present or the leader reads a text of sacred Scripture, for example:

Listen to the words of the Letter of St. Paul to Titus: 3:4–7

> But when the kindness and generous love
>   of God our savior appeared,
> not because of any righteous deeds we had done
>   but because of his mercy,
> he saved us through the bath of rebirth
>   and renewal by the holy Spirit,
> whom he richly poured out on us
>   through Jesus Christ our savior,
> so that we might be justified by his grace
>   and become heirs in hope of eternal life.

Or Ezekiel 17:22–24—*I will plant a tender shoot on the mountain heights of Israel.*

Reader: The Word of the Lord.
R/. Thanks be to God.

The intercessions are then said. The leader says:

Let us ask God to send his blessing upon us and upon this
sign of our faith in the Lord.
R/. Lord, give light to our hearts.

That this tree of lights may remind us of the tree of glory on
which Christ accomplished our salvation, let us pray to the
Lord. R/.

That the joy of Christmas may always be in our homes, let
us pray to the Lord. R/.

That the peace of Christ may dwell in our hearts and in the
world, let us pray to the Lord. R/.

After the intercessions the leader invites all present to
say the Lord's Prayer.

The leader says the prayer with hands joined:

Lord our God,
we praise you for the light of creation:
the sun, the moon, and the stars of the night.
We praise you for the light of Israel:
the Law, the prophets, and the wisdom of the Scriptures.
We praise you for Jesus Christ, your Son:
he is Emmanuel, God-with-us, the Prince of Peace,
who fills us with the wonder of your love.

Lord God,
let your blessing come upon us
as we illumine this tree.
May the light and cheer it gives
be a sign of the joy that fills our hearts.
May all who delight in this tree
come to the knowledge and joy of salvation.
We ask this through Christ our Lord.
R/. Amen.

> The lights of the tree are then illuminated.

[1590]

> The leader concludes the rite by signing himself or herself
> with the sign of the cross and saying:

**May the God of glory fill our hearts with peace and joy, now
    and forever.**
R/. Amen.

[1591]

> The blessing concludes with a verse from "O Come,
> O Come, Emmanuel":

**O come, thou dayspring, come and cheer
our spirits by thine advent here;
disperse the gloomy clouds of night
and death's dark shadow put to flight.
Rejoice! Rejoice! Emmanuel
shall come to thee, O Israel.**

—*From* Book of Blessings

Blessing of a Christmas Manger or Nativity Scene

[1541]

In its present form the custom of displaying figures depicting the birth of Jesus Christ owes its origin to St. Francis of Assisi, who made the Christmas crèche or manger for Christmas Eve of 1223.

[1542]

The blessing of the Christmas manger or nativity scene may take place on the Vigil of Christmas or at another suitable time.

[1545]

When the manger is set up in the home, it is appropriate that it be blessed by a parent or another family member.

[1566]

All make the sign of the cross as the leader says:

Our help is in the name of the Lord.
R/. Who made heaven and earth.

[1567]

One of those present or the leader reads a text of sacred Scripture, for example:

Listen to the words of the holy Gospel
according to Luke:

2:1–8

In those days a decree went out from Caesar
Augustus that the whole world should be
enrolled. This was the first enrollment, when
Quirinius was governor of Syria. So all went to
be enrolled, each to his own town. And Joseph
too went up from Galilee from the town of
Nazareth to Judea, to the city of David that is
called Bethlehem, because he was of the house
and family of David, to be enrolled with Mary,
his betrothed, who was with child. While they
were there, the time came for her to have her
child, and she gave birth to her firstborn son.
She wrapped him in swaddling clothes and
laid him in a manger, because there was no
room for them in the inn.

Now there were shepherds in that region
living in the fields and keeping the night watch
over their flock.

[1568]

Or Isaiah 7:10–15—*The birth of Emmanuel.*

Reader: The Gospel of the Lord.
R/. Praise to you, Lord Jesus Christ.

The leader prays with hands joined:

God of every nation and people,
from the very beginning of creation
you have made manifest your love:
when our need for a Savior was great
you sent your Son to be born of the Virgin Mary.
To our lives he brings joy and peace,
justice, mercy, and love.

Lord,
bless all who look upon this manger;
may it remind us of the humble birth of Jesus,
and raise our thoughts to him,
who is God-with-us and Savior of all,
and who lives and reigns forever and ever.
R/. Amen.

—*From* Book of Blessings

Prayer for the New Year

On New Year's Eve or New Year's Day, the household gathers at the table or at the Christmas tree or manger scene. Many people make New Year's Day a day of prayer for peace.

All make the sign of the cross. The leader begins:

Let us praise the Lord of days and seasons and years, saying:
Glory to God in the highest!
R/. And peace to his people on earth!

The leader may use these or similar words to introduce the blessing:

Our lives are made of days and nights, of seasons and years, for we are part of a universe of suns and moons and planets. We mark ends and we make beginnings and, in all, we praise God for the grace and mercy that fill our days.

Then the Scripture is read:

Listen to the words of the Book of Genesis: 1:14–19

> God said: "Let there be lights in the dome of
> the sky, to separate day from night. Let them
> mark the fixed times, the days and the years,
> and serve as luminaries in the dome of the
> sky, to shed light upon the earth." And so it
> happened: God made the two great lights, the
> greater one to govern the day, and the lesser
> one to govern the night; and he made the stars.

(continued)

God set them in the dome of the sky, to shed
light upon the earth, to govern the day and
the night, and to separate the light from the
darkness. God saw how good it was. Evening
came, and morning followed—the fourth day.

(The family's Bible may be used for an alternate reading
such as Psalm 90:1–4.)

Reader: The Word of the Lord.
R/. Thanks be to God.

After a time of silence, members of the household offer
prayers of thanksgiving for the past year, and of intercession
for the year to come. On January 1, it may be appropriate to
conclude these prayers with the Litany of the Blessed Virgin
Mary (in Part VII: Litanies) since this is the solemn feast of
Mary, Mother of God. In conclusion, all join hands for the
Lord's Prayer. Then the leader continues:

Let us now pray for God's blessing in the new year.

After a short silence, parents may place their hands on
their children in blessing as the leader says:

Remember us, O God;
from age to age be our comforter.
You have given us the wonder of time,
blessings in days and nights, seasons and years.

Bless your children at the turning of the year
and fill the months ahead with the bright hope
that is ours in the coming of Christ.

You are our God, living and reigning, forever and ever.
R/. Amen.

Another prayer for peace may be said:

Lord, make me an instrument of your peace:
where there is hatred, let me sow love;
where there is injury, pardon;
where there is doubt, faith;
where there is despair, hope;
where there is darkness, light;
where there is sadness, joy.

O divine Master, grant that I may not so much seek
to be consoled as to console,
to be understood as to understand,
to be loved as to love.
For it is in giving that we receive,
it is in pardoning that we are pardoned,
it is in dying that we are born to eternal life.
R/. Amen.

—Attributed to St. Francis of Assisi

The leader says:

Let us bless the Lord.

All respond, making the sign of the cross:

Thanks be to God.

The prayer may conclude with the singing of a Christmas
carol.

Blessing of the Home and Household on the Epiphany

The traditional date of Epiphany is January 6, but in the United States it is celebrated on the Sunday between January 2 and January 8.

[1601]

When all have gathered, a suitable song may be sung. The leader makes the sign of the cross, and all reply, "Amen."

[1603]

The leader greets those present in the following words:

Let us praise God, who fills our hearts and homes
    with peace.
Blessed be God forever.
R/. Blessed be God forever.

[1604]

In the following or similar words, the leader prepares those present for the blessing:

The Word became flesh and made his dwelling place among us. It is Christ who enlightens our hearts and homes with his love. May all who enter this home find Christ's light and love.

One of those present or the leader reads a text of sacred Scripture, for example:

Listen to the words of the holy Gospel according to Luke: 19:1–9

> Jesus came to Jericho and intended to pass through the town. Now a man there named Zacchaeus, who was a chief tax collector and also a wealthy man, was seeking to see who Jesus was; but he could not see him because of the crowd, for he was short in stature. So he ran ahead and climbed a sycamore tree in order to see Jesus, who was about to pass that way. When he reached the place, Jesus looked up and said to him, "Zacchaeus, come down quickly, for today I must stay at your house." And he came down quickly and received him with joy. When they all saw this, they began to grumble, saying, "He has gone to stay at the house of a sinner." But Zacchaeus stood there and said to the Lord, "Behold, half of my possessions, Lord, I shall give to the poor, and if I have extorted anything from anyone I shall repay it four times over." And Jesus said to him, "Today salvation has come to this house because this man too is a descendant of Abraham."

[1610]

The intercessions are then said:

Leader: The Son of God made his home among us. With thanks and praise let us call upon him.
R/. Stay with us, Lord.

Lord Jesus Christ, with Mary and Joseph you formed the Holy Family: remain in our home, that we may know you as our guest and honor you as our Head. We pray: **R/.**

Lord Jesus Christ, you had no place to lay your head, but in the spirit of poverty accepted the hospitality of your friends: grant that through our help the homeless may obtain proper housing. We pray: **R/.**

Lord Jesus Christ, the three kings presented their gifts to you in praise and adoration: grant that those living in this house may use their talents and abilities to your greater glory. We pray: **R/.**

[1611]

After the intercessions the leader invites all present to say the Lord's Prayer.

The leader says the prayer of blessing with hands joined:

Lord God of heaven and earth,
you revealed your only-begotten Son to every nation
by the guidance of a star.

Bless this house
and all who inhabit it.
Fill them (us) with the light of Christ,
that their (our) concern for others may reflect your love.

We ask this through Christ our Lord.
R/. Amen.

[1615]

The leader concludes the rite by signing himself or herself
with the sign of the cross and saying:

May Christ Jesus dwell with us,
keep us from all harm,
and make us one in mind and heart,
now and forever.
R/. Amen.

[1616]

It is preferable to end the celebration with a suitable song,
for example, "O Come, All Ye Faithful" or "We Three
Kings."

—*From* Book of Blessings

LENT

ASH WEDNESDAY

Blessing of the Season
and of a Place of Prayer

From Ash Wednesday to Easter, a place in the home is set aside for
prayer. The family's Bible is placed there with a crucifix or cross and a
candle, which is lighted when all have gathered.

All make the sign of the cross as the leader begins:

The Lord calls us to days of penance and mercy.
Blessed be the name of the Lord.
R/. Now and forever.

The leader may use these or similar words to introduce the
blessing:

Remember that we are but dust and ashes, yet by God's
grace we have died in Baptism and have put on the Lord
Jesus Christ. Each year we keep these Forty Days with
prayer and penance and the practice of charity so that we

may come to the Easter festival ready to renew once more the life-giving commitment of our Baptism. Through this Lent we shall gather here to read the Scriptures and ponder them and to intercede with God for our needs and for the needs of the Church and the world.

Then the Scripture is read:

Listen to the words of the Prophet Isaiah: 58:5–10

> Is this the manner of fasting I wish,
> of keeping a day of penance:
> That a man bow his head like a reed,
> and lie in sackcloth and ashes?
> Do you call this a fast,
> a day acceptable to the LORD?
> This, rather, is the fasting that I wish:
> releasing those bound unjustly,
> untying the thongs of the yoke;
> Setting free the oppressed,
> breaking every yoke;
> Sharing your bread with the hungry,
> sheltering the oppressed and the homeless;
> Clothing the naked when you see them,
> and not turning your back on your own.

(continued)

Then your light shall break forth like the dawn,
   and your wound shall quickly be healed;
Your vindication shall go before you,
   and the glory of the LORD shall be your rear guard.
Then you shall call, and the LORD will answer,
   you shall cry for help, and he will say: Here I am!
If you remove from your midst oppression,
   false accusation and malicious speech;
If you bestow your bread on the hungry
   and satisfy the afflicted;
Then light shall rise for you in the darkness,
   and the gloom shall become for you like midday.

(The family's Bible may be used for an alternate reading
such as Deuteronomy 30:15–20.)

Reader: The Word of the Lord.
R/. Thanks be to God.

After a time of silence, members of the household offer
prayers of intercession for the world, the Church and its
catechumens, and themselves. The leader then invites:

Let us kneel and ask God's blessing on us and on this holy
season.

After a short silence, the leader continues:

Merciful God,
you called us forth from the dust of the earth;
you claimed us for Christ in the waters of Baptism.
Look upon us as we enter these Forty Days
bearing the mark of ashes,
and bless our journey through the desert of Lent
to the font of rebirth.

May our fasting be hunger for justice;
our alms, a making of peace;
our prayer, the chant of humble and grateful hearts.

All that we do and pray is in the name of Jesus,
for in his Cross you proclaim your love
forever and ever.
R/. Amen.

> Each person then kisses the crucifix. All then stand, and
> the leader concludes:

All through these days let us be quiet and prayerful,
pondering the mysteries told in the Scriptures. In the Cross,
we have been claimed for Christ. In Christ, we make the
prayer that fills these days of mercy:

Our Father . . .

Leader: Let us bless the Lord.
R/. Thanks be to God.

> The blessing may conclude with an appropriate song.

LENTEN DISCIPLINES:
FASTING AND ALMSGIVING

For these Forty Days we are conscious of how we must sharpen our senses and focus mind and heart on the Reign of God. We are, above all, aware of those waters in which we were baptized into Christ's death. We died to sin and evil and began a new life in Christ. The waters of Baptism wait at Lent's end for the catechumens, but we are called to renew our Baptism as well.

The Church asks us to give ourselves to prayer and to the reading of Scripture, to fasting and to giving alms. The fasting that all do together on Fridays is but a sign of the daily lenten discipline of individuals and households: fasting for certain periods of time, fasting from certain foods, but also fasting from other things and activities. Likewise, the giving of alms is some effort to share this world equally—not only through the distribution of money, but through the sharing of our time and talents.

We Hunger and Thirst for Holiness

Blessed are you, Lord, God of all creation:
you make us hunger and thirst for holiness.
Blessed are you, Lord, God of all creation:
you call us to true fasting:
to set free the oppressed,
to share our bread with the hungry,
to shelter the homeless and to clothe the naked.

Psalm 102:5–8, 10, 13

Withered and dried up like grass is my heart;
    I forget to eat my bread.
Because of my insistent sighing
    I am reduced to skin and bone.
I am like a desert owl;
    I have become like an owl among the ruins.
I am sleepless, and I moan;
    I am like a sparrow alone on the housetop.
For I eat ashes like bread
    and mingle my drink with tears.
But you, O Lord, abide forever,
    and your name through all generations.

Before a Time of Solitude

Blessed are you, Lord, God of all creation:
you manifest yourself when we are silent.

Before Deeds of Charity

Blessed are you, Lord, God of all creation:
for all the earth is yours.

PENITENTIAL PSALMS

Lent is a time of penance and renewal. These seven psalms have traditionally been prayed in penitential times. Prayerfully reciting these psalms will help us to recognize our sinfulness, express our sorrow, and beg God for forgiveness.

Psalm 6

O LORD, reprove me not in your anger,
　　nor chastise me in your wrath.
Have pity on me, O LORD, for I am languishing;
　　heal me, O LORD, for my body is in terror;
My soul, too, is utterly terrified;
　　but you, O LORD, how long . . . ?

Return, O LORD, save my life;
　　rescue me because of your kindness,
For among the dead no one remembers you;
　　in the nether world who gives you thanks?

I am wearied with sighing;
　　every night I flood my bed with weeping;
　　I drench my couch with my tears.
My eyes are dimmed with sorrow;
　　they have aged because of all my foes.

Depart from me, all evildoers,
 for the LORD has heard the sound of my weeping;
The LORD has heard my plea;
 the LORD has accepted my prayer.
All my enemies shall be put to shame in utter terror;
 they shall fall back in sudden shame.

Psalm 32

Happy is he whose fault is taken away,
 whose sin is covered.
Happy the man to whom the LORD imputes not guilt,
 in whose spirit there is no guile.

As long as I would not speak, my bones wasted away
 with my groaning all the day,
For day and night your hand was heavy upon me;
 My strength was dried up as by the heat of summer.
Then I acknowledged my sin to you,
 my guilt I covered not.
I said, "I confess my faults to the LORD,"
 and you took away the guilt of my sin.
For this shall every faithful man pray to you
 in time of stress.
Though deep waters overflow,
 they shall not reach him.
You are my shelter; from distress you will preserve me;
 With glad cries of freedom you will ring me round.

(continued)

I will instruct you and show you the way you should walk;
    I will counsel you, keeping my eye on you.
Be not senseless like horses or mules:
    with bit and bridle their temper must be curbed,
    else they will not come near you.

Many are the sorrows of the wicked,
    but kindness surrounds him who trusts in the Lord.
Be glad in the Lord and rejoice, you just;
    exult, all you upright of heart.

Psalm 38

O Lord, in your anger punish me not,
    in your wrath chastise me not;
For your arrows have sunk deep in me,
    and your hand has come down upon me.
There is no health in my flesh because of your indignation;
    there is no wholeness in my bones because of my sin,
For my iniquities have overwhelmed me;
    they are like a heavy burden, beyond my strength.

Noisome and festering are my sores
    because of my folly,
I am stooped and bowed down profoundly;
    all the day I go in mourning,
For my loins are filled with burning pains;
    there is no health in my flesh.
I am numbed and severely crushed;
    I roar with anguish of heart.

O Lord, all my desire is before you;
    from you my groaning is not hid.
My heart throbs; my strength forsakes me;
    the very light of my eyes has failed me.
My friends and my companions stand back because
        of my affliction;
    my neighbors stand afar off.
Men lay snares for me seeking my life;
    they look to my misfortune, they speak of ruin,
    treachery they talk of all the day.

But I am like a deaf man, hearing not,
    like a dumb man who opens not his mouth.
I am become like a man who neither hears
    nor has in his mouth a retort.
Because for you, O Lord, I wait;
    you, O Lord my God, will answer
When I say, "Let them not be glad on my account
    who, when my foot slips, glory over me."

For I am very near to falling,
    and my grief is with me always.
Indeed, I acknowledge my guilt;
    I grieve over my sin.
But my undeserved enemies are strong;
    many are my foes without cause.
Those who repay evil for good
    harass me for pursuing good.
Forsake me not, O Lord;
    my God, be not far from me!
Make haste to help me,
    O Lord my salvation!

Psalm 51

Have mercy on me, O God, in your goodness;
    In the greatness of your compassion wipe
        out my offense.
Thoroughly wash me from my guilt
    And of my sin cleanse me.

For I acknowledge my offense,
    and my sin is before me always:
"Against you only have I sinned,
    and done what is evil in your sight"—
That you may be justified in your sentence,
    vindicated when you condemn.
Indeed, in guilt was I born,
    and in sin my mother conceived me;
Behold, you are pleased with sincerity of heart,
    and in my inmost being you teach me wisdom.

Cleanse me of sin with hyssop, that I may be purified;
    wash me, and I shall be whiter than snow.
Let me hear the sounds of joy and gladness;
    the bones you have crushed shall rejoice.
Turn away your face from my sins
    and blot out all my guilt.

A clean heart create in me, O God,
    and a steadfast spirit renew within me.
Cast me not out from your presence,
    and your holy spirit take not from me.
Give back the joy of your salvation,
    and a willing spirit sustain in me.

I will teach transgressors your ways,
   and sinners shall return to you.
Free me from blood guilt, O God, my saving God;
   then my tongue shall proclaim your praise.
For you are not pleased with sacrifices;
   should I offer a holocaust, you would not accept it.
My sacrifice, O God, is a contrite spirit;
   a heart contrite and humbled, O God, you will not spurn.

Be bountiful, O Lord, to Zion in your kindness
   by rebuilding the walls of Jerusalem;
Then shall you be pleased with due sacrifices,
   burnt offerings and holocausts;
      then shall they offer up bullocks on your altar.

Psalm 102

O Lord, hear my prayer,
   and let my cry come to you.
Hide not your face from me in the day of my distress.
Incline your ear to me;
   in the day when I call, answer me speedily.
For my days vanish like smoke,
   and my bones burn like fire.
Withered and dried up like grass is my heart;
   I forget to eat my bread.
Because of my insistent sighing
   I am reduced to skin and bone.
I am like a desert owl;
   I am become like an owl among the ruins.
I am sleepless, and I moan;
   I am like a sparrow alone on the housetop.

(continued)

All the day my enemies revile me;
     in their rage against me they make a curse of me.
For I eat ashes like bread
     and mingle my drink with tears,
Because of your fury and your wrath;
     for you lifted me up only to cast me down.
My days are like a lengthening shadow,
     and I wither like grass.

But you, O Lord, abide forever,
     and your name through all generations.
You will arise and have mercy on Zion,
     for it is time to pity her,
     for the appointed time has come.
For her stones are dear to your servants,
     and her dust moves them to pity.
And the nations shall revere your name, O Lord,
     and all the kings of the earth your glory,
When the Lord has rebuilt Zion
     and appeared in his glory;
When he has regarded the prayer of the destitute,
     and not despised their prayer.

Let this be written for the generation to come,
     and let his future creatures praise the Lord:
"The Lord looked down from his holy height,
     from heaven he beheld the earth,
To hear the groaning of the prisoners,
     to release those doomed to die"—
That the name of the Lord may be declared in Zion;
     and his praise, in Jerusalem,
When the peoples gather together,
     and the kingdoms, to serve the Lord.

He has broken down my strength in the way;
    he has cut short my days.
        I say: O my God,
Take me not hence in the midst of my days;
    through all generations your years endure.
Of old you established the earth,
    and the heavens are the work of your hands.
They shall perish, but you remain
    though all of them grow old like a garment.
Like clothing you change them, and they are changed,
    but you are the same, and your years have no end.
The children of your servants shall abide,
    and their posterity shall continue in your presence.

Psalm 130

Out of the depths I cry to you, O LORD;
    LORD, hear my voice!
Let your ears be attentive
    to my voice in supplication:

If you, O LORD, mark iniquities,
    LORD, who can stand?
But with you is forgiveness,
    that you may be revered.

I trust in the LORD;
    my soul trusts in his word.
My soul waits for the LORD
    more than sentinels wait for the dawn.

(continued)

More than sentinels wait for the dawn,
    let Israel wait for the LORD,
For with the LORD is kindness
    and with him is plenteous redemption;
And he will redeem Israel
    from all their iniquities.

Psalm 143

O LORD, hear my prayer;
    hearken to my pleading in your faithfulness;
    in your justice answer me.
And enter not into judgment with your servant,
    for before you no living man is just.

For the enemy pursues me;
    he has crushed me life to the ground;
    he has left me dwelling in the dark, like those long dead.
And my spirit is faint within me,
    my heart within me is appalled.
I remember the days of old;
    I meditate on all your doings,
    the works of your hands I ponder.
I stretch out my hands to you;
    my soul thirsts for you like parched land.

Hasten to answer me, O Lord,
    for my spirit fails me.
Hide not your face from me
    lest I become like those who go down into the pit.
At dawn let me hear of your kindness,
    for in you I trust.
Show me the way in which I should walk,
    for to you I lift up my soul.
Rescue me from my enemies, O Lord,
    for in you I hope.

Teach me to do your will,
    for you are my God.
May your good spirit guide me
    on level ground.
For your name's sake, O Lord, preserve me;
    in your justice free me from distress,
And in your kindness destroy my enemies;
    bring to nought all my foes
    for I am your servant.

PASSION SUNDAY
(THE BEGINNING OF HOLY WEEK)

Placing of Branches in the Home

The branches that are blessed and brought home on Passion (Palm)
Sunday are placed near the crucifix or the family Bible. They remind us
that Lent is the slow coming of spring to the earth, the renewal of life.
They are like the great "Hosanna" with which we hail the crucified and
risen Lord.

After dinner or at another time on Palm Sunday, the
household gathers where the palms have been placed.

All make the sign of the cross. The leader begins:

Hosanna in the highest!
Blessed is he who comes in the name of the Lord.
R/. Hosanna in the highest!

The leader may use these or similar words to introduce
the prayer:

We have come to the last days of Lent. Today we heard the
reading of the Passion. That story will remain with us as we
leave Lent behind on Holy Thursday and enter into the Three
Days when we celebrate the mystery of Christ's passing
through suffering and death to life at God's right hand.

Then the Scripture is read:

Listen to the words of the Second Letter of St. Paul
to the Corinthians: 4:10–11

> [We are] always carrying about in the body
> the dying of Jesus, so that the life of Jesus may
> also be manifested in our body. For we who
> live are constantly being given up to death for
> the sake of Jesus, so that the life of Jesus may
> be manifested in our mortal flesh.

Reader: The Word of the Lord.
R/. Thanks be to God.

After a time of silence, members of the household join
in prayers of intercession. Or the Litany of the Most
Precious Blood, in Part VII: Litanies, may be prayed. The
intercessions or litany are followed by the Lord's Prayer.
The leader continues:

Let us pray.
Blessed are you, God of Israel,
so rich in love and mercy.
Let these branches ever remind us of Christ's triumph.
May we who bear them rejoice in his Cross
and sing your praise forever and ever.
R/. Amen.

Together all take the palms to the place where they will be
kept through the coming year. When all have returned to
the starting point, the leader concludes:

Let us bless the Lord.

All respond, making the sign of the cross:

Thanks be to God.

HOLY WEEK
(DURING THE WEEK)

In the final days of Lent, our preparation intensifies. We give more freely, live more simply, and pray constantly. We take time to reflect on the abundant love of God, who gave his Son to open for us the way to eternal life. We strive to follow the path of Jesus, who humbled himself to save us. In these days, it is particularly appropriate to reflect on the four Songs of the Suffering Servant. The Church has interpreted these hymns, found in the Book of the prophet Isaiah, as speaking of Jesus, who suffered for our salvation.

Isaiah 42:1–7

Here is my servant whom I uphold,
    my chosen one with whom I am pleased,
Upon whom I have put my Spirit;
    he shall bring forth justice to the nations,
Not crying out, not shouting,
    not making his voice heard in the street.
A bruised reed he shall not break,
    and a smoldering wick he shall not quench,
Until he establishes justice on the earth;
    the coastlands will wait for his teaching.

Thus says God, the Lord,
    who created the heavens and stretched them out,
    who spreads out the earth with its crops,
Who gives breath to its people
    and spirit to those who walk on it:
I, the Lord, have called you for the victory of justice,
    I have grasped you by the hand;

I formed you, and set you
    as a covenant of the people,
    a light for the nations,
To open the eyes of the blind,
    to bring out prisoners from confinement,
    and from the dungeon, those who live in darkness.

Isaiah 49:1–6

Hear me, O islands,
    listen, O distant peoples.
The Lord called me from birth,
    from my mother's womb he gave me my name.
He made of me a sharp-edged sword
    and concealed me in the shadow of his arm.
He made me a polished arrow,
    in his quiver he hid me.
You are my servant, he said to me,
    Israel, through whom I show my glory.

Though I thought I had toiled in vain,
    and for nothing, uselessly, spent my strength,
Yet my reward is with the Lord,
    my recompense is with my God.
For now the Lord has spoken
    who formed me as his servant from the womb,
That Jacob may be brought back to him
    and Israel gathered to him;
And I am made glorious in the sight of the Lord,
    and my God is now my strength!

(continued)

It is too little, he says, for you to be my servant,
    to raise up the tribes of Jacob,
    and restore the survivors of Israel;
I will make you a light to the nations,
    that my salvation may reach to the ends of the earth.

Isaiah 50:4–9a

The Lord GOD has given me
    a well-trained tongue,
That I might know how to speak to the weary
    a word that will rouse them.
Morning after morning
    he opens my ear that I may hear;
And I have not rebelled,
    have not turned back.
I gave my back to those who beat me,
    my cheeks to those who plucked my beard;
My face I did not shield
    from buffets and spitting.

The Lord GOD is my help,
    therefore I am not disgraced;
I have set my face like flint,
    knowing that I shall not be put to shame.
He is near who upholds my right;
    if anyone wishes to oppose me,
    let us appear together.
Who disputes my right?
    Let him confront me.
See, the Lord GOD is my help;
    who will prove me wrong?

Isaiah 52:13–53:12

See, my servant shall prosper,
  he shall be raised high and greatly exalted.
Even as many were amazed at him—
  so marred was his look beyond that of man,
  and his appearance beyond that of mortals—
So shall he startle many nations,
  because of him kings shall stand speechless;
For those who have not been told shall see,
  those who have not heard shall ponder it.
Who would believe what we have heard?
  To whom has the arm of the Lord been revealed?
He grew up like a sapling before him,
  like a shoot from the parched earth;
There was in him no stately bearing to make us look at him,
  nor appearance that would attract us to him.
He was spurned and avoided by men,
  a man of suffering, accustomed to infirmity,
One of those from whom men hide their faces,
  spurned, and we held him in no esteem.

Yet it was our infirmities that he bore,
  our sufferings that he endured,
While we thought of him as stricken,
  as one smitten by God and afflicted.
But he was pierced for our offenses,
  crushed for our sins,
Upon him was the chastisement that makes us whole,
  by his stripes we were healed.
We had all gone astray like sheep,
  each following his own way;
But the Lord laid upon him
  the guilt of us all.

(continued)

Though he was harshly treated, he submitted
and opened not his mouth;
Like a lamb led to the slaughter
or a sheep before the shearers,
he was silent and opened not his mouth.
Oppressed and condemned, he was taken away,
and who would have thought any more of his destiny?
When he was cut off from the land of the living,
and smitten for the sin of his people,
A grave was assigned him among the wicked
and a burial place with evildoers,
Though he had done no wrong
nor spoken any falsehood.
[But the LORD was pleased
to crush him in infirmity.]

If he gives his life as an offering for sin,
he shall see his descendants in a long life,
and the will of the LORD shall be accomplished through him.
Because of his affliction
he shall see the light in fullness of days;
Through his suffering, my servant shall justify many,
and their guilt he shall bear.
Therefore I will give him his portion among the great,
and he shall divide the spoils with the mighty,
Because he surrendered himself to death
and was counted among the wicked;
And he shall take away the sins of many,
and win pardon for their offenses.

EASTER TRIDUUM

"Christ redeemed us all and gave perfect glory to
God principally through his paschal mystery: dying
he destroyed our death and rising he restored our
life. Therefore the Easter Triduum of the Passion and
Resurrection of Christ is the culmination of the entire
liturgical year. . . . The Easter Triduum begins with the
evening Mass of the Lord's Supper (on Holy Thursday),
reaches its high point in the Easter Vigil, and closes with
evening prayer on Easter Sunday. On Good Friday and, if
possible, also on Holy Saturday until the Easter Vigil, the
Easter fast is observed everywhere."

—*General Norms for the Liturgical Year*, nos. 18–19

Thus does the Church's calendar speak of these Three Days. Lent ends on
Holy Thursday. Friday and Saturday are days of private and communal
prayer. We fast from food, work, and entertainment in anticipation of
the great Vigil. We hold in special prayer the elect who will be baptized,
be confirmed, and join in the eucharistic banquet. Thus are the death
and Resurrection of Christ proclaimed in our midst. At various moments
from Thursday evening until Sunday, the community gathers for prayer
and vigil. In the times between these communal celebrations, we pray at
home, as individuals and as a family. The following texts come from the
liturgies of these days and are offered to help families prepare for fuller
participation in these special liturgies.

HOLY THURSDAY EVENING

Lent ends quietly on this evening as the Paschal Triduum begins. The liturgy of this night proclaims that we find glory in the Cross.

From Galatians 6:14

We should glory in the cross of our Lord Jesus Christ,
for he is our salvation, our life, and our resurrection;
through him we are saved and made free.

At the Holy Thursday liturgy, we recall Jesus' command to love each other as he has loved us. We embrace his call to become one with him in the Eucharist and to offer ourselves in loving service to all God's children.

From John 13:4, 5, 15

The Lord Jesus,
when he had eaten with his disciples,
poured water into a basin
and began to wash their feet, saying:
This example I leave you.

From John 13:14

If I, your Lord and Teacher, have washed your feet,
then surely you must wash one another's feet.

From John 13:34

I give you a new commandment:
love one another as I have loved you, says the Lord.

After the evening liturgy, it is customary to spend time in prayer before
the Blessed Sacrament. Appropriate prayers for this time can be found
elsewhere in this Part (Prayers for Corpus Christi) and also in Part I: Basic
Prayers (Prayers Before the Holy Eucharist).

During the time of individual reflection and prayer during the Triduum,
the following Scripture readings are especially appropriate for reading
and meditation: John 14–17, Psalm 22, and the Book of Lamentations.

GOOD FRIDAY

Today and tomorrow the Church takes on the Paschal Fast, the Easter Fast. This is a fast not of penance but of anticipation. We fast also from work and from all the usual distractions. Our minds and hearts grow hungry for God's Word. Our lives are filled with the mystery of Jesus' death and Resurrection and with how we ourselves take on that dying and rising, little by little becoming the image of Christ in this world. On Friday afternoon or evening, the parish community gathers to read the Passion, to pray, and to venerate the holy cross. These are prayers and songs of Good Friday.

Lord, Send Your Abundant Blessing

Lord, send your abundant blessing upon your people
who devoutly recall the death of your Son
in the sure hope of the Resurrection.
Grant us pardon; bring us comfort.
May our faith grow stronger
and our eternal salvation be assured.

We Worship You, Lord

We worship you, Lord,
we venerate your Cross,
we praise your Resurrection.
Through the Cross you brought joy to the world.

Holy Is God!

Holy is God!
Holy and strong!
Holy immortal One,
have mercy on us!

The Wood of the Cross

This is the wood of the Cross,
on which hung the Savior of the world.
Come, let us worship.

HOLY SATURDAY

The Paschal Fast begun on Thursday night continues today. The Church puts aside work and food to continue watching and praying. Some prayers for Holy Saturday are given here. The first text is from a centuries-old homily for Holy Saturday. The final prayer, next page, is for those who are to be baptized this night.

Ancient Homily for Holy Saturday

He has gone to search for our first parent, as for a lost sheep. Greatly desiring to visit those who live in darkness and in the shadow of death, he has gone to free from sorrow the captives Adam and Eve, he who is both God and the son of Eve. The Lord approached them bearing the Cross, the weapon that had won him the victory. At the sight of him Adam, the first man he had created, struck his breast in terror and cried out to everyone: "My Lord be with you all." Christ answered him: "And with your spirit." He took him by the hand and raised him up, saying, "Awake, O sleeper, and rise from the dead, and Christ will give you light."

Rise, let us leave this place. The enemy led you out of the earthly paradise. I will not restore you to that paradise, but I will enthrone you in heaven. I forbade you the tree that was only a symbol of life, but see, I who am life itself am now one with you. I appointed cherubim to guard you as slaves are guarded, but now I make them worship you as God. The throne formed by cherubim awaits you, its bearers swift and eager. The bridal chamber is adorned, the banquet is ready, the eternal dwelling places are prepared, the treasure houses of all good things lie open. The Kingdom of Heaven has been prepared for you from all eternity.

Baptism Prayer for Holy Saturday

O Christ,
you slept a life-giving sleep in the grave,
and did awaken humankind from the heavy sleep of sin.
All-powerful and ever-living God,
your only Son went down among the dead
and rose again in glory.
In your goodness raise up your faithful people
buried with him in Baptism,
to be one with him
in the eternal life of heaven.

Lord,
we pray to you for the elect,
who have now accepted for themselves
the loving purpose and the mysteries
that you revealed in the life of your Son.
May they have faith in their hearts
and accomplish your will in their lives.
We ask this through Christ our Lord.
R/. Amen.

THE EASTER VIGIL

Tonight, the Church gathers in the darkness and blesses a candle that symbolizes the Risen Christ, our Morning Star. We keep vigil, listening to the Scriptures unfold their stories of creation and freedom, their prophecies of God's bounty and love, their demand that we acknowledge our Baptism into the death of Christ. We sing the alleluia and listen to the Gospel of Jesus' Resurrection. Then the Church calls on all the saints and processes to the font. There, the elect reject evil and profess their faith in Father, Son, and Spirit. They are baptized and anointed with chrism. The whole Church rejoices. New Christians and old then join in the Eucharist. The texts below reflect various moments in the liturgy of this night.

Prayer for the Lighting of the Paschal Candle

May the light of Christ, rising in glory,
dispel the darkness of our hearts and minds.

Excerpts from the *Exsultet*

Rejoice, heavenly powers! Sing, choirs of angels!
Exult, all creation around God's throne!
Jesus Christ, our King, is risen!
Sound the trumpet of salvation!

Rejoice, O earth, in shining splendor,
radiant in the brightness of your King!
Christ has conquered! Glory fill you!
Darkness vanishes forever!

O happy fault, O necessary sin of Adam,
which gained for us so great a Redeemer!

The power of this holy night
dispels all evil, washes guilt away,
restores lost innocence, brings mourners joy;
it casts out hatred, brings us peace, and humbles earthy pride.

Night truly blessed when heaven is wedded to earth
and we are reconciled with God!

From the Blessing of Water

May all who are buried with Christ
in the death of Baptism
rise also with him to newness of life.

Easter Sunday and Easter Season

The Three Days of the Easter Triduum continue until the evening of Sunday. At the same time, the Church begins the Fifty Days of Easter, the time of rejoicing that ends on Pentecost. Here are songs and greetings for Easter Sunday and the Easter season.

This Is the Day the Lord Has Made

V/. This is the day the Lord has made;
R/. let us rejoice and be glad. Alleluia.

Christ Is Risen, Alleluia!

V/. Christ is risen, alleluia!
R/. Christ is truly risen, alleluia!

Easter Sequence: *Victimae Paschali Laudes*

Christians, to the Paschal Victim
    offer your thankful praises!
A Lamb the sheep redeems;
    Christ, who only is sinless,
    reconciles sinners to the Father.
Death and life have contended in that combat stupendous:
    the Prince of life, who died, reigns immortal.

Speak, Mary, declaring
   what you saw, wayfaring.
"The tomb of Christ, who is living,
   the glory of Jesus' Resurrection;
bright angels attesting,
   the shroud and napkin resting.
Yes, Christ my hope is arisen;
   to Galilee he goes before you."
Christ indeed from death is risen, our new life obtaining.
   Have mercy, victor King, ever reigning!
   Amen. Alleluia.

Blessing of Easter Foods

[1701]

The custom of blessing food for Easter arose from the discipline of fasting throughout Lent and the special Easter Fast during the Easter Triduum. Easter was the first day when meat, eggs, and other foods could again be eaten.

[1702]

According to custom, food may be blessed before or after the Easter Vigil on Holy Saturday or on Easter Sunday morning for consumption at the first meal of Easter, when fasting is ended and the Church is filled with joy.

[1708]

The leader greets those present in the following or other suitable words.

Before the Easter Vigil:

For our sake Christ became obedient, accepting even death, death on a Cross. Therefore God raised him on high and gave him the name above all other names. Blessed be God forever.
R/. Blessed be God forever.

After the Easter Vigil:

Christ is risen. Alleluia.
R/. He is risen indeed. Alleluia.

[1710]

One of those present or the leader reads a text of sacred Scripture: Deuteronomy 16:1–8—*The passover of the Lord*; or Isaiah 55:1–11—*Come all you who are thirsty*; or Luke 24:13–35—*They knew Christ in the breaking of the bread.*

[1716]

The leader says the prayer of blessing with hands joined.

God of glory,
the eyes of all turn to you
as we celebrate Christ's victory over sin and death.

Bless us and this food of our (first) Easter meal.
May we who gather at the Lord's table
continue to celebrate the joy of his Resurrection
and be admitted finally to his heavenly banquet.

Grant this through Christ our Lord.
R/. Amen.

—*From* Book of Blessings

The Chaplet of the Divine Mercy: Second Sunday of Easter (Divine Mercy Sunday)

You may wish to pray this chaplet today or on any Friday. To pray the chaplet, you use rosary beads. After making the sign of the cross, pray an Our Father, one Hail Mary, and the Apostles' Creed.

On the large bead before each decade pray the following:

Eternal Father, I offer You the Body and Blood, Soul and Divinity, of Your dearly beloved Son, our Lord Jesus Christ, in atonement for our sins and those of the whole world.

On the ten small beads of each decade:

For the sake of His sorrowful Passion, have mercy on us and on the whole world.

After five decades, pray the concluding doxology three times:

Holy God, Holy Mighty One, Holy Immortal One, have mercy on us and on the whole world.

Blessing of Homes During Eastertime

[1597]

The Easter season is a traditional time for the blessing of homes.

[1601]

When all have gathered, a suitable song may be sung. The leader makes the sign of the cross, and all reply, "Amen."

[1603]

The leader greets those present in the following words:

**Let us praise God, who fills our hearts and homes
with peace.
Blessed be God forever.
R/. Blessed be God forever.**

[1604]

In the following or similar words, the leader prepares those present for the blessing:

The Word became flesh and made his dwelling place among us. It is Christ, risen from the dead, who is our source of hope, joy, and comfort. May all who enter this home find Christ's light and love.

[1605]

One of those present or the leader reads a text of sacred Scripture, for example:

Listen to the words of the holy Gospel according
to Luke: 24:28–32

> As the disciples approached the village
> to which they were going, Jesus gave the
> impression that he was going on farther. But
> they urged him, "Stay with us, for it is nearly
> evening and the day is almost over." So he
> went in to stay with them. And it happened
> that, while he was with them at table, he took
> bread, said the blessing, broke it, and gave
> it to them. With that their eyes were opened
> and they recognized him, but he vanished
> from their sight. Then they said to each other,
> "Were not our hearts burning within us while
> he spoke to us on the way and opened the
> scriptures to us?"

[1610]

The intercessions are then said:

Leader: The Son of God made his home among us. With
thanks and praise let us call upon him.
R/. Stay with us, Lord.

Lord Jesus Christ, through you every dwelling is a temple
of holiness: build those who live in this house into the
dwelling place of God in the Holy Spirit. We pray: **R/.**

Lord Jesus Christ, the disciples recognized you in the
breaking of the bread: grant that the members of this family
may be open always to the presence of Christ in Word and
sacrament. We pray: **R/.**

Lord Jesus Christ, you appeared to the frightened Apostles
and said, "Peace be with you": grant that your abiding peace
may remain with the members of this family. We pray: **R/.**

[1611]

After the intercessions the leader invites all present to
say the Lord's Prayer.

[1612]

The leader says the prayer of blessing with hands joined:

Lord,
we rejoice in the victory of your Son over death:
by rising from the tomb to new life
he gives us new hope and promise.

Bless all the members of this household
and surround them with your protection,
that they may find comfort and peace
in Jesus Christ, the Paschal Lamb,
who lives and reigns with you and the Holy Spirit,
one God, forever and ever.
R/. Amen.

[1613]

The leader may sprinkle those present and the home with
holy water brought from the church. During the sprinkling
the leader may say:

Let this water call to mind our Baptism in Christ, who by his
death and Resurrection has redeemed us.

The leader concludes the rite by signing himself or herself
with the sign of the cross and saying:

May Christ Jesus dwell with us,
keep us from all harm,
and make us one in mind and heart,
now and forever.
R/. Amen.

The blessing may conclude with a suitable song.

—From Book of Blessings

Ascension Blessing over the People

May almighty God bless you on this day
when his only Son ascended into heaven
to prepare a place for you.

After his Resurrection, Christ was seen by his disciples.
When he appears as judge
may you be pleasing forever in his sight.

You believe that Jesus has taken his seat in majesty
at the right hand of the Father.
May you have the joy of experiencing
that he is also with you to the end of time.
according to his promise.

Pentecost Sequence: *Veni, Sancte Spiritus*

Come, Holy Spirit, come!
And from your celestial home
   shed a ray of light divine!
Come, Father of the poor!
Come, source of all our store!
   Come, within our bosoms shine.
You, of comforters the best;
you, the soul's most welcome guest;
   sweet refreshment here below;
in our labor, rest most sweet;
grateful coolness in the heat;
   solace in the midst of woe.
O most blessed light divine,
shine within these hearts of yours,
   and our inmost being fill!
Where you are not, we have naught,
nothing good in deed or thought,
   nothing free from taint of ill.
Heal our wounds, our strength renew;
on our dryness pour your dew;
   wash the stains of guilt away:
bend the stubborn heart and will;
melt the frozen, warm the chill;
   guide the steps that go astray.
On the faithful, who adore
and confess you, evermore
   in your sevenfold gift descend;
give them virtue's sure reward;
give them your salvation, Lord;
   give them joys that never end. Amen.
   Alleluia.

Feasts and Fasts of the Church

WEEK OF PRAYER FOR CHRISTIAN UNITY
(THIRD WEEK IN JANUARY)

See also the prayers in Part VI: Prayers for the Church and the World.

Prayer for Christian Unity

Let us pray
for all our brothers and sisters
who share our faith in Jesus Christ,
that God may gather and keep together in one Church
all those who seek the truth with sincerity.

Almighty and eternal God,
you keep together those you have united.
Look kindly on all who follow Jesus, your Son.
We are all consecrated to you by our common Baptism.
Make us one in the fullness of faith,
and keep us one in the fellowship of love.

We ask this through Christ our Lord.
R/. Amen.

CANDLEMAS
(FEBRUARY 2)

Receiving Blessed Candles at Home

On February 2, forty days after Christmas, the Church celebrates the Feast of the Presentation of the Lord (see Lk 2:22–40). Because it echoes the Christmas festival, this day is a celebration of light in darkness. Its Gospel tells of the old man Simeon's calling the infant Jesus a "light to the Gentiles and the glory of your people Israel."

For centuries, the Church has blessed candles on this day. Because of their simplicity and beauty, candles are used when the Church gathers for prayer, both in public places and in the home. Candles blessed at the Mass for this feast day may be brought into the home with the rite that follows. One or more of the candles is lighted; others are placed nearby. These candles are lighted at ordinary times (at dinner, for example) and at special times such as during the Anointing of the Sick or when Holy Communion is brought to a member of the family.

All make the sign of the cross. The leader begins:

Jesus Christ is the Light of the world,
a light no darkness can overpower.
Blessed be the name of the Lord.
R/. Now and forever.

The leader may use these or similar words to introduce the prayer:

These candles bring beauty and light to our home. In the darkness, they tell us of God's gift of light and of Christ, whose light we received at Baptism. As we bring these blessed candles into our home, we are reminded of our call to be the Light of the world.

Then the Scripture is read:

Listen to the words of the holy Gospel according to Luke: 2:25, 27–32

> There was a man in Jerusalem whose name was Simeon. This man was righteous and devout, awaiting the consolation of Israel, and the holy Spirit was upon him. . . . He came in the Spirit into the temple; and when the parents brought in the child Jesus to perform the custom of the law in regard to him, he took him into his arms and blessed God, saying:
>
> "Now, Master, you may let your servant go
>   in peace, according to your word,
> for my eyes have seen your salvation,
>   which you prepared in the sight of all the peoples:
> a light for revelation to the Gentiles,
>   and glory for your people Israel."

Reader: The Gospel of the Lord.
R/. Praise to you, Lord Jesus Christ.

After a time of silence, all hold lighted candles as the
leader continues:

Let us pray.
God of night and of day,
we praise you for the brightness of our sun,
for the softer light of the moon
and the splendor of the stars,
for the fires of earth that bring us light and warmth
even as they imperil all who use them.
By the great and small lights we mark our days and seasons,
we brighten the night and bring warmth to our winter,
and in these lights we see light:
Jesus, whose light we receive in Baptism,
whose light we carry by day and by night.

In the beauty of these candles,
keep us in quiet and in peace,
keep us safe and turn our hearts to you
that we may ourselves be light for our world.

All praise be yours through Christ,
the light of nations,
the glory of Israel,
forever and ever.
R/. Amen.

The leader says:

Let us bless the Lord.

All respond, making the sign of the cross:

Thanks be to God.

The service may conclude with song.

ST. PATRICK'S DAY
(MARCH 17)

St. Patrick's Breastplate

I bind to myself today
the strong virtue of the invocation of the Trinity:
I believe the Trinity in the Unity,
the Creator of the universe.

I bind to myself today
the virtue of the Incarnation of Christ with his Baptism,
the virtue of his crucifixion with his burial,
the virtue of his Resurrection with his Ascension,
the virtue of his coming on the Judgment Day.

I bind to myself today
the virtue of the love of seraphim,
in the obedience of angels,
in the hope of resurrection unto reward,
in prayers of patriarchs,
in predictions of prophets,
in preaching of apostles,
in faith of confessors,
in purity of holy virgins,
in deeds of righteous men.

(continued)

I bind to myself today
the power of heaven,
the light of the sun,
the brightness of the moon,
the splendor of fire,
the flashing of lightning,
the swiftness of wind,
the depth of sea,
the stability of earth,
the compactness of rocks.

I bind to myself today
God's power to guide me,
God's might to uphold me,
God's wisdom to teach me,
God's eye to watch over me,
God's ear to hear me,
God's word to give me speech,
God's hand to guide me,
God's way to lie before me,
God's shield to shelter me,
God's host to secure me,
against the snares of demons,
against the seductions of vices,
against the lusts of nature,
against everyone who meditates injury to me,
whether far or near,
whether few or with many.

I invoke today all these virtues
against every hostile merciless power
which may assail my body and my soul.

Christ, protect me today
against every poison, against burning,
against drowning, against death-wound,
that I may receive abundant reward.

Christ with me, Christ before me,
Christ behind me, Christ within me,
Christ beneath me, Christ above me,
Christ at my right, Christ at my left,
Christ in the fort,
Christ in the chariot seat,
Christ in the poop deck,
Christ in the heart of everyone who thinks of me,
Christ in the mouth of everyone who speaks to me,
Christ in every eye that sees me,
Christ in every ear that hears me.

I bind to myself today
the strong virtue of an invocation of the Trinity,
I believe the Trinity in the Unity,
the Creator of the universe.

SOLEMNITY OF ST. JOSEPH
(MARCH 19)

See also the Litany of St. Joseph, in Part VII: Litanies.

Blessing of St. Joseph's Table

[1679]

On the Solemnity of St. Joseph (March 19) it is the custom in some places to bless bread, pastries, and other food and give a large portion of it to the poor.

[1697]

All make the sign of the cross as the leader says:

Our help is in the name of the Lord.
R/. Who made heaven and earth.

[1698]

One of those present or the leader reads a text of sacred
Scripture, for example:

Listen to the words of the holy Gospel
according to Matthew: 1:18–23

> Now this is how the birth of Jesus Christ came
> about. When his mother Mary was betrothed
> to Joseph, but before they lived together, she
> was found with child through the holy Spirit.
> Joseph her husband, since he was a righteous

man, yet unwilling to expose her to shame,
decided to divorce her quietly. Such was his
intention when, behold, the angel of the Lord
appeared to him in a dream and said, "Joseph,
son of David, do not be afraid to take Mary
your wife into your home. For it is through the
holy Spirit that this child has been conceived
in her. She will bear a son and you are to name
him Jesus, because he will save his people from
their sins." All this took place to fulfill what the
Lord had said through the prophet:

"Behold, the virgin shall be with child and bear
a son, and they shall name him Emmanuel,"

which means "God is with us."

Or Matthew 13:54–58—*Is this not the carpenter's son?*

[1699]

[1700]

The leader says the prayer of blessing with the hands
joined:

All-provident God,
the good things that grace this table
remind us of your many good gifts.

Bless this food,
and may the prayers of St. Joseph,
who provided bread for your Son and food for the poor,
sustain us and all our brothers and sisters
on our journey towards your heavenly Kingdom.
We ask this through Christ our Lord.
R/. Amen.

—*From Book of Blessings*

ROGATION DAYS
(THREE DAYS BEFORE THE SOLEMNITY OF THE ASCENSION)

The Rogation Days were traditionally celebrated on the three days before the Solemnity of the Ascension. They may now be celebrated at any time when it is appropriate to ask that gardens, fields, and orchards be blessed during the coming season.

Blessing of Fields and Gardens

[966]

Through this rite the faithful express their grateful recognition of the blessings of God, who created the universe out of his inexpressible love and entrusted its care to human labor as the way of providing for common human needs.

[970]

All make the sign of the cross.

[972]

The leader begins:

Let us together praise the Lord, from whom we have rain from the heavens and abundance from the earth. Blessed be God now and forever.
R/. Amen.

In the following or similar words, the leader prepares
those present for the blessing:

Let us bless God, whose might has created the earth and
whose providence has enriched it. God has given us the
earth to cultivate, so that we may gather its fruits to
sustain life.

But as we thank God for his bounteousness, let us learn
also, as the Gospel teaches, to seek first his Kingship over
us, his way of holiness. Then all our needs will be given
us besides.

One of those present or the leader reads a text of sacred
Scripture:

Listen to the words of the
Book of Genesis: 1:1, 11–12, 29–31a

> In the beginning, when God created the
> heavens and the earth, . . . God said, "Let the
> earth bring forth vegetation: every kind of
> plant that bears seed and every kind of fruit
> tree on earth that bears fruit with its seed in
> it." And so it happened: the earth brought
> forth every kind of plant that bears seed and
> every kind of fruit tree on earth that bears fruit
> with its seed in it. God saw how good it was.
>   God also said: "See, I give you every seed-
> bearing plant all over the earth and every tree
> that has seed-bearing fruit on it to be your
> food; and to all the animals of the land, all the
> birds of the air, and all the living creatures that

crawl on the ground, I give all the green plants for food." And so it happened. God looked at everything he had made, and he found it very good. Evening came, and morning followed— the sixth day.

[976]

Or Matthew 6:25–34—*Learn a lesson from the way the wild flowers grow.*

Reader: The Word of the Lord.
R/. Thanks be to God.

[979]

The intercessions are then said:

Leader: The Lord and Father of us all, looking with benign providence on his children, gives them nourishment and growth by blessing the earth with the fruitfulness that sustains human life. As children of this heavenly Father, let us pray to him saying:
R/. Lord, hear our prayer.

You have told us that Christ is the vine and we are the branches; grant that by living in your Son we may produce much good fruit. For this we pray: **R/.**

You bless the earth and abundance flows in its pastures; grant that by your blessing our fields may yield the food we need. For this we pray: **R/.**

You make the wheat grow that provides our daily bread and the gift of the Eucharist; give us a crop made rich by abundant rain and fertile soil. For this we pray: **R/.**

The leader says the prayer of blessing with hands joined.

O God,
from the very beginning of time
you commanded the earth to bring forth vegetation
and fruit of every kind.
You provide the sower with seed and give bread to eat.
Grant, we pray, that this land,
enriched by your bounty and cultivated by human hands,
may be fertile with abundant crops.
Then your people, enriched by the gifts of your goodness,
will praise you unceasingly now and for ages unending.

We ask this through Christ our Lord.
R/. Amen.

The leader concludes the rite by signing himself or herself
with the sign of the cross and saying:

May God, the source of every good,
bless us and give success to our work,
that we may receive the joy of his gifts
and praise his name now and forever.
R/. Amen.

The blessing may conclude with a suitable song.

—From Book of Blessings

CORPUS CHRISTI: SOLEMNITY OF THE BODY AND BLOOD OF CHRIST
(SECOND SUNDAY AFTER PENTECOST)

On the Solemnity of the Body and Blood of Christ, we give special honor to Jesus, truly present in the most Blessed Sacrament of the altar. As Catholics, we worship the presence of Jesus Christ in the Eucharist, both during Mass and outside of Mass. We are encouraged to spend time in prayer before the Lord in the Eucharist. Many parishes offer regular exposition of the Blessed Sacrament in a monstrance. We may also choose to visit the church at other times to adore the Blessed Sacrament reserved in the tabernacle.

In his apostolic exhortation *The Sacrament of Charity*, Pope Benedict XVI observed that "the personal relationship which the individual believer establishes with Jesus present in the Eucharist constantly points beyond itself to the whole communion of the Church and nourishes a fuller sense of membership in the Body of Christ" (*Sacramentum Caritatis*, no. 68). It is, therefore, appropriate to hold in prayer the special needs of our community and our world. You may choose from the following groups of prayers, Scripture readings, and intercessions, interspersed with times of silence, for your time of prayer before the Blessed Sacrament.

A Holy Hour of Prayer for Life

PRAYERS

A

Lord Jesus Christ,
we worship you living among us
in the Sacrament of your Body and Blood.

May we offer to our Father in heaven
a solemn pledge of undivided love.
May we offer to our brothers and sisters
a life poured out in loving service of that Kingdom
where you live with the Father and the Holy Spirit,
one God, forever and ever.

Or:

B
Lord our God,
in this great Sacrament
we come into the presence of Jesus Christ, your Son,
born of the Virgin Mary
and crucified for our salvation.
May we who declare our faith in this fountain of love
  and mercy
drink from it the water of everlasting life.
We ask this through Christ our Lord.
R/. Amen.

SCRIPTURE READINGS

These or other appropriate readings may be read from
your Bible: Genesis 9:1–7; Psalm 139; John 6:51–58.

INTERCESSIONS

R/. Lord, hear our prayer.

That justice, truth, and a love for the gift of life might
inspire all legislators, governors, and our president, we pray
to the Lord: **R/.**

For all who do not embrace the rights of the unborn: that, in love, they may come to know the dignity of every person in the eyes of God, we pray to the Lord: **R/.**

For those preparing to receive the Sacrament of Marriage: that they might embrace their role as sharers in God's creative love, we pray to the Lord: **R/.**

For all who touch the lives of the condemned, the old, and the forgotten: that they might have compassion, respect, and appreciation for the dignity of all human life, we pray to the Lord: **R/.**

For the dying: that through the love, care, and devotion of others, they may know the beauty of life in their dying moments, we pray to the Lord: **R/.**

For all the victims of the culture of death: that like Lazarus, forgotten and poor, they may be welcomed into God's eternal peace, we pray to the Lord: **R/.**

Our Father . . .

CONCLUDING PRAYER

Lord Jesus Christ,
you gave us the Eucharist
as the memorial of your suffering and death.
May our worship of this Sacrament of your Body and Blood
help us to experience the salvation you won for us
and the peace of the Kingdom
where you live with the Father and the Holy Spirit,
one God, forever and ever.
R/. Amen.

A Holy Hour of Prayer for Vocations

PRAYERS

A

Lord Jesus Christ,
you promised always to give your Church shepherds.
In faith, we know your promise cannot fail.
Trusting in the power of the Holy Spirit at work in
    the Church,
we pray you raise up sacred ministers from your
    holy people,
that the Sacrifice in which you give your Body and Blood
may be daily renewed in the world until we come to
    that Kingdom
where you live with the Father and the Holy Spirit,
one God, forever and ever.

    Or:

B

Lord,
hear the prayers of your people
gathered here before you.
By this Sacrament of love
bring to maturity
the seeds you have sown
in the field of your Church;
may many of your people choose to serve you
by devoting themselves to the service of their brothers
    and sisters.
We ask this through Christ our Lord.
R/. Amen.

SCRIPTURE READINGS

These or other appropriate readings may be read from
your Bible: 1 Samuel 3:1–10; Psalm 16; John 1:35–42.

INTERCESSIONS

R/. Lord, hear our prayer.

As you called Abram to be the father of many nations,
inspire young people to answer your call. **R/.**

As you called Moses, tending the flocks of Jethro, provide
worthy pastors to your flock in our day. **R/.**

As you called Aaron to serve your temple, call men to serve
your Church in the image of Christ. **R/.**

As you spoke to awaken Samuel with your call, open the
ears of your chosen ones. **R/.**

As every High Priest was taken from among men, so call
men to offer the holy and living Sacrifice. **R/.**

As Elisha was anointed by the prophet Elijah, give those you
call strength to follow you without looking back. **R/.**

As you called the Apostles to be ambassadors for Christ, so
send us fervent preachers to strengthen our spirits. **R/.**

Our Father . . .

CONCLUDING PRAYER

Lord Jesus Christ,
we worship you living among us
in the Sacrament of your Body and Blood.
May we offer to our Father in heaven
a solemn pledge of undivided love.
May we offer our brothers and sisters
a life poured out in loving service of that Kingdom
where you live with the Father and the Holy Spirit,
one God, forever and ever.
R/. Amen.

A Holy Hour of Prayer for Peace

PRAYERS

A

Lord,
you give us the Body and Blood of your Son
and renew our strength.
Fill us with the spirit of love,
that we may work effectively to establish
Christ's farewell gift of peace.
We ask this through Christ our Lord.
R/. Amen.

Or:

B

Father,
you satisfy our hunger with one bread
that gives strength to mankind.

(continued)

Help us to overcome war and violence,
and to establish your law of love and justice.
We ask this through Christ our Lord.
R/. Amen.

SCRIPTURE READINGS

These or other appropriate readings may be read from
your Bible: James 3:13–18; Psalm 122; John 14:23–29.

INTERCESSIONS

R/. Lord, hear our prayer.

For Christians and all people of good will, may they never
lose hope in the possibility of peace, we pray to the Lord: **R/.**

For government leaders, may they hear and respond to their
peoples' plea for peace and justice, we pray to the Lord: **R/.**

For the young everywhere, may they grow in courage to
seek the peace God offers the world, we pray to the Lord: **R/.**

For those serving in the military, may the Lord guide them
and protect them, we pray to the Lord: **R/.**

For those who have died, especially those who have died in
war, may the Lord accept them into his loving presence, we
pray to the Lord: **R/.**

Our Father . . .

CONCLUDING PRAYER

Lord our God,
teach us to cherish in our hearts
the Paschal Mystery of your Son
by which you redeemed the world.
Watch over the gifts of grace
your love has given us
and bring them to fulfillment
in the glory of heaven.
We ask this through Christ our Lord.
R/. Amen.

ASSUMPTION DAY
(AUGUST 15)

On August 15, or another appropriate day, the produce of fields, gardens, and orchards may be blessed. Those who take part should assemble in an appropriate place around the grains, fruits, and vegetables to be blessed. A Blessing on the Occasion of Thanksgiving for the Harvest is found in Part V: Prayers for Catholic Living and may be used on this day.

MEMORIAL OF ST. FRANCIS
(OCTOBER 4)

On October 4, or another appropriate day, the household may join in the blessing of pets and other animals. The blessing takes place wherever the animals can be gathered.

Blessing of Animals

[946]

All make the sign of the cross.

[948]

The leader greets those present in the following words:

God has done all things wisely, let us praise his name, now and forever.
R/. Amen.

[949]

In the following or similar words, the leader prepares those present for the blessing.

The animals of God's creation inhabit the skies, the earth, and the sea. They share in the fortunes of human existence and have a part in human life. God, who confers his gifts on all living things, has often used the service of animals or made them symbolic reminders of the gifts of salvation. We therefore invoke the divine blessing on these animals through the intercession of St. Francis.

One of those present or the leader reads a text of sacred Scripture.

Listen to the words of the Book of Genesis: 1:1, 20–25

In the beginning, when God created the heavens and the earth, God said, "Let the water teem with an abundance of living creatures, and on the earth let birds fly beneath the dome of the sky." And so it happened: God created the great sea monsters and all kinds of swimming creatures with which the water teems, and all kinds of winged birds. God saw how good it was, and God blessed them, saying, "Be fertile, multiply, and fill the water of the seas; and let the birds multiply on the earth." Evening came and morning followed— the fifth day.

Then God said, "Let the earth bring forth all kinds of living creatures: cattle, creeping things, and wild animals of all kinds." And so it happened: God made all kinds of wild animals, all kinds of cattle, and all kinds of creeping things of the earth. God saw how good it was. Then God said, "Let us make man in our image, after our likeness. Let them have dominion over the fish of the sea, the birds of the air, and the cattle, and over all the wild animals and all the creatures that crawl on the ground."

(continued)

God created man in his image;
  in the image of God he created him;
  male and female he created them.

God blessed them, saying: "Be fertile and
multiply; fill the earth and subdue it. Have
dominion over the fish of the sea, the birds of
the air, and all the living things that move on
the earth."

[952]

Or Isaiah 11:6–10—*Animals will be tame and there shall
be no harm or ruin on all my holy mountain.*

Reader: The Word of the Lord.
R/. Thanks be to God.

[957]

The leader says the prayer of blessing with hands joined.

[958]

O God,
you have done all things wisely;
in your goodness you have made us in your image
and given us care over other living things.

Reach out with your right hand
and grant that these animals may serve our needs
and that your bounty in the resources of this life
may move us to seek more confidently
the goal of eternal life.

We ask this through Christ our Lord.
R/. Amen.

The leader concludes the rite by saying:

[960]

May God, who created the animals of this earth as
    a help to us,
continue to protect and sustain us
with the grace his blessing brings,
now and forever.
R/. Amen.

[961]

The blessing may conclude with a song.

—*From* Book of Blessings

ALL SAINTS DAY AND ALL SOULS DAY
(NOVEMBER 1, 2)

See also the Prayer for the Dead and other appropriate prayers in Part IV: Family Prayers from Birth to Death.

Visiting a Grave

Some or all of the following prayers and readings may be used when visiting the grave of a family member or friend. The month of November, especially All Saints Day and All Souls Day (Commemoration of the Faithful Departed), is a traditional time for visiting graves, as is the anniversary of death and, in many cultures, the Lunar New Year. Other appropriate prayers are on pages 161, 268, and 274.

All make the sign of the cross. The leader begins:

Praise be to God our Father, who raised Jesus Christ from the dead.
Blessed be God forever.
R/. Blessed be God forever.

One or more of the following Scripture texts may be read:

2 Corinthians 5:1

We know that if our earthly dwelling, a tent,
should be destroyed, we have a building from
God, a dwelling not made with hands, eternal
in heaven.

Romans 8:38–39

I am convinced that neither death, nor life, nor
angels, nor principalities, nor present things,
nor future things, nor powers, nor height,
nor depth, nor any other creature will be able
to separate us from the love of God in Christ
Jesus our Lord.

After a time of silence, all join in prayers of intercession,
or in one of the litanies (see Part VII: Litanies). All
then join hands for the Lord's Prayer. Then the leader
continues:

Lord God,
whose days are without end
and whose mercies beyond counting,
keep us mindful
that life is short and the hour of death unknown.
Let your Spirit guide our days on earth
in the ways of holiness and justice,
that we may serve you
in union with the whole Church,
sure in faith, strong in hope, perfected in love.
And when our earthly journey is ended,
lead us rejoicing into your Kingdom,
where you live forever and ever.
R/. Amen.

V/. Eternal rest grant unto them, O Lord,
R/. and let perpetual light shine upon them.
V/. May they rest in peace.
R/. Amen.
V/. May their souls and the souls of all the faithful departed,
through the mercy of God, rest in peace.
R/. Amen.

All make the sign of the cross as the leader concludes:

May the peace of God,
which is beyond all understanding,
keep our hearts and minds
in the knowledge and love of God
and of his Son, our Lord Jesus Christ.
R/. Amen.

MONTH OF NOVEMBER

During November, the Church celebrates the communion of saints, intercedes for those who have died, and prepares to welcome the one whom St. Francis called "Sister Death." These prayers are appropriate all through November. The Litany of the Saints may be found in Part VII: Litanies. Other appropriate prayers are on pages 268 and 274.

O Lord, Support Us All the Day Long

O Lord, support us all the day long,
until the shadows lengthen,
and the evening comes,
and the busy world is hushed,
and the fever of life is over,
and our work is done.

Then in your mercy,
grant us a safe lodging,
and a holy rest,
and peace at the last.

—*Cardinal John Henry Newman*

Psalm 103:1–2, 11–18

Bless the LORD, O my soul;
 and all my being, bless his holy name.
Bless the LORD, O my soul,
 and forget not all his benefits.

(*continued*)

For as the heavens are high above the earth,
  so surpassing is his kindness toward those who fear him.
As far as the east is from the west,
  so far has he put our transgressions from us.
As a father has compassion on his children,
  so the Lord has compassion on those who fear him,
For he knows how we are formed;
  he remembers that we are dust.
Man's days are like those of grass;
  like a flower of the field he blooms;
The wind sweeps over him and he is gone,
  and his place knows him no more.
But the kindness of the Lord is from eternity
  to eternity toward those who fear him,
And his justice toward children's children
  among those who keep his covenant
  and remember to fulfill his precepts.

I Know That My Redeemer Lives

The following verses may be sung to any appropriate tune
such as "The Old Hundredth" ("Praise God from Whom
All Blessings Flow"):

I know that my Redeemer lives,
and on that final day of days,
his voice shall bid me rise again:
unending joy, unceasing praise!

This hope I cherish in my heart:
to stand on earth, my flesh restored,
and, not a stranger but a friend,
behold my Savior and my Lord.

IMMACULATE CONCEPTION
(DECEMBER 8)

See an appropriate Immaculate Conception prayer and other prayers to Mary in Part I: Basic Prayers.

FEAST OF OUR LADY
OF GUADALUPE
(DECEMBER 12)

Prayer to Our Lady of Guadalupe

God of power and mercy,
you blessed the Americas at Tepeyac
with the presence of the Virgin Mary of Guadalupe.
May her prayers help all men and women
to accept each other as brothers and sisters.
Through your justice present in our hearts
may your peace reign in the world.

We ask this through our Lord Jesus Christ, your Son,
who lives and reigns with you and the Holy Spirit,
one God, forever and ever.
R/. Amen.

EMBER DAYS

For many centuries, the Church kept three days (Wednesday, Friday, and Saturday) near the beginning of each season as times of special penance and intercession. Ember days are not part of the present calendar, but local churches may set aside appropriate days for fasting, works of charity, and prayer. Households may wish to observe seasonal penitential days that focus on sins that are all too prevalent in the contemporary world.

On such days, the members of the family may wish to offer their prayer, fasting, and almsgiving in reparation for their own sins and the sins of the world. On these days, we turn our attention to our dependence on God, who alone fulfills our hungers and brings healing to a wounded world.

The following psalm may be used on any of the ember days, either as part of morning prayer or at table.

Psalm 102:2–5, 13

O LORD, hear my prayer,
    and let my cry come to you.
Hide not your face from me
    in the day of my distress.
Incline your ear to me;
    in the day when I call, answer me speedily.
For my days vanish like smoke,
    and my bones burn like fire.
Withered and dried up like grass is my heart;
    I forget to eat my bread.

But you, O LORD, abide forever,
    and your name through all generations.

Winter: Reparation for Sins Against Life

January 22: The Anniversary of Roe v. Wade. In the United States, this day is observed as a particular day of penance for violations to the dignity of the human person committed through acts of abortion, and of prayer for the full restoration of the legal guarantee of the right to life. (Additional prayers for this observance may be found in this Part [see the Holy Hour for Life] and in Part VI: Prayers for the Church and the World [Prayers for a Culture of Life].)

A
Heavenly Father,
your holiness, revealed in Jesus,
challenges us to renounce violence,
to forsake revenge,
and to love without discrimination, without measure.

Teach us the surpassing truth of the Gospel,
which puts worldly wisdom to shame,
that we may recognize as one with us
even our enemies and persecutors
and see all people as your children.
We ask this through Christ our Lord.
R/. Amen.

B
God our Creator,
guardian of our homes and source of all blessings,
your Son, begotten before the dawn of creation,
entered the human family
and was entrusted to the care of Mary and Joseph.

(continued)

Confirm in us a reverence
for the gift and mystery of life,
so that parents and children,
like the Holy Family of Nazareth,
may cherish one another and be heartened by your love.

We ask this through Christ our Lord.
R/. Amen.

Spring: Reparation for Sins of Hatred and Prejudice

Yom HaShoah: Twelve Days After Passover. This day remembers the six million Jews and others who perished in the Holocaust (the *Shoah*). This systematic effort to exterminate an entire people, not for what they had done nor for any threat they posed, but simply for being who they were—whether young or old; every last man, woman, and child—is an attempt at evil on a nearly unimaginable scale. The *Shoah* raises in a most awful way the darkest questions that the mystery of evil has put to the human family in our time.

A
God of our fathers,
you chose Abraham and his descendants
to bring your Name to the Nations:
we are deeply saddened by the behavior of those
who in the course of history

have caused these children of yours to suffer,
and asking your forgiveness we wish to commit ourselves
to genuine brotherhood
with the people of the Covenant.
We ask this through Christ our Lord.
R/. Amen.

*—Prayer of Pope John Paul II at the Western Wall of
the Temple in Jerusalem, March 26, 2000*

B

In the sight of this evil, words fail;
   in the end, there can only be a dread silence—
A silence which is itself a heartfelt cry to God:
   Why, Lord, did you remain silent?
   How could you tolerate all this?

In silence, then, we bow our heads
   before the endless line of those who suffered and
      were put to death;
We beg for forgiveness and reconciliation
   and that God may never let this happen again.

God of compassion,
draw men and women to conversion
and help them to see that violence does not bring peace.

*—Adapted from a speech by Pope Benedict XVI at
Auschwitz, May 28, 2006*

C

PSALM 44:14, 23–27

You made us the reproach of our neighbors,
   the mockery and the scorn of those around us.
Yet for your sake we are being slain all the day:
   we are looked upon as sheep to be slaughtered.

(continued)

Awake! Why are you asleep, O Lᴏʀᴅ?
  Arise! Cast us not off forever!
Why do you hide your face,
  forgetting our woe and our oppression?
For our souls are bowed down to the dust,
  our bodies pressed to the earth.
Arise, help us!
  Redeem us for your kindness.

Summer: Reparation for Sins of Violence

Anniversaries of the Bombings of Hiroshima and Nagasaki: August 6 and August 9. In 1945, the United States dropped atomic bombs on the cities of Hiroshima and Nagasaki, Japan. The effects were devastating and long-lasting. By observing these two days with fasting and prayer, we express sorrow for this event and pray for an end to all violence and the coming of a Kingdom of justice and peace.

Above the clamor of our violence
your Word of truth resounds,
O God of majesty and power.
Over nations enshrouded in despair
your justice dawns.

Grant your household
a discerning spirit and a watchful eye
to perceive the hour in which we live.
Hasten the advent of that day
when the weapons of war shall be banished,
our deeds of darkness cast off,
and all your scattered children gathered into one.

We ask this through him whose coming is certain,
whose Day draws near:
your Son, our Lord Jesus Christ,
who lives and reigns with you and the Holy Spirit,
one God, forever and ever.
R/. Amen.

Autumn: Reparations for Sins Against the Poor

The Weekdays Before Thanksgiving. The Thanksgiving holiday is
associated with special efforts for the hungry and for economic justice.
As we give thanks for God's abundant blessings, we remember those who
have little. Our consciousness of the great inequality that pervades the
world, and of how we are to give thanks in such a world, would grow
if these days before Thanksgiving were set aside for deeds of charity, for
penance, and for prayer.

Almighty God,
to you belongs the sea, for you made it,
and the dry land shaped by your hand.
We hold the riches of the universe only in trust.

Make us honest stewards of your creation,
careful of the good earth you have given us,
compassionate and just in sharing its bounty
with the whole human family.
We ask this through Christ our Lord.
R/. Amen.

ON FRIDAY

In memory of Christ's suffering and death, the Church prescribes making each Friday throughout the year a penitential day. All of us are urged to prepare appropriately for that weekly Easter that comes with each Sunday.

Penitential practices take many forms: apologizing to an injured party, healing divisions within our families, fasting, graciously accepting the menial tasks of life, or performing some work of mercy. The purpose of penance is not to diminish life but to enrich it. For Christians, suffering and joy are not incompatible.

One or more of the following prayers may be used on Friday morning or at Friday dinner.

Isaiah 58:6–7, 9–10

This, rather, is the fasting that I wish:
    releasing those bound unjustly,
    untying the thongs of the yoke;
Setting free the oppressed,
    breaking every yoke;
Sharing your bread with the hungry,
    sheltering the oppressed and the homeless;
Clothing the naked when you see them,
    and not turning your back on your own.

If you remove from your midst oppression,
    false accusation and malicious speech;
If you bestow your bread on the hungry
    and satisfy the afflicted;
Then light shall rise for you in the darkness,
    and the gloom shall become for you like midday.

We Ask Your Forgiveness

Lord Jesus Christ,
you died on the Cross
for the salvation of the world.
We ask your forgiveness for the sins of our past
and your protection from all future evil.
Bring us to the peace and joy of that Kingdom
where you live forever and ever.

We Offer Ourselves

God our Father,
you brought salvation to all human beings
through the suffering of Christ, your Son.
May we strive to offer ourselves to you as a living sacrifice
and be filled with the abundance of your love.
We ask this through Christ our Lord.
R/. Amen.

National Holidays

Presidents' Day (Third Monday in February)

Almighty and eternal God,
you have revealed your glory to all nations.
God of power and might, wisdom and justice,
through you authority is rightly administered,
laws are enacted, and judgment is decreed.

Assist with your spirit of counsel and fortitude
the president of these United States,
that his/her administration
may be conducted in righteousness,
and be eminently useful to your people
over whom he/she presides.
May he/she encourage due respect for virtue and religion.
May he/she execute the laws with justice and mercy.
May he/she seek to restrain crime, vice, and immorality.

We, likewise, commend to your unbounded mercy
all who dwell in the United States.
Bless us and all people with the peace
which the world cannot give.
We pray to you, who are Lord and God, forever and ever.
R/. Amen.

—*Archbishop John Carroll*

Mother's Day (Second Sunday in May)

The following prayer may be used prior to the Grace Before Meals or at the conclusion of dinner.

All may stretch out their hands over the mother(s) in a gesture of blessing.

May God,
the source of life,
give you joy in the love, growth,
and holiness of your children.
R/. Amen.

The following prayer may also be appropriate:

Loving God,
as a mother gives life and nourishment to her children,
so you watch over your Church.
Bless our mother.
Let the example of her faith and love shine forth.
Grant that we, her family,
may honor her always
with a spirit of profound respect.
Grant this through Christ our Lord.
R/. Amen.

Memorial Day (Last Monday in May)

God of power and mercy,
you destroy war and put down earthly pride.
Banish violence from our midst and wipe away our tears,
that we may all deserve to be called your sons
    and daughters.
Keep in your mercy those men and women
who have died in the cause of freedom
and bring them safely
into your kingdom of justice and peace.
We ask this through Jesus Christ our Lord.
R/. Amen.

Father's Day (Third Sunday in June)

The following prayer may be used prior to the Grace Before Meals or at the conclusion of dinner.

All may stretch out their hands over the father(s) in a gesture of blessing.

May God, who gives life on earth and in heaven,
lead you to walk by the light of faith
and so help your children attain the good things
Christ has promised us.
R/. Amen.

The following prayer may also be appropriate:

God our Father,
in your wisdom and love you made all things.
Bless our father.
Let the example of his faith and love shine forth.
Grant that we, his family,
may honor him always
with a spirit of profound respect.
Grant this through Christ our Lord.
R/. Amen.

Independence Day (July 4)

God, source of all freedom,
this day is bright with the memory
of those who declared that life and liberty
are your gift to every human being.
Help us to continue a good work begun long ago.
Make our vision clear and our will strong:
that only in human solidarity will we find liberty,
and justice only in the honor that belongs
to every life on earth.
Turn our hearts toward the family of nations:
to understand the ways of others,
to offer friendship,
and to find safety only in the common good of all.
We ask this through Christ our Lord.
R/. Amen.

Labor Day (First Monday in September)

God our Creator,
we are the work of your hands.
Guide us in our work,
that we may do it, not for self alone,
but for the common good.
Make us alert to injustice,
ready to stand in solidarity,
that there may be dignity for all
in labor and in labor's reward.
Grant this through Christ our Lord.
R/. Amen.

V/. Joseph, patron of laborers,
R/. pray for us.

Thanksgiving Day (Fourth Thursday in November)

When all have gathered at table, the following prayer and song may be used. An extended table blessing follows on the next page.

Lord, we thank you
for the goodness of our people
and for the spirit of justice
that fills this nation.
We thank you for the beauty and fullness of the
land and the challenge of the cities.

We thank you for our work and our rest,
for one another, and for our homes.
We thank you, Lord:
accept our thanksgiving on this day.
We pray and give thanks through Jesus Christ our Lord.
R/. Amen.

> An appropriate song such as "Now Thank We All Our God" (page 60) may then be sung.

EXTENDED THANKSGIVING TABLE BLESSING

On Thanksgiving Day, families and friends gather to give thanks to God for the many blessings we have received. In sharing our abundance, it is most fitting to remember those who do not have the basic necessities of life.

> When all have gathered at table, they make the sign of the cross.

Leader: God has filled us with every good thing.
R/. Blessed be the name of the Lord.

> Then the Scripture is read:

Listen to the words of the Letter of St. Paul
to the Colossians: 3:12–17

> Brothers and sisters:
> Put on, as God's chosen ones, holy and
> beloved, heartfelt compassion, kindness,
> humility, gentleness, and patience, bearing
> with one another and forgiving one another,
> if one has a grievance against another; as the
> Lord has forgiven you, so must you also do.
> And over all these put on love, that is, the
> bond of perfection. And let the peace of Christ
> control your hearts, the peace into which you
> were also called in one Body. And be thankful.
> Let the word of Christ dwell in you richly, as
> in all wisdom you teach and admonish one
> another, singing psalms, hymns, and spiritual
> songs with gratitude in your hearts to God.
> And whatever you do, in word or in deed,
> do everything in the name of the Lord Jesus,
> giving thanks to God the Father through him.

(The family's Bible may be used for an alternate reading such as 1 Corinthians 1:3–9.)

Reader: The Word of the Lord.
R/. Thanks be to God.

After a time of silence, the leader prays:

Lord, we thank you
for the goodness of our people
and for the spirit of justice
that fills this nation.
We thank you for the beauty and fullness of the land
and the challenge of the cities.
We thank you for our work and our rest,
for one another, and for our homes.
We thank you, Lord:

(Pause for those gathered to offer their prayers of thanksgiving.)

For all that we have spoken
and for all that we keep in our hearts,
accept our thanksgiving on this day.

Keep us ever mindful of those who lack the necessities of life
and make us generous in sharing all that we have.

We pray and give thanks through Jesus Christ our Lord.
R/. Amen.

All make the sign of the cross as the leader concludes:

May God bless the food and friendship that we share
and fill our hearts with gratitude and generous love.
R/. Amen.

PART IV
FAMILY PRAYERS
FROM BIRTH
TO DEATH

FAMILY PRAYERS
FROM BIRTH
TO DEATH

*T*he *Christian family is* . . . where God's children learn to pray 'as the Church' and to persevere in prayer" (*Catechism of the Catholic Church*, no. 2685). In addition to the prayer that frames each day, this section offers special blessings and prayers for important moments in the life of a family. Whether in times of joy or times of grief, God is always with us.

General Blessing for a Family or Household

[42]

The celebration of the blessing provided here is a suitable means of fostering the Christian life in the members of a family.

[46]

All make the sign of the cross.

[48]

The leader greets those present in the following words:

**The grace of our Lord Jesus Christ be with us all,
now and forever.
R/. Amen.**

[49]

In the following or similar words, the leader prepares those present for the blessing:

From the Sacrament of Marriage the family has received newness of life and the grace of Christ. The family is specially important to the Church and to civil society, for it is the primary life-giving community.

In our celebration today we call down the Lord's blessing upon you (us), so that you (we) may continually be instruments of God's grace to one another and witnesses to faith in all the circumstances of life.

With God as our help you (we) fulfill your (our) mission by conforming your (our) entire life to the Gospel and so witness to Christ before the world.

One of those present or the leader reads a text of sacred Scripture.

Listen to the words of the First Letter of St. Paul to the Corinthians: 12:12–14

> As a body is one though it has many parts, and all the parts of the body, though many, are one body, so also Christ. For in one Spirit we were all baptized into one body, whether Jews or Greeks, slaves or free persons, and we were all given to drink of one Spirit.
> Now the body is not a single part, but many.

Or Ephesians 4:1–6—*Bear with one another lovingly*;
Romans 12:4–16—*Love each other with mutual affection*.

Reader: The Word of the Lord.
R/. Thanks be to God.

The intercessions are then said.

Leader: Christ the Lord, the Word coeternal with the Father, lived among us and chose to be part of a family and to enrich it with his blessings. Let us humbly ask his favor and protection on this family.
R/. Lord, keep our family in your peace.

Through your own obedience to Mary and Joseph you consecrated family life; make this family holy by your presence. For this we pray: **R/.**

You made your own family the model of prayer, of love, and of obedience to your Father's will; by your grace make this family holy and make it rich with your gifts. For this we pray: **R/.**

[56]

After the intercessions the leader invites all present to say the Lord's Prayer.

[57]

The leader says the prayer of blessing with hands joined:

O God,
you have created us in love and saved us in mercy,
and through the bond of marriage
you have established the family
and willed that it should become a sign
of Christ's love for his Church.

Shower your blessings on this family
gathered here in your name.
Enable those who are joined by one love
to support one another
by their fervor of spirit and devotion to prayer.
Make them responsive to the needs of others
and witnesses to the faith in all they say and do.
We ask this through Christ our Lord.
R/. Amen.

[59]

The leader may sprinkle all with holy water brought home from the church.

[60]

The leader concludes by saying:

May the Lord Jesus,
who lived with his Holy Family in Nazareth,
dwell also with your (our) family,
keep it from all evil,
and make all of you (us) one in heart and mind.
R/. Amen.

[61]

The blessing may conclude with singing "Now Thank We All Our God" (page 60) or another appropriate song.

—From Book of Blessings

Prayers and Blessings for Family Members

Prayer for Families

We bless your name, O Lord,
for sending your own incarnate Son,
to become part of a family,
so that, as he lived its life,
he would experience its worries and its joys.

We ask you, Lord,
to protect and watch over this family,
so that in the strength of your grace
its members may enjoy prosperity,
possess the priceless gift of your peace,
and, as the Church alive in the home,
bear witness in this world to your glory.
We ask this through Christ our Lord.
R/. Amen.

Prayer for Mothers

Loving God,
as a mother gives life and nourishment to her children,
so you watch over your Church.
Bless our mother.

Let the example of her faith and love shine forth.
Grant that we, her family,
may honor her always
with a spirit of profound respect.
Grant this through Christ our Lord.
R/. Amen.

Prayer for Fathers

God, you are the giver of all life,
human and divine.
Bless our father.
May he be the best of teachers for his children,
bearing witness to the faith
by what he says and does,
in Christ Jesus our Lord.
R/. Amen.

Prayers for Children

PRAYER FOR BAPTIZED CHILDREN

[151]

Lord Jesus Christ,
you loved children so much that you said:
"Whoever welcomes a child welcomes me."

Hear our prayers and, with your unfailing protection,
watch over these children (this child)
whom you have blessed with the grace of Baptism.

(continued)

When they (he/she) have (has) grown to maturity,
grant that they (he/she) will confess your name in
willing faith,
be fervent in charity,
and persevere courageously in the hope of reaching
your Kingdom,
where you live and reign forever and ever.
R/. Amen.

At the conclusion of the prayer, the parents, godparents,
grandparents, etc., may trace the sign of the cross on each
child's forehead.

PRAYER FOR A CHILD NOT YET BAPTIZED

[166]

All-powerful God and Father,
you are the source of all blessings, the protector of infants,
whose gift of children enriches and brightens a marriage.
Look with favor on this child
and, when he/she is reborn of water and the Holy Spirit,
bring him/her into your own spiritual family, the Church,
there to become a sharer in your Kingdom
and with us to bless your name forever.
We ask this through Christ our Lord.
R/. Amen.

At the conclusion of the prayer, the parents, godparents-
to-be, grandparents, etc., may trace the sign of the cross
on each child's forehead.

—From Book of Blessings

Blessing of Grandparents

This blessing may be used at special family visits (such as for holidays), at the beginning or end of a visit, or at another appropriate time. If possible, the oldest grandchild might serve as the leader.

When the grandparents, parents, and children have gathered, all make the sign of the cross.

Leader: Blessed be God, who is faithful through all generations.
R/. Blessed be God forever.

The leader introduces the blessing in these or similar words:

Grandparents are cherished members of our family. They bring gifts of wisdom, experience, and love and share with us their life of faith. We thank God for their example and ask that he bless them with happiness and good health.

Then the Scripture is read:

Listen to the words of Psalm 128:

> Happy are you who fear the Lord,
>   who walk in his ways!
> For you shall eat the fruit of your handiwork;
>   happy shall you be, and favored.
> Your wife shall be like a fruitful vine
>   in the recesses of your home;
> Your children like olive plants
>   around your table.

(continued)

Behold, thus is the man blessed
    who fears the Lord.
The Lord bless you from Zion:
    may you see the prosperity of Jerusalem
    all the days of your life.
May you see your children's children.
    Peace be upon Israel!

(The family Bible may be used for an alternate reading,
such as Ezekiel 37:24b–27.)

Reader: The Word of the Lord.
R/. Thanks be to God.

After a time of silence, all join in prayers of intercession
and in the Lord's Prayer. Then the leader prays:

Lord God almighty,
bless our grandparents with long life, happiness, and health.
May they remain constant in your love
and be living signs of your presence
to their children and grandchildren.
We ask this through Christ our Lord.
R/. Amen.

All make the sign of the cross as the leader concludes:

May God bless us and keep us
all the days of our lives.
R/. Amen.

Blessing on Birthdays

[323]

It is always appropriate to give thanks to God, but especially so on the occasion of a birthday. The birthday celebration provides an opportunity for acknowledging and giving thanks to God as the author and giver of life.

[324]

A birthday is also an appropriate occasion for children to express love and thanks to their parents, who have shared the gift of life and love with them.

[340]

All make the sign of the cross as the leader says:

Blessed be the name of the Lord.
R/. Now and forever.

[341]

One of those present or the leader reads a text of sacred Scripture, for example:

[342]

Listen to the words of the First Letter of Paul
to the Thessalonians: 3:9–11

> What thanksgiving, then, can we render to
> God for you, for all the joy we feel on your
> account before our God? Night and day we
> pray beyond measure to see you in person and

(continued)

to remedy the deficiencies of your faith. Now
may God himself, our Father, and our Lord
Jesus direct our way to you.

Reader: The Word of the Lord.
R/. Thanks be to God.

[341–342]

Or Philippians 1:3–11—*Thanks be to God*;
Matthew 5:1–12—*The beatitudes.*

[343]

The leader says the prayer of blessing with hands joined.

God of all creation,
we offer you grateful praise for the gift of life.
Hear the prayers of N., your servant,
who recalls today the gift of his/her birth
and rejoices in your gifts of life and love, family and friends.

Bless him/her with your presence
and surround him/her with your love
that he/she may enjoy many happy years,
all of them pleasing to you.

We ask this through Christ our Lord.
R/. Amen.

Or, for children:

Loving God,
you created all the people of the world,
and you know each of us by name.
We thank you for N.,
who celebrates his/her birthday.

Bless him/her with your love and friendship
that he/she may grow in wisdom, knowledge, and grace.
May he/she love his/her family always
and be ever faithful to his/her friends.
Grant this through Christ our Lord.
R/. Amen.

—*From Book of Blessings*

The blessing may conclude with a suitable song, such as
the following:

O God, our help in ages past,
our hope for years to come,
our shelter from the stormy blast,
and our eternal home.
Before the hills in order stood,
or earth received its frame,
from everlasting you are God,
to endless years the same.

—*Isaac Watts*

BLESSINGS FOR THE HOUSEHOLD

Blessing for New Beginnings

When someone in the household is ready to begin some new undertaking, the family may bless the person by placing hands on the person's head and saying this prayer.

May the Lord bless you and keep you.
R/. Amen.

May the Lord's face shine upon you,
and be gracious to you.
R/. Amen.

May the Lord look upon you with kindness,
and give you peace.
R/. Amen.

Prayer for Safety

Strong and faithful God,
keep our son/daughter safe from injury and harm
and make him/her a blessing to all he/she meets today.
R/. Amen.

Prayer for Strength

God,
we pray for our young people,
growing up in an unsteady and confusing world.
Show them that your ways give more life
than the ways of the world,
and that following you is better
than chasing after selfish goals.
Help them to take failure,
not as a measure of their worth,
but as a chance for a new start.
Give them strength to hold their faith in you,
and to keep alive their joy in your creation.
We ask this through Christ our Lord.
R/. Amen.

Prayers for Times of Trouble

When there is difficulty in the life of the family or one of its members,
one of the following prayers may be prayed at table or at bedside. At
times, parents may pray these prayers silently for an older child.

A
Praised be God, the Father of our Lord Jesus Christ,
the Father of mercies and the God of all consolation,
who comforts us in all our afflictions.

B

May God, the source of all patience and encouragement,
enable us to live in perfect harmony with one another
according to the spirit of Christ Jesus.
R/. Amen.

C

May the Lord make us overflow with love for one another
and for all.
May God strengthen our hearts.
R/. Amen.

D

God of all our days:
like a parent you forgive us,
and like a child you love us.
May we love and forgive one another.

Blessing of Those Who Are Homebound

Those who are confined at home or in a nursing home need their brothers and sisters in Christ to help them feel that they are still part of the family and the ecclesial community. This blessing is a mark of respect, affection, and solidarity from the Christian community. It may be used when visiting someone who is homebound, at the beginning or end of a visit to a nursing home, or when carrying the Holy Eucharist to someone who is homebound.

When the household and visitors have gathered, all make the sign of the cross.

Leader: Blessed be God now and forever.
R/. Amen.

The leader introduces the blessing in these or similar words:

People who are ill or homebound share in Christ's suffering in a special way. Each day, they must take up their cross and follow Jesus. Let us join them in asking God to keep their hopes high and strengthen their trust in him.

Then the Scripture is read:

Listen to the words of the Second Letter of Paul
to the Corinthians: 4:10–18

> Brothers and sisters:
>   We always carry about in the body the
> dying of Jesus, so that the life of Jesus may
> also be manifested in our body. For we who
> live are constantly being given up to death for

the sake of Jesus, so that the life of Jesus may be manifested in our mortal flesh.

So death is at work in us, but life in you. Since, then, we have the same spirit of faith, according to what is written, "I believed, therefore I spoke," we too believe and therefore we speak, knowing that the one who raised the Lord Jesus will raise us also with Jesus and place us with you in his presence. Everything indeed is for you, so that the grace bestowed in abundance on more and more people may cause the thanksgiving to overflow for the glory of God.

Therefore, we are not discouraged; rather, although our outer self is wasting away, our inner self is being renewed day by day. For this momentary light affliction is producing for us an eternal weight of glory beyond all comparison, as we look not to what is seen but to what is unseen; for what is seen is transitory, but what is unseen is eternal.

(The family's Bible may be used for an alternate reading such as Isaiah 53:1-5, 10-11.)

Reader: The Word of the Lord.
R/. Thanks be to God.

After a time of silence, all join in prayers of intercession and in the Lord's Prayer. Then the leader invites:

Let us pray for God's blessing upon our brother(s)/sister(s) who are homebound.

After a short silence, the leader prays, with hands joined:

[357]

Lord, our God,
you have given these your faithful
the grace to maintain their hope in you
through all life's changes
and to taste and see your goodness.
We bless you for the gifts you have showered on them.
We ask that they may find joy in a renewed strength
    of spirit,
that they may have good health,
and that they may inspire us by the example of their
    serene way of life.

We ask this through Christ our Lord.
R/. Amen.

[358]

Or:

All-powerful and ever-living God,
in whom we live and move and have our being,
we thank you and praise you
for N. and N. (or: the members of this community).

(continued)

Grant that they may have the loving support of their friends
    and relatives,
that in good health they may be cheerful,
and in poor health not lose hope.
Sustained by the help of your blessing,
let them spend their days giving praise to your name.

We ask this through Christ our Lord.
R/. Amen.

[361]

All make the sign of the cross as the leader concludes:

May the Lord bless us,
protect us from all evil,
and bring us to everlasting life.
R/. Amen.

—From Book of Blessings

MOVING INTO
AND OUT OF A HOME

Prayer Before Moving from a Home

When a family is about to leave a house or apartment where they have lived, they may wish to mark the departure with thanksgiving and intercession. The prayer may begin by walking together through the rooms and speaking of the life lived in each. Then all gather before a cross or icon that is still in place.

All make the sign of the cross. The leader begins:

Blessed be the Lord,
a merciful and gracious God,
rich in kindness and fidelity.
Blessed be God forever.
R/. Blessed be God forever.

The leader may use these or similar words to introduce the prayer:

As we leave this home, we give thanks to God for all the blessings found here. We ask forgiveness for the wrong we have done one another. Let us pray now that God will guide us on our way.

Psalm 23 or Psalm 121 may be read by one or by all together. Then all may join in prayers of thanksgiving and intercession and in the Lord's Prayer. The leader then speaks the closing prayer:

Lord our God,
you called your servant Abraham
to go forth from his home to a new land.
As we go forth from this home,
we ask you to be with us on the journey
and to stay with us always
for, apart from your love,
we can never be at home.
R/. Amen.

The cross or icon is taken from its place and all reverence it with a kiss. All then make the sign of the cross as the leader concludes:

Let us bless the Lord.
R/. Thanks be to God.

Blessing When Moving into a New Home

[660]

Moving into a new home provides a special opportunity for a gathering of members of the community to mark the joyful event and to thank God, from whom all blessings come, for the gift of a new home.

[664]

All make the sign of the cross.

[666]

The leader greets those present in the following words:

May the God whom we glorify with one heart and voice enable us, through the Spirit, to live in harmony as followers of Christ Jesus, now and forever.
R/. Amen.

[667]

In the following or similar words, the leader prepares those present for the blessing:

When Christ took flesh through the Blessed Virgin Mary, he made his home with us. Let us now pray that he will enter this home and bless it with his presence. May he always be here among you (us); may he nurture your (our) love for each other, share in your (our) joys, comfort you (us) in your (our) sorrows. Inspired by his teachings and example, (let us) seek to make your (our) new home before all else a dwelling place of love, diffusing far and wide the goodness of Christ.

[668]

One of those present or the leader reads a text of sacred
Scripture.

[669]

Listen to the words of the holy Gospel
according to Luke: 10:38–42

> As they continued their journey [Jesus] entered
> a village where a woman whose name was
> Martha welcomed him. She had a sister named
> Mary [who] sat beside the Lord at his feet
> listening to him speak. Martha, burdened with
> much serving, came to him and said, "Lord,
> do you not care that my sister has left me by
> myself to do the serving? Tell her to help me."
> The Lord said to her in reply, "Martha, Martha,
> you are anxious and worried about many
> things. There is need of only one thing. Mary
> has chosen the better part and it will not be
> taken from her."

[668–669]

Or Mark 1:29–30—*Jesus went straight to Simon's house*;
Luke 10:5–9—*Peace to this house.*

Reader: The Gospel of the Lord.
R/. Praise to you, Lord Jesus Christ.

The intercessions are then said.

Leader: The Son of God, Lord of heaven and earth, made his home among us. With thankfulness and gladness let us call upon him, saying:
R/. Stay with us, Lord.

Lord Jesus Christ, by your life with Mary and Joseph you sanctified the life of the home; dwell with us in our home, so that we may have you as our guest and honor you as our Head. For this we pray: **R/.**

In you every dwelling grows into a holy temple; grant that those who live in this house may be built up together into the dwelling place of God in the Holy Spirit. For this we pray: **R/.**

You taught your followers to build their houses upon solid rock; grant that the members of this family may hold fast to you teachings and, free of all discord, serve you with their whole heart. For this we pray: **R/.**

The leader says the prayer of blessing with hands joined.

Lord,
be close to your servants
who move into this home (today)
and ask for your blessing.
Be their (our) shelter when they (we) are at home,
their (our) companion when they (we) are away,
and their (our) welcome guest when they (we) return.

(continued)

And at last receive them (us)
into the dwelling place you have prepared for them (us)
in your Father's house,
where you live forever and ever.
R/. Amen.

[675]

> After the prayer of blessing, the leader sprinkles those
> present and the new home with holy water brought from
> the church.

[676]

> The leader concludes the rite by saying:

May the peace of Christ rule in our hearts,
and may the Word of Christ in all its richness dwell in us,
so that whatever we do in word and in work,
we will do in the name of the Lord.
R/. Amen.

[677]

> The blessing may conclude with a suitable song.

—From Book of Blessings

PRAYERS DURING SICKNESS OR INFIRMITY

In times of serious illness, a priest, deacon, or a lay minister will come to visit and bless the sick and to bring Holy Communion. A family should advise the parish priest when a family member is seriously ill or injured so that the person may be anointed. It is fitting that the sick be blessed, perhaps daily, by other members of the household. Sometimes, this may be simply the prayer of blessing or the short form of blessing that concludes the following rite. At other times, the inclusion of a suitable Scripture reading and time for prayers of intercession will be appropriate. Prayers for a sick child are on page 240.

Blessing of the Sick

[376]

The blessing of the sick is a very ancient custom, having its origins in the practice of Christ himself and his Apostles. The primary concern should be to show the sick how much Christ and his Church are concerned for them.

[403]

The leader says:

Our help is in the name of the Lord.
R/. Who made heaven and earth.

One of those present or the leader reads a text of sacred
Scripture.

A
Listen to the words of the Second Letter of St. Paul
to the Corinthians: 1:3–4

> Blessed be the God and Father of our Lord
> Jesus Christ, the Father of compassion and the
> God of all encouragement, who encourages us
> in our every affliction, so that we may be able
> to encourage those who are in any affliction
> with the encouragement with which we
> ourselves are encouraged by God.

Reader: The Word of the Lord.
R/. Thanks be to God.

Or:

B
Listen to the words of the holy Gospel
according to Matthew: 11:28–29

> Jesus said: "Come to me, all you who labor
> and are burdened, and I will give you rest.
> Take my yoke upon you and learn from me, for
> I am meek and humble of heart; and you will
> find rest for yourselves."

Reader: The Gospel of the Lord.
R/. Praise to you, Lord Jesus Christ.

The leader may wish to make the sign of the cross on the sick person's forehead while saying the prayer.

Lord and Father, almighty and eternal God,
by your blessing you give us strength and support in our frailty:
turn with kindness toward this your servant, N.
Free him/her from all illness and restore him/her to health,
so that in the sure knowledge of your goodness
he/she will gratefully bless your holy name.

We ask this through Christ our Lord.
R/. Amen.

—*From Book of Blessings*

Short Prayers for the Sick

Sometimes, a short blessing is used alone, especially at the end of the day.

A
May the Lord bless us,
protect us from all evil,
and bring us to everlasting life.
R/. Amen.

Or:

B
May the almighty and merciful God bless and protect us,
the Father, and the Son, and the Holy Spirit.
R/. Amen.

Communion of the Sick or Elderly

When a minister of the Church (who may be a priest, deacon, or extraordinary minister of Holy Communion) brings Communion, the sick or elderly person shares in the eucharistic meal of the community. A member of the family, with the permission of the parish pastor, may serve as an extraordinary minister of Holy Communion. This Holy Communion manifests the support and concern of the community for its members who are not able to be present. This Holy Communion is a bond to the community as well as union with Christ. When the Eucharist is brought to the home, the family should prepare a table with a cloth and lighted candle. All members of the household may receive Communion with the sick person according to the usual norms. The following texts are among many that may be chosen from the Rite of Communion of the Sick.

All make the sign of the cross. The minister of Communion speaks the following or a similar greeting:

Peace be with this house and with all who live here.
R/. And also with you.

The Blessed Sacrament is placed on the table. The sick person and all present may be sprinkled with holy water. Before this sprinkling, the minister of Communion says:

Let this water call to mind our Baptism into Christ, who by his death and Resurrection has redeemed us.

The minister of Communion then invites all to join in the penitential rite:

My brothers and sisters, let us turn with confidence to the Lord and ask forgiveness for all our sins.

After a brief silence, all may recite the "I confess" prayer
(the *Confiteor*, in Part I: Basic Prayers) or the minister may
speak the following invocations, to which all respond.

Lord Jesus, you healed the sick: Lord, have mercy.
R/. Lord, have mercy.

Lord Jesus, you forgave sinners: Christ, have mercy.
R/. Christ, have mercy.

Lord Jesus, you give us yourself to heal us and to bring us
   strength: Lord, have mercy.
R/. Lord, have mercy.

Then the minister concludes the penitential rite:

May almighty God have mercy on us,
forgive us our sins,
and bring us to everlasting life.
R/. Amen.

Then the Scripture is read. An appropriate reading should
be selected and prepared by the family or the minister
of Communion. The following Scripture readings are
appropriate but should not limit the choice of a reading.

A
Listen to the words of the holy Gospel
according to John: 15:5

I am the vine, you are the branches. Whoever
remains in me and I in him will bear much
fruit, because without me you can do nothing.

Reader: The Gospel of the Lord.
R/. Praise to you, Lord Jesus Christ.

Or:

B
Listen to the words of the First Letter of St. John: 4:16

> We have come to know and to believe in the
> love God has for us.
>   God is love, and whoever remains in love
> remains in God and God in him.

Reader: The Word of the Lord.
R/. Thanks be to God.

Following a time of silence, all join in prayers of
intercession. Then, in preparation for Holy Communion,
all recite the Lord's Prayer. After this, the minister shows
the eucharistic bread to those present, saying:

A
This is the bread of life.
Taste and see that the Lord is good.

Or:

B
This is the Lamb of God
who takes away the sins of the world.
Happy are those who are called to his supper.

All who are to receive Communion respond:

Lord, I am not worthy to receive you,
but only say the word and I shall be healed.

The minister gives Communion, saying, "The Body of Christ," "The Blood of Christ," as appropriate. The sick person answers, "Amen." All who wish receive Communion in the usual way.

After a time of silence, the minister says the following or another prayer:

All-powerful and ever-living God,
may the Body and Blood of Christ, your Son,
be for our brother/sister N.
a lasting remedy for body and soul.
We ask this through Christ our Lord.
R/. Amen.

The rite concludes with a blessing:

A
May the Lord bless us,
protect us from all evil,
and bring us to everlasting life.
R/. Amen.

Or:

B
May the almighty and merciful God bless and protect us,
the Father, and the Son, and the Holy Spirit.
R/. Amen.

Anointing of the Sick

When a family member is seriously ill, faces serious surgery, or becomes frail due to old age, a priest may be asked to celebrate the Sacrament of the Anointing of the Sick. The sacrament may be celebrated in the home, the hospital, or the parish church. If a person's condition worsens, the sacrament may be repeated.

> The Lord himself showed great concern for the bodily and spiritual welfare of the sick and commanded his followers to do likewise. . . .
>
> Those who are seriously ill need the special help of God's grace in this time of anxiety, lest they be broken in spirit and, under the pressure of temptation, perhaps weakened in their faith. . . .
>
> Through the Sacrament of Anointing, Christ strengthens the faithful who are afflicted by illness, providing them with the strongest means of support. . . .
>
> This sacrament gives the grace of the Holy Spirit to those who are sick: by this grace the whole person is helped and saved, sustained by trust in God, and strengthened against the temptations of the Evil One and against anxiety over death. Thus the sick person is able not only to bear suffering bravely, but also to fight against it. A return to physical health may follow the reception of this sacrament if it will be beneficial to the sick person's salvation. If necessary, the sacrament also provides the sick person with the forgiveness of sins and the completion of Christian penance. . . .
>
> Because of its very nature as a sign, the Sacrament of the Anointing of the Sick should be celebrated with members of the family and other representatives of the Christian community whenever this is possible. Then the sacrament is seen for what it is—a part of the prayer of the Church and an encounter with the Lord.
>
> —*Pastoral Care of the Sick*

The Anointing of the Sick begins much as the Communion of the Sick on page 212. After the reading of Scripture (and homily), the following litany is prayed. All respond "Lord, have mercy" to each petition.

The priest says:

My brother and sisters, in our prayer of faith let us appeal to God for our brother/sister N.

Come and strengthen him/her through this holy anointing: Lord, have mercy. **R/.**

Free him/her from all harm: Lord, have mercy. **R/.**

Free him/her from sin and all temptations: Lord, have mercy. **R/.**

Relieve the sufferings of all the sick: Lord, have mercy. **R/.**

Assist all those dedicated to the care of the sick: Lord, have mercy. **R/.**

Give life and health to our brother/sister N., on whom we lay our hands in your name: Lord, have mercy. **R/.**

After the laying on of hands, the priest gives thanks over the oil of the sick, then anoints the forehead and hands of the sick person. He may also anoint other parts of the body, for example, the area of pain or injury. A prayer follows the anointing, then all join in the Lord's Prayer. If the sick person is to receive Communion, others present may also receive. The anointing concludes with the blessing of the sick person and of all present.

Prayers of the Sick

Those who are sick should make use of many of the prayers throughout
this book. Sometimes, short prayers, repeated slowly over and over, are
most appropriate. (See also the Pious Invocations in Part I: Basic Prayers.)

Lord Jesus Christ,
Son of the living God,
have mercy on me.

Praised be Jesus Christ.

Lord, I hope in you.

Your will be done.

Strengthen me, Lord.

Lord, have mercy.

Sacred Heart of Jesus, have mercy on us.

My Lord and my God.

Jesus, Mary, and Joseph.

Pray for us, holy Mother of God,
that we may become worthy of the promises of Christ.

Holy Mary, pray for us.

Prayer for Those Who Care for the Sick

Lord Jesus, our brother,
you showed your compassion for the sick
when you reached out in love to them.
We praise you for the saving love
that is exercised among those who care for the sick.
Conform them more and more to your image,
that they may be your healing touch to the sick,
and share the peace
of your Holy Spirit with all they meet.

Glory and praise to you, Christ Jesus,
the Incarnation of the Father's love,
you are Lord forever and ever.
R/. Amen.

Blessing of a Person Suffering from Addiction

[407]

Addiction to alcohol, drugs, and other controlled substances causes great disruption in the life of an individual and his or her family. This blessing is intended to strengthen the addicted person in the struggle to overcome addiction and to assist his or her family and friends.

[408]

This blessing may also be used for individuals who, although not addicted, abuse alcohol or drugs and wish the assistance of God's blessing in their struggle.

[412]

When the household and friends have gathered, all make the sign of the cross.

[414]

The leader greets those present in the following words.

Let us praise God our Creator, who gives us courage and strength, now and forever.
R/. Amen.

[415]

In the following or similar words, the leader prepares those present for the blessing.

God created the world and all things in it and entrusted them into our hands, that we might use them for our good and for the building up of the Church and human society.

Today we pray for N., that God may strengthen him/her
in his/her weakness and restore him/her to the freedom
of God's children. We pray also for ourselves that we may
encourage and support him/her in the days ahead.

[416]

One of those present or the leader reads a text of sacred
Scripture.

[417]

Listen to the words of the Letter of Paul
to the Romans: 8:18–25

> Brothers and sisters:
>   I consider that the sufferings of this present
> time are as nothing compared with the glory
> to be revealed for us. For creation awaits
> with eager expectation the revelation of the
> children of God; for creation was made subject
> to futility, not of its own accord but because
> of the one who subjected it, in hope that
> creation itself would be set free from slavery to
> corruption and share in the glorious freedom
> of the children of God. We know that all
> creation is groaning in labor pains even until
> now; and not only that, but we ourselves, who
> have the firstfruits of the Spirit, we also groan
> within ourselves as we wait for adoption, the
> redemption of our bodies. For in hope we were
> saved. Now hope that sees for itself is not
> hope. For who hopes for what one sees? But
> if we hope for what we do not see, we wait
> with endurance.

Or 2 Corinthians 4:6–9—*We are afflicted, but not crushed.* [416]

Reader: The Word of the Lord.
R/. Thanks be to God.

The intercessions are then said. [420]

Leader: Our God gives us life and constantly calls us to new life; let us pray to God with confidence.
R/. Lord, hear our prayer.

For those addicted to alcohol/drugs, that God may be their strength and support, we pray. **R/.**

For N., bound by the chains of addiction/substance abuse, that we encourage and assist him/her in his/her struggle, we pray. **R/.**

For N., that he/she may trust in the mercy of God, through whom all things are possible, we pray. **R/.**

After the intercessions the leader invites all present to say the Lord's Prayer. [421]

The leader says the prayer of blessing with hands joined:

God of mercy,
we bless you in the name of your Son, Jesus Christ,
who ministered to all who came to him.
Give your strength to N., your servant,
enfold him/her in your love
and restore him/her to the freedom of God's children.

Lord,
look with compassion on all those
who have lost their health and freedom.
Restore to them the assurance of your unfailing mercy,
strengthen them in the work of recovery,
and help them to resist all temptation.

To those who care for them,
grant patient understanding and a love that perseveres.

We ask this through Christ our Lord.
R/. Amen.

The leader concludes the rite by signing himself or herself
with the sign of the cross and saying:

May our all-merciful God, Father, Son, and Holy Spirit, bless
us and embrace us in love forever.
R/. Amen.

—From Book of Blessings

Blessings and Prayers Before and After Birth or Adoption

Prayer for Those Hoping to Conceive or Adopt a Child

For couples who hope to conceive or adopt a child, this psalm and prayer can be joined to table prayers or used at other times.

PSALM 145:13–21

The Lord is faithful in all his words
    and holy in all his works.
The Lord lifts up all who are falling
    and raises up all who are bowed down.

The eyes of all look hopefully to you,
    and you give them their food in due season;
You open your hand
    and satisfy the desire of every living thing.
The Lord is just in all his ways
    and holy in all his works.
The Lord is near to all who call upon him,
    to all who call upon him in truth.

He fulfills the desire of those who fear him,
    he hears their cry and saves them.
The LORD keeps all who love him,
    but all the wicked he will destroy.
May my mouth speak the praise of the LORD,
    and may all flesh bless his holy name forever and ever.

PRAYER

God our Creator,
by your love the world is filled with life,
through your generosity one generation
gives life to another,
and so are your wonders told and your praises sung.
We look to you in our love and in our need:
may it be your will that we bear (adopt) a child
to share our home and faith.
Loving God, be close to us
as we pray to love and do your will.
You are our God, nourishing us forever and ever.
R/. Amen.

BLESSINGS FOR PREGNANCY

When a pregnancy is first confirmed and at various times during the pregnancy (when the extended family is present, for example), these blessings are appropriate. They may take place at the beginning or end of a family gathering or as part of the blessing at table, using the Scripture reading and prayer of blessing before joining in the Grace Before Meals. A blessing of the mother only, page 234, may be used when it is more appropriate. The leader may be a priest, deacon, lay minister, friend, or member of the family.

Blessing of Parents Before Childbirth

All make the sign of the cross. [218]

The leader greets those present in the following words: [220]

Let us bless the Lord Jesus, who in the womb of the Virgin Mary became like us. Blessed be God forever.
R/. Blessed be God forever.

In the following or similar words, the leader prepares those present for the blessing. [221]

God, the Lord of life, brings every human creature into being and rules and sustains the life of each one of us. He has particular care for those born of a Christian marriage, since through the Sacrament of Baptism they will receive the gift of divine life itself. These parents-to-be are partners in God's

love and seek his blessing because they already cherish the child they have conceived and because they await the hour of their child's birth in faith and hope.

[222]

One of those present or the leader reads a text of sacred Scripture.

[223]

Listen to the words of the holy Gospel according to Luke: 1:39–45

> During those days Mary set out and traveled
> to the hill country in haste to a town of Judah,
> where she entered the house of Zechariah
> and greeted Elizabeth. When Elizabeth heard
> Mary's greeting, the infant leapt in her womb,
> and Elizabeth, filled with the holy Spirit, cried
> out in a loud voice and said, "Most blessed are
> you among women, and blessed is the fruit
> of your womb. And how does this happen
> to me, that the mother of my Lord should
> come to me? For at the moment the sound of
> your greeting reached my ears, the infant in
> my womb leapt for joy. Blessed are you who
> believed that what was spoken to you by the
> Lord would be fulfilled."

Reader: The Gospel of the Lord.
R/. Praise to you, Lord Jesus Christ.

The litany is then said.

Leader: Christ the Lord, the blessed fruit of Mary's womb, by the mystery of his Incarnation filled the world with his grace and goodness. Let us therefore raise our voices to praise him, saying:
R/. Blessed are you, O Lord, for your loving kindness.

Christ our Lord, you assumed our nature in order that we may be reborn as children of God. We pray: **R/.**

Christ the Lord, you give the example of Mary and Joseph to N. and N. that they may be loving parents. We pray: **R/.**

Christ our Lord, through the ministry of parents you fill the Church with joy by enriching it with new children. We pray: **R/.**

After the litany the leader invites all present to say the Lord's Prayer.

The leader says the prayer of blessing with hands joined:

Gracious Father,
your Word, spoken in love, created the human family
and, in the fullness of time,
your Son, conceived in love, restored it to your friendship.
Hear the prayers of N. and N.,
who await the birth of their child.

Calm their fears when they are anxious.
Watch over and support these parents
and bring their child into this world
safely and in good health,
so that as members of your family
they may praise you and glorify you
through your Son, our Lord Jesus Christ,
now and forever.
R/. Amen.

[230]

The leader concludes the rite by signing himself or herself
with the sign of the cross and saying:

May God, who chose to give us the joys of eternal salvation
through the motherhood of the Virgin Mary and the
protection of Joseph, bless us and keep us in his care, now
and forever.
R/. Amen.

—From Book of Blessings

Blessing Before Childbirth: For the Mother

[236]

The blessing before childbirth provided here may be celebrated for an individual mother, particularly in the company of her own family. It may also be celebrated for several mothers together.

[240]

When the household and friends have gathered, all make the sign of the cross.

[242]

The leader greets those present in the following words:

Let us bless the Lord Jesus, who in the womb of the Virgin Mary became one of us. Blessed be God forever.
R/. Blessed be God now and forever.

[243]

In the following or similar words, the leader prepares those present for the blessing.

God, the Lord of life, brings every human creature into being and rules and sustains the life of every one of us. The reason for the blessing of a mother-to-be is that she may await her hour of delivery in faith and hope and, as the partner of God's own love, may already cherish with her maternal love the child in her womb.

One of those present or the leader reads a text of sacred
Scripture.

Listen to the words of the holy Gospel
according to Luke: 1:39–45

> During those days Mary set out and traveled
> to the hill country in haste to a town of Judah,
> where she entered the house of Zechariah
> and greeted Elizabeth. When Elizabeth heard
> Mary's greeting, the infant leapt in her womb,
> and Elizabeth, filled with the holy Spirit, cried
> out in a loud voice and said, "Most blessed are
> you among women, and blessed is the fruit
> of your womb. And how does this happen
> to me, that the mother of my Lord should
> come to me? For at the moment the sound of
> your greeting reached my ears, the infant in
> my womb leapt for joy. Blessed are you who
> believed that what was spoken to you by the
> Lord would be fulfilled."

Reader: The Gospel of the Lord.
R/. Praise to you, Lord Jesus Christ.

The intercessions are then said.

Leader: Christ the Lord, the blessed fruit of Mary's womb,
by the mystery of his Incarnation filled the world with his
grace and goodness. Let us therefore raise our voices to
praise him, saying:
R/. Blessed be God forever.

You were born of a woman, so that we might become God's adopted children. Let us bless the Lord: **R/.**

You took life from Mary and willed that the womb that bore you and the breasts that nursed you would be called blessed. Let us bless the Lord: **R/.**

Through the ministry of mothers you increase the joy and exultation of the Church by enriching it with new children. Let us bless the Lord: **R/.**

[249]

The leader says the prayer of blessing with hands joined:

Lord God,
Creator of the human race,
your Son, through the working of the Holy Spirit,
was born of a woman,
so that he might pay the age-old debt of sin
and save us by his redemption.

Receive with kindness the prayer of your servant
as she asks for the birth of a healthy child.
Grant that she may safely deliver a son or daughter
to be numbered among your family,
to serve you in all things,
and to gain eternal life.

We ask this through Christ the Lord.
R/. Amen.

After the prayer of blessing, the leader invites all present to pray for the protection of the Blessed Virgin. (See the Prayers to Mary in Part I: Basic Prayers.)

The leader invokes God's blessing on the mother and all present by signing himself or herself with the sign of the cross and saying:

May God, who chose to make known and to send
the blessings of eternal salvation
through the motherhood of the Blessed Virgin,
bless us and keep us in his care,
now and forever.
R/. Amen.

—*From* Book of Blessings

BLESSINGS AND PRAYERS NEAR THE TIME OF BIRTH

Blessing of the Mother

God of love and compassion,
look with favor on your daughter
who anxiously awaits the birth of her child.
Be with her in her labor
that she may deliver her child safely
and rest always in you.
We ask this through Christ our Lord.
R/. Amen.

Prayer of the Mother

Lord God,
you made us out of nothing
and redeemed us by the precious Blood of your only Son.

Preserve the work of your hands,
and defend both me and the tender fruit of my womb
from all perils and evils.
I beg of you, for myself,
your grace, protection, and a happy delivery.
Sanctify my child
and make this child yours forever.
Grant this through Christ our Lord.
R/. Amen.

Blessing of the Father

Heavenly Father,
We thank you for this new life
and humbly pray to be worthy of your gift.

Grant N. the strength and courage
to pass through this time of waiting and of change,
as Joseph did with Mary.
May your grace shine upon N.,
and may you grant him your wisdom and love in
    the days ahead.
We ask this through Christ our Lord.
R/. Amen.

Prayer of the Father

Heavenly Father, Creator of all life,
we praise you that you have given life to our child,
and we rejoice with our family and friends
as we prepare for its birth.

Protect (my wife,) N.,
as she carries our child in her womb,
and bring her to a safe delivery.

May our child be baptized into the life of Jesus,
and live in the community of your people,
and proclaim your praise and glory.
We ask this through Jesus Christ our Lord.
R/. Amen.

PRAYERS AFTER THE ARRIVAL OF A CHILD

Thanksgiving for a Newborn or Newly Adopted Young Child

On first holding a newborn or newly adopted child, on bringing the child into the home for the first time, and on other occasions before the child's Baptism, this blessing may be given by the parents.

A

God, our Creator, cherish this child.
Jesus, our Savior, protect him/her.
Holy Spirit, our comforter, strengthen him/her.

Or:

B

Source of all blessings, protector of infants,
look with favor on this child, N.

Hold him/her gently in your hands.
When he/she is reborn of water and the Holy Spirit,
bring him/her into the Church,
there to share in your kingdom
and with us to bless your name forever.
We ask this through Christ our Lord.
R/. Amen.

The parents trace the sign of the cross on the child's forehead.

N., may the Lord Jesus, who loved children,
bless you and keep you in his love,
now and forever.
R/. Amen.

Thanksgiving for Adoption of an Older Child

Heavenly Father, lover of all,
we praise you for giving us Jesus as our Savior:
he blessed the children who came to him,
and welcomes those who come to him now.

Look with favor upon N., our son/daughter,
and embrace him/her with your love.
May he/she grow in assurance of our love,
in the wisdom and knowledge of your Son, Jesus,
and in the strength of the Holy Spirit.
May he/she be one with us
as we praise you for your presence.

We ask this through your beloved Son,
Jesus Christ our Lord.
R/. Amen.

Parents' Thanksgiving

O God, we give you thanks for N.,
whom you have welcomed into our family.
Bless this family.

(continued)

Confirm a lively sense of your presence with us,
and grant us patience and wisdom,
that our lives may show forth the love of Christ,
as we bring N. up to love all that is good.
We ask this through Christ our Lord.
R/. Amen.

Prayer on Bringing a Child into the Home

Good Lord,
you have tenderly loved us,
and given us this home and good friends.
May we make a true home for this child
where he/she will learn trust in us and in you.
(May his/her brothers and sisters rejoice
in their own growing up
as they help to care for this child.)
We ask this through Christ our Lord.
R/. Amen.

Parent's Blessing of a Child When Nursing or Feeding

God,
you are like a mother to us all,
nourishing all creatures with food and with blessing.
Strengthen my child with (my milk/this food)
and with the warmth of our nearness.

Or:

Blessed are you, Lord, God of all creation:
you nourish all your children.

BLESSINGS DURING CHILDHOOD

Daily Blessing of a Child

One of the following short blessings may be said by the parent at various times, such as when a child is going to play or to school, but especially when the child is going to bed each night. The parent makes the sign of the cross on the child's forehead or heart and says one of the following blessings.

May God bless you.

May God keep you safe.

God be with you.

God be in your heart.

May God bless and protect you.

Prayer When a Child Is Sick

When a child is ill, parents and others may bless him or her. When the illness is more serious, the parish priest should be asked to visit and to join the family in prayer and perhaps in the Sacrament of the Anointing of the Sick (page 216). A longer blessing of the sick will be found on page 209.

When the parents wish to give a simple blessing, they may place a hand on the child's head and say one of the following prayers:

A
God of love,
ever caring, ever strong,
stand by us in our time of need.
Watch over N., who is sick;
look after him/her in every danger,
and grant him/her your healing and peace.
We ask this in the name of Jesus the Lord.
R/. Amen.

B
N., when you were baptized,
you were marked with the cross of Jesus.
I (we) make this cross + on your forehead
and ask the Lord to bless you
and restore you to health.
R/. Amen.

C
May the Lord Jesus watch over you
and keep you in peace.
R/. Amen.

Godparent's Blessing of a Child

At Baptism, godparents promise to help parents in their duties as Christian mothers and fathers. Throughout the years of childhood it is appropriate for a godparent to bless his or her godchild, perhaps with a cross traced on the child's forehead. One of the following short blessings may be prayed.

N., blessed be God who chose you in Christ.

N., may Christ's peace reign in your heart.

BLESSINGS FOR SPECIAL OCCASIONS OF CHILDHOOD

The following are Scripture texts and prayers of blessing appropriate for the various occasions. They may often be used as part of the blessing at table when the family gathers to celebrate the event. During the blessing, those present place their hands over or on the one being blessed.

Blessing on a Child's Birthday

FROM JEREMIAH 1:5

The Lord said to Jeremiah:
Before I formed you in the womb I knew you,
    before you were born I dedicated you.

May God, in whose presence our ancestors walked,
bless you.
R/. Amen.

May God, who has been your shepherd from birth until
now, keep you.
R/. Amen.

May God, who saves you from all harm, give you peace.
R/. Amen.

Blessing on a Child's Name Day

On the feast of the saint for whom a child is named, the following blessing may be used. The life of the saint may also be related.

God of glory,
whom we name in many ways,
when we brought this child to your Church
we were asked, "What name do you give this child?"
We answered, "N." (or: "N. N.").

May St. N. ever pray for him/her,
may he/she guard him/her
so that N. might overcome all evil
and come at last to that place
where his/her name is written in the book of life.

We ask this through Christ our Lord.
R/. Amen.

Blessing on the Anniversary of Baptism

On this day, or yearly on Easter Sunday, the baptismal garment may be displayed, the baptismal candle lighted, and holy water (brought from the church) placed in a bowl.

N., on this day the Christian community
welcomed you with great joy.
You were baptized in the name of the Father,
and of the Son, and of the Holy Spirit.
You put on the Lord Jesus.
Today we sign you again with the cross
by which you were claimed for Christ,
and we pray that God's blessing be upon you.

Each person signs the forehead of the one celebrating the anniversary and says:

Blessed be God who chose you in Christ.

In conclusion, all may sign themselves with holy water, saying:

In the name of the Father, and of the Son, and of the Holy Spirit.
R/. Amen.

Blessing Before Confirmation

During the months when a candidate is preparing for Confirmation, and especially on the day of the celebration, the parents and sponsor may bless the candidate.

N., in Baptism you were claimed for Christ.
May God bless you now and watch over you.

Blessing Before First Communion

During the months when a child is preparing for first Holy Communion, and especially as the day approaches, parents may bless the candidate.

N., may the Lord Jesus touch your ears to receive his Word,
and your mouth to proclaim his faith.
May you come with joy to his supper
to the praise and glory of God.
R/. Amen.

Prayer Before a Child's Graduation

Blessed are you, Lord our God,
for you begin all things and bring them to conclusion.
At the dawn of creation you created all things
and placed this earth under our care;
you sent your Son Jesus
to be the way, the truth, and the life;
and through the gift of the Holy Spirit
guide our way to the glory of your Kingdom.

We praise you for our son/daughter:
you have guided him/her to this proud moment.
As we celebrate his/her graduation,
we ask you to continue your gracious guidance
in his/her life.

Open new doors and lead him/her
to marvel at the wonders of creation and life.
May your Spirit help him/her to see
his/her many gifts,
and teach him/her how to share these
in your Church and for the benefit of others.

Continue to bless our family and our children,
and grant that we
may always rejoice in your gift of love.

We ask this through Jesus Christ our Lord,
in the unity of the Holy Spirit,
one God, forever and ever.
R/. Amen.

BLESSINGS RELATED TO MARRIAGE

Blessing of an Engaged Couple

[195]

The betrothal of a Christian couple is a special occasion for their families, who should celebrate it together with prayer and a special rite. In this way, they ask God's blessing that the happiness promised by the engagement will be brought to fulfillment.

[196]

When the engagement is celebrated within the circle of the two families, one of the parents should preside.

[199]

When the families have gathered, all make the sign of the cross.

[201]

The leader greets those present in the following words:

Brothers and sisters, let us praise our Lord Jesus Christ, who loved us and gave himself for us. Let us bless him now and forever.
R/. Blessed be God forever.

[202]

In the following or similar words, the leader prepares
those present for the blessing.

We know that all of us need God's blessing at all times; but
at the time of their engagement to be married, Christians
are in particular need of grace as they prepare themselves to
form a new family.

Let us pray, then, for God's blessing to come upon this
couple: that as they await the day of their wedding, they will
grow in mutual respect and in their love for one another;
that through their companionship and prayer together they
will prepare themselves rightly and chastely for marriage.

[203]

One of those present or the leader reads a text of sacred
Scripture.

[204]

Listen to the words of the First Letter of
St. Paul to the Corinthians: 13:4–13

> Love is patient, love is kind. It is not jealous,
> love is not pompous, it is not inflated, it is
> not rude, it does not seek its own interests, it
> is not quick-tempered, it does not brood over
> injury, it does not rejoice over wrongdoing
> but rejoices with the truth. It bears all things,
> believes all things, hopes all things, endures
> all things.
>   Love never fails. If there are prophecies,
> they will be brought to nothing; if tongues,
> they will cease; if knowledge, it will be
> brought to nothing. For we know partially and

we prophesy partially, but when the perfect comes, the partial will pass away. When I was a child, I used to talk as a child, think as a child, reason as a child; when I became a man, I put aside childish things. At present we see indistinctly, as in a mirror, but then face to face. At present I know partially; then I shall know fully, as I am fully known. So faith, hope, love remain, these three; but the greatest of these is love.

[203]

Or John 15:9–12—*This is my commandment: love one another as I have loved you.*

Reader: The Word of the Lord.
R/. Thanks be to God.

[208]

The intercessions are then said.

Leader: God our Father has so loved us that in Christ he makes us his children and the witnesses of his love before the entire world. Let us, therefore, call upon him in all confidence, saying:
R/. Lord, help us to remain always in your love.

God our Father, you willed that your true children, brothers and sisters in Christ, should be known by their love for one another. **R/.**

You place upon us the sweet demands of love so that we may find happiness by responding to them. **R/.**

You call N. and N. to the communion of life and love that
binds the Christian family together, mind and heart. **R/.**

[209]

The engaged couple may exchange rings or some other
gift that signifies their pledge to each other.

[210]

One of the parents may bless these gifts:

N. and N., in due course may you honor the
sacred pledge symbolized by these gifts which
you now exchange.
R/. Amen.

[211]

The leader says the prayer of blessing with hands joined.

We praise you, Lord,
for your gentle plan draws together your children,
   N. and N.,
in love for one another.
Strengthen their hearts,
so that they will keep faith with each other,
please you in all things,
and so come to the happiness of celebrating the sacrament
   of their marriage.

We ask this through Christ our Lord.
R/. Amen.

The leader concludes the rite by signing himself or herself
with the sign of the cross and saying:

May the God of love and peace
abide in you, guide your steps,
and confirm your hearts in his love,
now and forever.
R/. Amen.

The blessing may conclude with a suitable song.

—*From* Book of Blessings

Prayer of a Future Husband

ADAPTED FROM TOBIT 8:5–7

Blessed are you, O God of our ancestors,
and blessed too is your name forever.
Let the heavens bless you for evermore
and all the things you have made.

It was you who created Adam,
you who created Eve his wife
to be his help and support;
and from these two the human race was born.
It was you who said,
"It is not good for the man to be alone;
let us make him a partner like himself."

I take N.
in sincerity of heart.
Have mercy on her and on me
and allow us to live together to a happy old age.

Prayer of a Future Wife

ADAPTED FROM PSALM 16

Keep me, O God, for in you I take refuge;
  I say to the Lord, "My God are you.
  Apart from you I have no good."

I bless the Lord who counsels me;
  even in the night my heart exhorts me.
I set the Lord ever before me;
  with him at my right hand I shall not be disturbed.
Therefore my heart is glad and my soul rejoices,
  my body abides in confidence.

You, O Lord, will show me the path to life,
  fullness of joys in your presence,
  the delights at your right hand forever.

Blessing of a Son or Daughter Before Marriage

In the days immediately before the wedding, the family may gather around its member who is to be married, perhaps at a special meal in the family's home.

All make the sign of the cross. A parent begins:

Let us bless the Lord,
by whose goodness we live
and by whose grace we love one another.
Blessed be God forever.
R/. Blessed be God forever.

Then the Scripture is read:

Listen to the words of the Book of Deuteronomy:　　6:4–7

> Hear, O Israel! The LORD is our God, the LORD
> alone! Therefore, you shall love the LORD, your
> God, with all your heart, and with all your soul,
> and with all your strength. Take to heart these
> words which I enjoin on you today. Drill them
> into your children. Speak of them at home and
> abroad, whether you are busy or at rest.

Reader: The Word of the Lord.
R/. Thanks be to God.

The parents may give a Bible or crucifix to the one who is to be married. Then all join in prayers of intercession for the couple to be married and for the world. After the Lord's Prayer, the parents and other family members place their hands on the head of their son or daughter as one or both parents speak the blessing.

May the Lord, who gave you into our care
and made you a joy to our home,
bless you and keep you.
R/. Amen.

May the Lord, who turns the hearts of parents
    to their children
and the hearts of children to their parents,
smile on you and be kind to you.
R/. Amen.

May the Lord, who delights in our love for one another,
turn toward you and give you peace.
R/. Amen.

All make the sign of the cross as the leader concludes:

May the God of love and peace
abide in you, guide your steps,
and confirm your heart in his love,
now and forever.
R/. Amen.

Table Blessing for Weddings

This blessing may be used before the meal at a wedding reception. A member of the wedding party or one of the parents of the newly married couple may serve as the leader.

When everyone has gathered at table and the meal is ready to be served, all make the sign of the cross.

Leader: Blessed be God who has brought us together in joy.
R/. Blessed be God forever.

The leader introduces the blessing in these or similar words:

We have gathered here to celebrate the love of N. and N. God has brought them together, and we pray that God will hold them in his love always. As the food we share will strengthen our bodies, may our time together strengthen the love that binds us.

After a time of silence, the leader prays:

Let us pray.

Lord God,
you sustain all creatures
and never cease to give your children the food they need.
We bless you for bringing us together
in the love that unites us around this table
where the food we take strengthens our bodies.
We pray that, nourished by your Word,
we may grow ever stronger in faith
as we strive for the coming of your Kingdom.

We ask this through Christ our Lord.
R/. Amen.

—*From* Book of Blessings

Blessing on Anniversaries

[117]
When the household and friends have gathered, all make the sign of the cross.

[119]
The leader greets those present in the following words:

Blessed be the God of all consolation, who has shown us his great mercy. Blessed be God now and forever.
R/. Blessed be God forever.

[120]
In the following or similar words, the leader prepares those present for the blessing.

We have come together to celebrate the anniversary of the marriage of our brother and sister. As we join them in their joy, we join them also in their gratitude. God has set them among us as a sign of his love and through the years they have remained faithful (and have fulfilled their responsibilities as parents). Let us give thanks for all the favors N. and N. have received during their married life. May God keep them in their love for each other, so that they may be more and more of one mind and one heart.

[121]
One of those present or the leader reads a text of sacred Scripture.

Listen to the words of the First Letter of St. Paul
to the Corinthians: 1:4–9

> I give thanks to my God always on your
> account for the grace of God bestowed on
> you in Christ Jesus, that in him you were
> enriched in every way, with all discourse and
> all knowledge, as the testimony to Christ was
> confirmed among you, so that you are not
> lacking in any spiritual gift as you wait for the
> revelation of our Lord Jesus Christ. He will
> keep you firm to the end, irreproachable on the
> day of our Lord Jesus Christ. God is faithful,
> and by him you were called to fellowship with
> his Son, Jesus Christ our Lord.

Reader: The Word of the Lord.
R/. Thanks be to God.

[127]

The intercessions are then said.

Leader: In the tender plan of his providence, God our
almighty Father has given married love, its faithfulness,
(and its fruitfulness,) a special significance in the history of
salvation. Let us therefore call upon him, saying:
R/. Lord, hear our prayer.

Father all-holy, you have made marriage the great symbol of
Christ's love for his Church; bestow on these your servants
the fullness of your own love. For this we pray: **R/.**

Father all-holy, the faithful one, you ask for and respond to fidelity to your covenant; fill with your blessings your servants who are celebrating their wedding anniversary. For this we pray: **R/.**

It is your will that all married life should be a lesson in Christian living; grant that all husbands and wives may be witnesses to the wonders of your Son's love. For this we pray: **R/.**

[128]

The leader says the prayer of blessing with hands joined.

A

Lord God and Creator,
we bless and praise your name.
In the beginning you made man and woman,
so that they might enter a communion of life and love.
You likewise blessed the union of N. and N.,
so that they might reflect the union of Christ with
    his Church:
look with kindness on them today.
Amid the joys and struggles of their life
you have preserved the union between them;
renew their marriage covenant,
increase your love in them,
and strengthen their bond of peace,
so that (surrounded by their children)
they may always rejoice in the gift of your blessing.

We ask this through Christ our Lord.
R/. Amen.

B

Almighty and eternal God,
you have so exalted the unbreakable bond of marriage
that it has become the sacramental sign
of your Son's union with the Church as his spouse.
Look with favor on N. and N.,
whom you have united in marriage,
as they ask for your help
and the protection of the Virgin Mary.
They pray that in good times and in bad
they will grow in love for each other;
that they will resolve to be of one heart
in the bond of peace.
Lord, in their struggles let them rejoice
that you are near to help them;
in their needs let them know
that you are there to rescue them;
in their joys let them see
that you are the source and completion of every happiness.

We ask this through Christ our Lord.
R/. Amen.

[130]

The leader concludes the rite by signing himself or herself
with the sign of the cross and saying:

May the God of hope fill us with every joy in believing.
May the peace of Christ abound in our hearts.
May the Holy Spirit enrich us with his gifts,
now and forever.
R/. Amen.

—From Book of Blessings

PRAYERS FOR DEATH AND GRIEVING

Blessing of Parents After a Miscarriage or Stillbirth

[279]

In times of death and grief the Christian turns to the Lord for consolation and strength. This is especially true when a child dies before birth. This blessing is provided to assist the parents in their grief and console them with the blessing of God.

[284]

All make the sign of the cross. The leader begins:

Let us praise the Father of mercies,
the God of all consolation.
Blessed be God forever.
R/. Blessed be God forever.

[285]

In the following or similar words, the leader prepares those present for the blessing.

For those who trust in God,
in the pain of sorrow there is consolation,
in the face of despair there is hope,
in the midst of death there is life.

(continued)

N. and N., as we mourn the death of your child, we place ourselves in the hands of God and ask strength, for healing, and for love.

[286]

One of those present or the leader reads a text of sacred Scripture.

Listen to the words of the Book
of Lamentations: 3:17–18, 21–24

My soul is deprived of peace,
    I have forgotten what happiness is;
I tell myself my future is lost,
    all that I hoped for from the LORD.

But I will call this to mind,
    as my reason to have hope:
The favors of the LORD are not exhausted,
    his mercies are not spent;
They are renewed each morning,
    so great is his faithfulness.
My portion is the LORD, says my soul;
    therefore I will hope in him.

Reader: The Word of the Lord.
R/. Thanks be to God.

[290]

The intercessions are then said.

Leader: Let us pray to God, who throughout the ages has heard the cries of parents.
R/. Lord, hear our prayer.

For N. and N., who know the pain of grief, that they may be comforted, we pray: **R/.**

For this family, that it may find new hope in the midst of suffering, we pray: **R/.**

For all who have suffered the loss of a child, that Christ may be their support, we pray: **R/.**

[291]
After the intercessions the leader invites all present to say the Lord's Prayer.

[292]
The leader says the prayer of blessing with hands joined.

Compassionate God,
soothe the hearts of N. and N.,
and grant that through the prayers of Mary,
who grieved by the Cross of her Son,
you may enlighten their faith,
give hope to their hearts,
and peace to their lives.

Lord, grant mercy to all the members of this family
and comfort them with the hope
that one day we will all live with you,
with your Son Jesus Christ, and the Holy Spirit,
forever and ever.
R/. Amen.

Or:

Lord,
God of all creation
we bless and thank you for your tender care.
Receive this life you created in love
and comfort your faithful people in their time of loss
with the assurance of your unfailing mercy.

We ask this through Christ our Lord.
R/. Amen.

The leader concludes the rite by signing himself or herself
with the sign of the cross and saying:

May God give us peace in our sorrow,
consolation in our grief,
and strength to accept his will in all things.
R/. Amen.

—*From* Book of Blessings

PRAYERS AT THE TIME OF DEATH

Viaticum

Viaticum is the sacrament of the dying. "Communion in the body and blood of Christ, received at this moment of 'passing over' to the Father, has a particular significance and importance. It is the seed of eternal life and the power of resurrection" (*Catechism of the Catholic Church*, no. 1524).

Viaticum is celebrated in the same manner as Communion of the Sick (page 212), but after giving Communion, the minister says:

May the Lord Jesus Christ protect you
and lead you to eternal life.
R/. Amen.

The concluding prayer follows:

God of peace,
you offer eternal healing to those who believe in you;
you have refreshed your servant N.
with food and drink from heaven:
lead him/her safely into the Kingdom of light.
We ask this through Christ our Lord.
R/. Amen.

Prayers with the Dying

The *Catechism of the Catholic Church* teaches that "the Christian meaning of death is revealed in the light of the Paschal mystery of the death and resurrection of Christ in whom resides our only hope. The Christian who dies in Christ Jesus is 'away from the body and at home with the Lord' (2 Cor 5:8)" (no. 1681). The following prayers may be recited with the dying person, alternating with times of silence. Sometimes, the same prayer should be repeated many times. When the dying person cannot take part, those who are present continue to pray. In such prayers, the paschal character of a Christian's death is made manifest. The Our Father, Hail Mary, Glory Be, and many of the prayers in Part I are also appropriate. The dying person may be signed on the forehead with the cross, as was done at Baptism.

SHORT TEXTS

What will separate us from the love of Christ? (Rom 8:35)

Whether we live or die, we are the Lord's. (Rom 14:8)

We shall always be with the Lord. (1 Thess 4:17)

To you I lift up my soul, O Lord. (Ps 25:1)

Even though I walk in the dark valley,
    I fear no evil; for you are at my side. (Ps 23:4)

Into your hands, Lord, I commend my spirit. (Ps 31:5a)

Jesus, remember me when you come into your
    kingdom. (Lk 23:42)

Lord Jesus, receive my spirit. (Acts 7:59)

Holy Mary, pray for me.
St. Joseph, pray for me.
Jesus, Mary, and Joseph,
assist me in my last agony.

SCRIPTURE READINGS

Among many appropriate Scripture readings are the following:
Job 19:23–27; Psalm 23; Psalm 25; Psalm 91; Psalm 121; 1 John 4:16;
Revelation 21:1–7; Matthew 25:1–13; Luke 22:39–46; Luke 23:44–49;
Luke 24:1–8; John 6:37–40; John 14:16, 23, 27. Those gathered might
take turns reading these passages from the family Bible.

PRAYERS OF COMMENDATION

As the time of death approaches, this prayer may be said.

Go forth, Christian soul, from this world
in the name of God the almighty Father,
who created you,
in the name of Jesus Christ, Son of the living God,
who suffered for you,
in the name of the Holy Spirit,
who was poured out upon you,
go forth, faithful Christian.

May you live in peace this day,
may your home be with God in Zion,
with Mary, the Virgin Mother of God,
with Joseph, and all the angels and saints.

PRAYERS AFTER DEATH

Prayer for the Dead

Into your hands, O Lord,
we humbly entrust our brothers and sisters.
In this life you embraced them with your tender love;
deliver them now from every evil
and bid them enter eternal rest.

The old order has passed away:
welcome them into paradise,
where there will be no sorrow,
   no weeping nor pain,
but fullness of peace and joy
with your Son and the Holy Spirit
forever and ever.
R/. Amen.

Prayers Immediately After Death

The following prayers may be recited immediately after death and may be
repeated in the hours that follow.

Saints of God, come to his/her aid!
Come to meet him/her, angels of the Lord!
R/. Receive his/her soul and present him/her to God the
   Most High.

May Christ, who called you, take you to himself;
may angels lead you to Abraham's side. **R/.**
Give him/her eternal rest, O Lord,
and may your light shine on him/her forever. **R/.**

Let us pray.
All-powerful and merciful God,
we commend to you N., your servant.
In your mercy and love,
blot out the sins he/she has committed
through human weakness.
In this world he/she has died:
let him/her live with you forever.
We ask this through Christ our Lord.
R/. Amen.

These verses may also be used.

V/. Eternal rest grant unto him/her, O Lord.
R/. And let perpetual light shine upon him/her.
V/. May he/she rest in peace.
R/. Amen.
V/. May his/her soul and the souls of all the
    faithful departed,
through the mercy of God,
rest in peace.
R/. Amen.

Gathering in the Presence of the Body

When the family first gathers around the body, before or after it is prepared for burial, all or some of the following prayers may be used. It is most fitting that, where possible, family members take part in preparing the body for burial.

All make the sign of the cross. Then one member of the family reads:

My brothers and sisters, Jesus says: "Come to me, all you who labor and are overburdened, and I will give you rest. Shoulder my yoke and learn from me, for I am gentle and humble in heart, and you will find rest for your souls. Yes, my yoke is easy and my burden light."

The body may then be sprinkled with holy water:

The Lord God lives in his holy temple yet abides in
   our midst.
Since in Baptism N. became God's temple
and the Spirit of God lived in him/her,
with reverence we bless his/her mortal body.

Then one member of the family may say:

With God there is mercy and fullness of redemption; let us pray as Jesus taught us:

Our Father . . .

Then this prayer is said:

Into your hands, O Lord,
we humbly entrust our brother/sister N.
In this life you embraced him/her with your tender love;
deliver him/her now from every evil
and bid him/her enter eternal rest.

The old order has passed away:
welcome him/her then into paradise,
where there will be no sorrow, no weeping nor pain,
but the fullness of peace and joy
with your Son and the Holy Spirit
forever and ever.
R/. Amen.

All may sign the forehead of the deceased with the sign of
the cross. One member of the family says:

Blessed are those who have died in the Lord;
let them rest from their labors
for their good deeds go with them.

V/. Eternal rest grant unto him/her, O Lord.
R/. And let perpetual light shine upon him/her.
V/. May he/she rest in peace.
R/. Amen.
V/. May his/her soul and the souls of all the
   faithful departed,
through the mercy of God,
rest in peace.
R/. Amen.

(continued)

All make the sign of the cross as one member of the
family says:

May the love of God and the peace of the Lord Jesus Christ
bless and console us
and gently wipe every tear from our eyes:
in the name of the Father,
and of the Son, and of the Holy Spirit.
R/. Amen.

Prayers for Mourners

The final prayer from the previous section ("May the love of God") or one
of the following prayers may be used by those in mourning.

A
Lord God,
you are attentive to the voice of our pleading.
Let us find in your Son
comfort in our sadness,
certainty in our doubt,
and courage to live through this hour.
Make our faith strong
through Christ our Lord.
R/. Amen.

B

Lord,
N. is gone now from this earthly dwelling,
and has left behind those who mourn his/her absence.
Grant that we may hold his/her memory dear,
never bitter for what we have lost
nor in regret for the past,
but always in hope of the eternal Kingdom
where you will bring us together again.

We ask this through Christ our Lord.
R/. Amen.

For those who mourn the death of a child:

C

O Lord, whose ways are beyond understanding,
listen to the prayers of your faithful people:
that those weighed down by grief
at the loss of this little child
may find reassurance in your infinite goodness.

We ask this through Christ our Lord.
R/. Amen.

Prayers at Graveside

During the time of mourning, the following prayers my be recited at the graveside. The prayers given on page 158 are appropriate whenever visiting a grave.

A

Lord Jesus Christ,
by your own three days in the tomb,
you hallowed the graves of all who believe in you
and so made the grave a sign of hope
that promises resurrection
even as it claims our mortal bodies.

Grant that our brother/sister, N., may sleep here in peace
until you awaken him/her to glory,
for you are the resurrection and the life.
Then he/she will see you face to face
and in your light will see light
and know the splendor of God,
for you live and reign forever and ever.
R/. Amen.

B

O God,
by whose mercy the faithful departed find rest,
send your holy Angel to watch over this grave.

We ask this through Christ our Lord.
R/. Amen.

Byzantine Prayer for the Deceased

God of the spirits and of all flesh, who have destroyed death and annihilated the devil and given life to your world, may you yourself, O Lord, grant to the soul of your deceased servant N. rest in a place of light, a verdant place, a place of freshness, from where suffering, pain, and cries are far removed. Do you, O good and compassionate God, forgive every fault committed by him/her in word, work, or thought; because there is no man who lives and does not sin. You alone are without sin, and your justice is justice throughout the ages, and your Word is truth.

Since you, O Christ our God, are the resurrection, the life, and the repose of your deceased servant N., we give you glory together with your un-begotten Father with your most holy, good, and vivifying Spirit, now and always and forever and ever.

PART V
PRAYERS FOR
CATHOLIC
LIVING

PRAYERS FOR
CATHOLIC
LIVING

*I*n Baptism, Christians begin their life in Christ. As we go through life, celebrating the sacraments, most especially the Eucharist, we grow in our ability to live as Jesus' disciples, following his path. The prayers in this section help us to seek God's counsel and consolation in the questions, struggles, and transitions of life.

PRAYERS FOR DISCERNMENT AND DECISION MAKING

Novena in Honor of St. Jude Thaddeus

St. Jude is the patron saint of hopeless causes. If ever faced with grave difficulties, you may wish to seek the intercession of St. Jude by using this novena. Traditionally, a novena is prayed for nine days. You may pray on nine consecutive days, on the same day (e.g., Tuesday) for nine consecutive weeks, or on the same day (e.g., the First Friday) for nine consecutive months.

Glorious St. Jude Thaddeus,
by those sublime privileges with which you were adorned in
    your lifetime,
namely, your relationship with our Lord Jesus Christ
    according to the flesh,
and your vocation to be an apostle,
and by that glory which now is yours in heaven
as the reward of your apostolic labors and your martyrdom,
obtain for me from the Giver of every good and perfect gift
all the graces of which I stand in need:

(Mention your request.)

May I treasure up in my heart
the divinely inspired doctrines that you have given us in
    your epistle:
build my edifice of holiness upon our most holy faith,
by praying for the grace of the Holy Spirit;
keep myself in the love of God,
looking for the mercy of Jesus Christ unto eternal life;
to strive by all means to help those who go astray.

May I thus praise the glory and majesty,
the dominion and power of him who is able to keep me
    without sin
and to present me spotless with great joy at the coming of
    our Divine Savior,
the Lord Jesus Christ.
Amen.

CONSECRATION TO ST. JUDE

St. Jude, apostle of Christ and glorious martyr,
I desire to honor you with a special devotion.
I choose you as my patron and protector.
To you I entrust my soul and my body,
all my spiritual and temporal interests,
as well as those of my family.
To you I consecrate my mind
so that in all things it may be enlightened by faith;
my heart so that you may keep it pure
and fill it with love for Jesus and Mary;
my will so that, like yours, it may always be one with the
    will of God.

(continued)

I beg you to help me to master my evil inclinations
and temptations
and to avoid all occasions of sin.
Obtain for me the grace of never offending God,
of fulfilling faithfully all the duties of my state of life,
and of practicing all those virtues that are needful for
my salvation.

Pray for me, my holy patron and helper,
so that, being inspired by your example and assisted by
your prayers,
I may live a holy life, die a happy death,
and attain to the glory of heaven,
there to love and thank God forever.
Amen.

PRAYER

O God, you made your name known to us through
the Apostles.
By the intercession of St. Jude,
let your Church continue to grow
with an increased number of believers.
Grant this through Christ our Lord. Amen.

Litany of the Way: Prayer for the Journey

As Jesus sought the quiet of the desert,
teach us to pray.

As Jesus washed the feet of his disciples,
teach us to love.

As Jesus promised paradise to the thief on the cross,
teach us to hope.

As Jesus called Peter to walk to him across the water,
teach us to believe.

As the child Jesus sat among the elders in the temple,
teach us to seek answers.

As Jesus in the garden opened his mind and heart to God's will,
teach us to listen.

As Jesus reflected on the Law and the prophets,
teach us to learn.

As Jesus used parables to reveal the mysteries of
the Kingdom, teach us to teach.

PRAYERS FOR LEAVING OR DEPARTURES

Blessing Before Leaving Home for School, Employment, Deployment, or Ministry

When a member of the household prepares to move away or leave for a prolonged time, such as for a military deployment, this blessing may be part of the prayer at table or at some other time.

All make the sign of the cross. The leader begins:

The Lord will guard your coming and your going. Blessed be the name of the Lord.
R/. Now and forever.

The leader may use these or similar words to introduce the blessing:

Gathering all our memories of good times and difficulties together, and full of hope and concern for the days ahead, let us ask God's blessing on N.

Then the Scripture is read:

Listen to the words of the holy Gospel
according to John: 14:5–6

> Thomas said to [Jesus], "Master, we do not
> know where you are going; how can we know
> the way?" Jesus said to him, "I am the way
> and the truth and the life. No one comes to the
> Father except through me."

(The family's Bible may be used for an alternate reading
such as Genesis 12:1–9.)

Reader: The Gospel of the Lord.
R/. Praise to you, Lord Jesus Christ.

All join in prayers of intercession and in the Lord's Prayer.
A Bible or other religious article may be given by the
family to the one who is leaving. Then all may extend
their hands toward the one who is leaving as the leader
speaks the blessing:

A
O God, you led your servant Abraham from his home
and guarded him in all his wanderings.
Guide this servant of yours, N.
Be a refuge on the journey, shade in the heat,
shelter in the storm, rest in weariness,
protection in trouble, and a strong staff in danger.
For all our days together, we give you thanks:
bind us together now, even though we may be far apart.

May your peace rest upon this house,
and may it go with your servant always.

Grant this through Christ our Lord.
R/. Amen.

The following prayer is appropriate for one leaving to work in Christian ministry:

B

God our Father,
you will that all people be saved
and come to the knowledge of the truth.
Send workers into your great harvest,
that the Gospel may be preached to every creature
and your people, gathered together by the Word of life
and strengthened by the power of the sacraments,
may advance in the way of salvation and love.

Grant this through Christ our Lord.
R/. Amen.

A sign of God's peace may be extended to the one who is leaving. All make the sign of the cross as the leader concludes:

Let us bless the Lord.
R/. Thanks be to God.

The blessing may conclude with a song.

Blessing at Retirement

All praise and glory are yours,
almighty and eternal God.
You created this earth and all it contains
and placed creation within our care
so that by the work of human hands
we might share in your creative power
and build up human society.

Look with kindness and blessing
upon N., our co-worker,
who has contributed to our community/company
and who is now retiring/has retired.
Allow him/her the time
to survey all that he/she has accomplished
and give him/her satisfaction and fulfillment
for all his/her labors,
as you did on the seventh day,
when you rested and saw that all you had made was good.

Give him/her peace and help him/her
in this period of adjustment.
Reassure him/her of your love
and open new ways for him/her
to share his/her gifts for the benefit of others.

We praise you, God of love,
through Jesus Christ our Lord.
R/. Amen.

Blessing of Travelers

[617]

The practice of having special prayers to ask for God's protection upon travelers, a custom often mentioned in the Bible, should be respected.

[620]

When the household and visitors have gathered, all make the sign of the cross.

[622]

The leader greets those present in the following words:

**May the Lord turn his face toward us
and guide our feet into the way of peace,
now and forever.
R/. Amen.**

[623]

In the following or similar words, the leader prepares those present for the blessing.

Let us entrust those who are leaving to the hands of the Lord. Let us pray that he will give them a prosperous journey and that as they travel they will praise him in all his creatures; that they will experience God's own goodness in the hospitality they receive and bring the Good News of salvation to all those they meet; that they will be courteous toward all; that they will greet the poor and afflicted with kindness and know how to comfort and help them.

One of those present or the leader reads a text of sacred
Scripture. [624]

Listen to the words of the Book of Deuteronomy: 6:4–9 [625]

> Hear, O Israel! The LORD is our God, the LORD
> alone! Therefore, you shall love the LORD, your
> God, with all your heart, and with all your
> soul, and with all your strength. Take to heart
> these words which I enjoin on you today. Drill
> them into your children. Speak of them at
> home and abroad, whether you are busy or at
> rest. Bind them at your wrist as a sign and let
> them be as a pendant on your forehead. Write
> them on the doorposts of your houses and on
> your gates.

Or John 14:1–11—*I am the way, the truth, and the life.* [626]

Reader: The Word of the Lord.
R/. Thanks be to God.

Leader: Lord, teach us your ways: Lord, have mercy. [630]
R/. Lord, have mercy.

Lord, send help from your sanctuary: Lord, have mercy. **R/.**

Lord, save your servants, for they hope in you: Lord, have
mercy. **R/.**

A leader who is not going to accompany the travelers says
the following prayer, with hands joined:

All-powerful and merciful God,
you led the children of Israel on dry land, parting the waters
   of the sea;
you guided the Magi to your Son by a star.
Help these our brothers and sisters and give them a
   safe journey.
Under your protection let them reach their destination
and come at last to the eternal haven of salvation.

We ask this through Christ our Lord.
R/. Amen.

A leader who is to accompany the travelers says the
following prayer, with hands joined:

All-powerful and ever-living God,
when Abraham left his own land
and departed from his own people,
you kept him safe all through his journey.
Protect us, who also are your servants:
walk by our side to help us;
be our companion and our strength on the road
and our refuge in every adversity.
Lead us, O Lord,
so that we will reach our destination in safety
and happily return to our homes.

We ask this through Christ our Lord.
R/. Amen.

The leader invokes God's blessing on the travelers and all present by signing himself or herself with the sign of the cross and saying:

**May almighty God bless us
and hear our prayers for a safe journey.
R/. Amen.**

—From Book of Blessings

Blessing of Those Going on a Mission Trip

Mission trips offer an opportunity to put faith into action and to stand in solidarity with our brothers and sisters in need.

When the community has gathered, all make the sign of the cross.

Leader: Blessed be the name of the Lord, who guards our coming and our going.
R/. Now and forever.

The leader introduces the blessing in these or similar words:

As we (you) set out, we remember that this mission trip is a time to grow in our desire to serve God and our brothers and sisters. We must try to bring our example of faith, hope, and love as a witness to God's power and mercy.

Then the Scripture is read.

Listen to the words of the Second Letter of
Paul to the Corinthians: 5:6–10

So we are always courageous, although we
know that while we are at home in the body
we are away from the Lord, for we walk by
faith, not by sight. Yet we are courageous, and
we would rather leave the body and go home
to the Lord. Therefore, we aspire to please him,
whether we are at home or away. For we must
all appear before the judgment seat of Christ,
so that each one may receive recompense,
according to what he did in the body, whether
good or evil.

(The family's Bible may be used for an alternate reading
such as Isaiah 2:2–5.)

Reader: The Word of the Lord.
R/. Thanks be to God.

After a time of silence, all join in prayers of intercession
and in the Lord's Prayer. Then the leader prays:

[603]

All-powerful God,
you always show mercy toward those who love you
and you are never far away for those who seek you.
Remain with your servants as they travel
and guide their way in accord with your will.
Shelter them with your protection by day,

give them the light of your grace by night,
and, as their companion on the journey,
bring them to their destination in safety.

We ask this through Christ our Lord.
R/. Amen.

All make the sign of the cross as the leader concludes:

[604]

May the Lord grant that this journey
will end happily through his protection.
R/. Amen.

—From Book of Blessings

Prayers for Arriving or Returns

Prayer for Welcoming Guests

When the household welcomes guests, Psalm 23 (see Part VIII: God's Word in Times of Need) may be prayed at table or another time. It should be followed with a blessing of the guests:

May grace be yours
and peace in abundance from God,
now and forever.
R/. Amen.

Prayer at a Family Celebration or Reunion

Lord Jesus Christ,
you are the presence of God on earth
and the revelation of his love.
You welcomed all people who came to you
and joined in the festivities of their meals.
Be with us and bless our family gathering
with your presence.
Keep us always in your love
and grant us the joy of celebrating
the mystery of your love in each other.
Bless our time together
(and make us thankful for the food we share).

Accept our prayer, Jesus.
You live and reign forever and ever.
R/. Amen.

Prayer upon Returning from a Journey

When one or several members of the household have been away for some time, prayer is appropriate upon their return. The prayer may take place at table or at another time. If all the members of the household have been gone, the words are changed accordingly.

All make the sign of the cross. The leader begins:

**Peace be with this house and with all who live here.
Blessed be the name of the Lord.
R/. Now and forever.**

The leader may use these or similar words to introduce the prayer:

Join now in praising God for a journey safely ended and for the home we share, for all that we have seen of God's goodness and for all those we met on our way. Remember that God commands us to welcome the homeless and to shelter the stranger.

Then the Scripture is read:

Listen to the words of the holy Gospel according to Matthew: 11:28–30

> [Jesus said:] "Come to me, all you who labor
> and are burdened, and I will give you rest.
> Take my yoke upon you and learn from me, for

I am meek and humble of heart; and you will
find rest for yourselves. For my yoke is easy,
and my burden light."

Reader: The Gospel of the Lord.
R/. Praise to you, Lord Jesus Christ

After a time of silence, all may join in prayers of
thanksgiving and intercession and in the Lord's Prayer.
The leader then speaks the concluding prayer:

Blessed are you, Lord our God,
for you lead us by separate ways,
and you return us to one another.
In loving kindness you have given us a place to be at home.
Keep us in your care through all our pilgrimage
until we find our home with you.

We ask this through Christ our Lord.
R/. Amen.

All make the sign of the cross as the leader concludes:

Let us bless the Lord.
R/. Thanks be to God.

Blessing of Those Returning from a Mission Trip

When the household has gathered, all make the sign of the cross.

Leader: Blessed be the name of the Lord.
R/. Now and forever.

The leader introduces the blessing in these or similar words:

[608]

Our (Your) mission trip was a privileged period of grace given by God. As we (you) return home, let us (may you) live up to the vocation God has given us (you): to everywhere proclaim the goodness of him who called us from darkness into his marvelous light.

[609]

Then the Scripture is read:

[610]

Listen to the words of the holy Gospel according to Luke: 24:28–35

> As they approached the village to which they were going, he gave the impression that he was going on farther. But they urged him, "Stay with us, for it is nearly evening and the day is almost over." So he went in to stay with them. And it happened that, while he was with

them at table, he took bread, said the blessing, broke it, and gave it to them. With that their eyes were opened and they recognized him, but he vanished from their sight. Then they said to each other, "Were not our hearts burning within us while he spoke to us on the way and opened the Scriptures to us?" So they set out at once and returned to Jerusalem where they found gathered together the Eleven and those with them who were saying, "The Lord has truly been raised and has appeared to Simon!" Then the two recounted what had taken place on the way and how he was made known to them in the breaking of the bread.

(The family's Bible may be used for an alternate reading such as Matthew 5:13–16.)

Reader: The Gospel of the Lord.
R/. Praise to you, Lord Jesus Christ.

After a time of silence, all join in prayers of intercession and in the Lord's Prayer. Then the leader prays:

[614]

Blessed are you, O God,
Father of our Lord Jesus Christ.
From all races of the earth
you have chosen a people dedicated to you,
eager to do what is right.

Your grace has moved the hearts of these, your friends,
to love you more deeply and to serve you more generously.
We ask you to bless them,
so that they may tell of your wonderful deeds
and give proof of them in their lives.

We ask this through Christ our Lord.
R/. Amen.

All make the sign of the cross as the leader concludes:

[615]

May God, whose goodness inspires in you
all that you desire and achieve,
strengthen your devotion by his blessing.
R/. Amen.

—*From* Book of Blessings

Prayers for School, Work, and Other Endeavors

SCHOOL

Prayers to Begin a School Year/Semester

Blessed are you, Lord God,
Creator of body and mind and heart;
you have sent the Spirit of wisdom and knowledge
to guide your people in all their ways.

At the beginning of this new school year (or semester/term),
we implore your mercy:
bless the students, teachers, and staff of N.,
that together we may grow in faith, hope, and love
as we learn from you and each other
how to follow your Son Jesus.

Expand the horizons of our minds,
that we may grow in wisdom,
understanding, and knowledge;
deepen our commitment to seek the truth of your ways;
and enliven our faith to reach out to those in need.

Glory and praise to you, Lord God,
in the Church and in Christ Jesus forever and ever.
R/. Amen.

Or:

God of wisdom and might,
we praise you for the wonders of our being,
for mind, body, and spirit.
Be with our children as they begin
a new school year (or semester/term).
Bless them and their teachers and staff.

Give them strength and grace as their bodies grow;
wisdom and knowledge to their minds
as they search for understanding;
and peace and zeal to their spirits.

We ask this through Jesus Christ our Lord.
R/. Amen.

Prayer to End a School Year/Semester

God of wisdom,
we thank you for all the gifts you have given us
throughout this school year (or semester/term).
We praise you for giving us life,
for saving us in Christ,
and for choosing us to be your people.

As we come to the end of this school year (or semester/term),
we voice our gratitude
for the good things you have done in us,
and we praise you for all who have shared
in the work of this school.

We ask you to bless them in your love
and give them refreshment and peace.

(continued)

We praise you, God,
through Jesus Christ our Lord,
who lives and reigns forever and ever.
R/. Amen.

Prayer for Students

Lord our God,
in your wisdom and love
you surround us with the mysteries of the universe.

Send your Spirit upon these students
and fill them with your wisdom and blessings.
Grant that they may
devote themselves to their studies
and draw ever closer to you,
the source of all knowledge.

We ask this through Christ our Lord.
R/. Amen.

Prayer for Teachers

Lord God,
your spirit of wisdom fills the earth
and teaches us your ways.

Look upon these teachers.
Let them strive to share their knowledge with gentle patience
and endeavor always to bring the truth to eager minds.

Grant that they may follow Jesus Christ,
the way, the truth, and the life,
forever and ever.
R/. Amen.

WORK

Prayer to St. Joseph, Model for Workers

Silent and well-known carpenter in Nazareth,
model of workers, by the work of your hands,
you gave your contribution to the work of the Creator,
you earned your living,
and you provided for the needs of the Holy Family.
Intercede for all workers, in the difficulties of their daily lives,
especially for the unemployed, in their anxieties
    for tomorrow,
so that, through the guidance of God,
the great Architect and Builder,
they all may use their strength and their talents
to make visible his Kingdom, his new creation,
to offer a concrete service to society,
and to earn wages worthy of their efforts.

Prayer for Those Seeking Work

Loving God,
you created the human race
and you know each one of us by name.
Through Christ you have chosen us
to be your sons and daughters
and to build up your Kingdom on earth.

Give N. the work he/she seeks
so that he/she may share his/her talents with others
and know the dignity and satisfaction
that you give us through our work.

(continued)

Give him/her patience while you open doors,
and grant him/her the wisdom to see your will.

Keep our family in your care
and provide for all our needs.
Never let stress diminish our love for each other
nor the desire for material things
lessen our love for you.

With confidence and trust, loving God,
we make this prayer through Jesus Christ our Lord.
R/. Amen.

Prayer of Workers

Blessed are you, Lord God,
from eternity you have called us to be your people,
and to sing your praises at all times.

Bless us in our work and prayer,
and grant that our lives may give you glory
through our words, our witness, and our worship.
We give you praise, Creator God,
through Jesus Christ our Lord,
in the communion of the Holy Spirit,
one God, forever and ever.
R/. Amen.

Blessing of Workers

Blessed are you, Lord our God,
Creator of the universe and Father of humanity.
We praise you for your mighty works
and for the wonders of your love.

Hear our prayers today
and grant your blessings to all workers.
Let our work contribute to the good
of all members of this community
and to your glory forever and ever.
R/. Amen.

Prayers Before Meetings

[552]

We stand before you, Holy Spirit,
conscious of our sinfulness
but aware that we gather in your name.

Come to us, remain with us,
and enlighten our hearts.

Give us light and strength
to know your will,
to make it our own,
and to live it in our lives.

Guide us by your wisdom,
support us by your power,
for you are God,
sharing the glory of Father and Son.

You desire justice for all:
enable us to uphold the rights of others;
do not allow us to be misled by ignorance
or corrupted by fear or favor.

Unite us to yourself in the bond of love
and keep us faithful to all that is true.

(continued)

As we gather in your name
may we temper justice with love,
so that all our decisions
may be pleasing to you,
and earn the reward
promised to good and faithful servants.

You live and reign with Father and Son,
one God, forever and ever.
R/. Amen.

—Used before every session of the Second Vatican Council;
from Book of Blessings

Or:

Blessed are you, bounteous God,
maker of heaven and earth,
you have chosen us to be your people
and to give you glory in everything we do.
Be with us during our meeting,
which will bring many people together.
Help us to meet one another in joy
and to work together for your glory
and the benefit of our community.

We praise your name forever and ever.
R/. Amen.

Prayers After Meetings

[572]

In you, Lord our God,
all things have their beginning, continuation, and end.
Grace us with your saving presence,
aid us with your constant help,
and let us glorify you,
now and forever.
R/. Amen.

—*From Book of Blessings*

Or:

Father of us all,
look upon us in your love, and bless us.
Protect us from sin and harm,
and guide us with your light
until we come together again.

All praise, glory, and honor to you, Father,
through Christ our Lord.
R/. Amen.

Blessing of Farms and Farmworkers

All praise and glory are yours, Lord our God,
Creator of the universe and Father of all:
we give you thanks for your mercy
and for your loving care of creation.

Continue to shower your blessings on this farm:
on the people who live and work here,
on the animals and plants,
on the buildings and machinery.

Let your people live and work in happiness
and enjoy the fruits of their labors.
Let the plants and animals flourish
and be protected from all harm.
Let these buildings and machines
continue to be of service to all.

Almighty God, we bless and glorify your name
now and always and forever.
R/. Amen.

Blessing at Planting Time

[986]

At the beginning of the planting season it is customary for farmers or gardeners to seek God's blessing on their crops. As the seeds are planted, God is asked to protect them from disease and destruction and to bring forth from them an abundant yield.

~

[989]

When the community has gathered, all make the sign of the cross.

[991]

The leader greets those present in the following words:

Let us praise God, who plants the seeds and reaps the harvest. Blessed be God forever.
R/. Blessed be God forever.

[992]

In the following or similar words, the leader prepares those present for the blessing.

Today we seek God's blessing on these seeds and the crops they will produce. Christ reminds us that, unless the seed is planted in the earth and dies, it will not yield fruit. As these seeds grow and are cared for, may they be signs of the new life that comes from God.

[993]

One of those present or the leader reads a text of sacred Scripture.

[994]

Listen to the words of the holy Gospel
according to John: 12:23–25

> Jesus answered the disciples, "The hour has
> come for the Son of Man to be glorified. Amen,
> amen, I say to you, unless a grain of wheat
> falls to the ground and dies, it remains just
> a grain of wheat; but if it dies, it produces
> much fruit. Whoever loves his life loses it,
> and whoever hates his life in this world will
> preserve it for eternal life."

Or Isaiah 55:10–13—*God gives seed to the one who sows.*

Reader: The Gospel of the Lord.
R/. Praise to you, Lord Jesus Christ.

[997]

The litany is then said.

Leader: The Lord of the harvest sustains us, let us
call upon him:
R/. Deliver us, O Lord.

From despair in times of drought: **R/.**

From wastefulness in times of plenty: **R/.**

From neglect of those in need: **R/.**

From hunger and thirst: **R/.**

[998]

After the litany the leader invites all present to say the Lord's Prayer.

[999]

The leader says the prayer of blessing with hands joined.

Lord of the harvest,
you placed the gifts of creation in our hands
and called us to till the earth and make it fruitful.

We ask your blessing
as we prepare to place these seeds in the earth.
May the care we show these seeds
remind us of your tender love for your people.

We ask this through Christ our Lord.
R/. Amen.

[1001]

The leader concludes the rite by signing himself or herself with the sign of the cross and saying:

May God nourish us and care for us, now and forever.
R/. Amen.

—*From* Book of Blessings

Blessing on the Occasion of Thanksgiving for the Harvest

[1007]

The symbolic offering of first fruits of the harvest to God, in order to praise him for this gift, is a custom that should be maintained. It is a reminder of the debt of gratitude owed to God for all his favors and it continues a tradition that is mentioned in the Old Testament.

[1010]

When the household and friends have gathered, all make the sign of the cross.

[1012]

The leader greets those present in the following words:

Let us forever praise God, who in his all-embracing providence gives us food from the fruits of the earth. Blessed be God now and forever.
R/. Amen.

[1013]

In the following or similar words, the leader prepares those present for the blessing.

Let us now bless the Lord, who has once again bestowed on us the fruits of the earth. Abel offered his first fruits to God; let us also learn to share our blessings for the good of those in need, so that we may be true children of the Father, who bestows his gifts for the benefit of all the peoples of the earth.

[1014]

One of those present or the leader reads a text of sacred Scripture.

Listen to the words of the Acts of the Apostles: 14:15b–17

> Paul shouted to the crowd: "We proclaim to
> you good news that you should turn from
> these idols to the living God, 'who made
> heaven and earth and sea and all that is
> in them.' In past generations he allowed
> all Gentiles to go their own ways; yet, in
> bestowing his goodness, he did not leave
> himself without witness, for he gave you
> rains from heaven and fruitful seasons, and
> filled you with nourishment and gladness for
> your hearts."

[1015]

Or Luke 12:15–21—*Your life is not made secure by what you own, even when you have more than you need.*

Reader: The Word of the Lord.
R/. Thanks be to God.

[1020]

The leader says the prayer of blessing with hands joined.

[1021]

Let us pray:
All-powerful God,
we appeal to your tender care,
that even as you temper the winds and rains
to nurture the fruits of the earth
you will also send upon them
the gentle shower of your blessing.
Fill the hearts of your people with gratitude,
that from the earth's fertility
the hungry may be filled with good things
and the poor and needy proclaim the glory of your name.

We ask this through Christ our Lord.
R/. Amen.

[1022]

The leader concludes the rite by saying:

Let us bless God,
forever let us praise and extol the name
of Father, Son, and Holy Spirit.
R/. Amen.

—*From* Book of Blessings

OTHER ENDEAVORS

Blessing Before an Athletic Event

[1024]

This blessing is intended for those who participate in an athletic event. The blessing asks that God may protect the athletes from injury and that throughout the event they may show respect for one another.

[1026]

All make the sign of the cross as the leader says:

Blessed be the name of the Lord.
R/. Now and forever.

[1027]

One of those present or the leader reads a text of sacred Scripture.

Listen to the words of the Second Letter of St. Paul to Timothy:

4:6–8

> For I am already being poured out like a libation, and the time of my departure is at hand. I have competed well; I have finished the race; I have kept the faith. From now on the crown of righteousness awaits me, which the Lord, the just judge, will award to me on that day, and not only to me, but to all who have longed for his appearance.

[1028]

Or 1 Corinthians 9:24–27—*We win a crown that is imperishable.*

Reader: The Word of the Lord.
R/. Thanks be to God.

[1029]

The leader says the prayer of blessing with hands joined.

Strong and faithful God,
as we come together for this contest,
we ask you to bless these athletes.

Keep them safe from injury and harm,
instill in them respect for each other,
and reward them for their perseverance.

Lead us all to the rewards of your Kingdom
where you live and reign forever and ever.
R/. Amen.

—*From Book of Blessings*

Prayer When Gathering to Meet or Study

When the household hosts a meeting, faith-sharing group, or study group, various prayers may be chosen, as appropriate, from Part I: Basic Prayers or Part II: Daily Prayers. Praying Evening Prayer together is especially appropriate if the meeting has a spiritual purpose. In addition, the invocation of the Holy Spirit (see the Pentecost Sequence in Part III: Days and Seasons) may be a fitting prayer.

If the purpose of the meeting is the study of Scripture, the following prayer is appropriate:

Lord our God,
we bless you.
As we come together to ponder the Scriptures,
we ask you in your kindness
to fill us with the knowledge of your will
so that, pleasing you in all things,
we may grow in every good work.
We ask this through Christ our Lord.
R/. Amen.

Any meeting may conclude with this blessing:

May God, the source of all patience and encouragement,
enable us to live in perfect harmony with one another
in the spirit of Christ Jesus.
With one heart and one voice
may we glorify God,
now and forever.
R/. Amen.

The Lord's Prayer may follow.

Blessing Before and After a Bible Study or Prayer Meeting

[509]

Whenever Christians come together in the name of Christ, he himself is present in their midst. Those taking part in the meeting should wish to offer prayers in praise of Christ and in petition for the divine help needed to achieve the purpose for which they have gathered.

BEGINNING OF THE MEETING

When the participants have gathered, all make the sign of the cross.

The leader introduces the blessing in these or similar words:

We have gathered today to pray (study) together, that we may grow in our understanding of the mystery of faith and follow God's path ever more closely.

After a time of silence, the leader prays:

Lord,
pour out on us the spirit of understanding, truth, and peace.
Help us to strive with all our hearts
to know what is pleasing to you,
and when we know your will
make us determined to do it.

We ask this through Christ our Lord.
R/. Amen.

END OF THE MEETING

[513]
The leader introduces the prayer in these or similar words:

Through this meeting Jesus himself has spoken to us. Since
our task is to conform our lives to the Word we have heard,
let us raise our minds and hearts to God, praying that he
may guide us through the Holy Spirit and give us the power
always to do what is pleasing to him.

[514]
After a time of silence, all join in prayers of intercession
and in the Lord's Prayer.

[516]
The leader says the prayer of blessing with hands joined.

We thank you and bless you, Lord our God.
In times past you spoke in many varied ways through
    the prophets,
but in this, the final age, you have spoken through your Son
to reveal to all nations the riches of your grace.
May we who have met to ponder the Scriptures
be filled with the knowledge of your will
in all wisdom and spiritual understanding,
and, pleasing you as we should in all things,
may we bear fruit in every good work.
We ask this through Christ our Lord.
R/. Amen.

All make the sign of the cross as the leader concludes:

God, the Father of mercies, has sent his Son into the world.
Through the Holy Spirit, who will teach us all truth,
may he make us messengers of the Gospel
and witnesses of his love to the world.
R/. Amen.

—From Book of Blessings

Prayers for an Interfaith Gathering

Blessed are you, Lord, God of all creation,
whose goodness fills our hearts with joy.
Blessed are you,
who have brought us together this day
to work in harmony and peace.
Strengthen us with your grace and wisdom
for you are God forever and ever.
R/. Amen.

Or:

Lord,
may everything we do
begin with your inspiration
and continue with your help,
so that all our prayers and works
may begin in you
and by you be happily ended.
Glory and praise to you,
forever and ever.
R/. Amen.

Or:

[573]

May God strengthen you and bring your work
    to completion.
May hope accompany your journey through the
    days to come.
May God's abiding presence be with you
all the days of your life.
R/. Amen.

—From Book of Blessings

Prayer When Planning a Special Project

The following prayer may be adapted by adding a description of the project. The alternate prayer may also be used at the conclusion of an event or project meeting.

Blessed are you, Lord God,
ruler of all creation:
you know our hearts and our plans,
and guide all that we do for your glory.
Bless us as we continue to do our work: *(brief description)*
and bless all that we do for you.
Help us to carry out all our activities
for your honor and glory
and for the salvation of your people.
Guide us in all we do;
help us to build up your Kingdom
and come to our reward.

We praise your name forever and ever.
R/. Amen.

Or:

Lord, direct our actions by your inspiration
and carry them out by your assistance.
May our every prayer and work
always begin with you
and through you come to a successful completion.
R/. Amen.

BLESSINGS FOR OBJECTS

Prayer for Placing Objects for Prayer and Devotion

This prayer may be used when placing blessed icons and other images, or other objects used in the household's prayer.

> Appropriate Scriptures include Colossians 1:12–20;
> Luke 1:42–50; Ephesians 3:14–19; 2 Corinthians 3:17–18;
> Romans 8:26–31; 1 Corinthians 13:8–13; Luke 11:5–13;
> Psalm 150.

Lord,
you are blessed and the source of every blessing.
Be with us now
and whenever we use this symbol of our faith.
May we strive always to be transformed
into the likeness of Christ, your Son,
who lives and reigns forever and ever.
R/. Amen.

General Blessings for Objects

Sometimes, tools or objects provide an occasion to give thanks and ask God's blessing. In these prayers, we recognize the joy and responsibility of human labor, recreation, and devotion.

For each kind of object named below, an appropriate Scripture reading is suggested and a short prayer of blessing is provided. The blessing begins with the sign of the cross and these words:

Let us praise and bless the Lord, the fountain of all goodness. Blessed be God now and forever.
R/. Amen.

The leader may prepare those present for the blessing with a brief introduction.

Then one of those present or the leader reads a text of sacred Scripture. Suggested Scripture texts are given for each type of blessing below. Then the leader says "Let us pray" followed by a moment of silence and the appropriate blessing. Any of these blessings may conclude with a suitable song.

FOR THE PRODUCTS OF NATURE

Appropriate Scriptures include 1 Timothy 4:4–5 and Wisdom 13:1–7.

[2000]

Blessed are you, O God,
Creator of the universe,
who have made all things good
and given the earth for us to cultivate.

Grant that we may always use created things gratefully
and share your gifts with those in need,
out of the love of Christ our Lord,
who lives and reigns with you forever and ever.
R/. Amen.

—From Book of Blessings

FOR THE PRODUCTS OF HUMAN LABOR

Appropriate Scriptures include Romans 8:24–28 and
Sirach 18:1–9.

[2003]

Almighty and ever-living God,
you have made us stewards over the created world,
so that in all things we might honor the demands of charity.
Graciously hear our prayers,
that your blessing may come upon all those
who use these objects for their needs.
Let them always see you as the good surpassing every good
and love their neighbor with upright hearts.
We ask this through Christ our Lord.
R/. Amen.

—From Book of Blessings

FOR TOOLS FOR WORK

[929]

Appropriate Scriptures include Job 28:1–28;
Proverbs 31:10–31; Sirach 38:24–34; Isaiah 28:23–29;
Acts 18:1–5; Matthew 13:1–9; Luke 5:3–11.

[934]

O God,
the fullness of blessing comes down from you,
to you our prayers of blessing rise up.

(continued)

In your kindness protect your servants,
who stand here before you devout and faithful,
bearing the tools of their trade.

Grant that their hard work may contribute
to the perfecting of your creation
and provide a decent life for themselves and their families.
Help them to strive for a better society
and to praise and glorify your holy name always.
We ask this through Christ our Lord.
R/. Amen.

—From Book of Blessings

In some cases, the following prayers may be appropriate.

FOR THE WORK OF AN ARTIST OR CRAFTSPERSON

Appropriate Scriptures include Genesis 1; Job 38–39;
Psalm 8; Revelation 21:1–4.

God our Creator,
the heavens declare your glory,
and earth proclaims your handiwork.
We praise you for the work of creation,
manifest in the imagination and skill
of artists and craftspeople
who bring beauty and delight,
challenge and vision to our lives.

May your blessing be upon all who share this work:
may we all become heralds of your reign
when beauty shall be the companion of justice and peace.
We ask this through Christ our Lord.
R/. Amen.

FOR OBJECTS FOR USE OR ENTERTAINMENT

Appropriate Scriptures include Psalm 104 and Psalm 150.

God,
we praise you for the work of human hands.
Bless us when these *(name the objects)*
are used to renew our spirits,
to help us in our work,
or to bring us knowledge of our neighbors,
our community, and our world.
Give us wisdom and humility
to be good stewards of the earth and of our days.
We ask this through Christ our Lord.
R/. Amen.

BLESSINGS FOR TRANSPORTATION

Blessing of a Family Vehicle

[851]

The quality of life is enhanced by the various means of overcoming distance and of making it possible for people to come together for meetings, visits, and other forms of social contact.

[857]

When the household has gathered, all make the sign of the cross.

[859]

The leader greets those present in the following words:

With one heart and one mind let us bless the Lord Jesus Christ, who is the way, the truth, and the life. Blessed be God now and forever.
R/. Amen.

[860]

In the following or similar words, the leader prepares those present for the blessing.

Christ, the Son of God, came into the world to gather those who were scattered. Whatever contributes to bringing us closer together therefore is in accord with God's plan. Let us call on God to protect those who will ride in this car.

[861]

Then the Scripture is read:

Listen to the words of the holy Gospel
according to John: 14:6-7

> Jesus said to Thomas, "I am the way and the
> truth and the life. No one comes to the Father
> except through me. If you know me, then you
> will also know my Father. From now on you
> do know him and have seen him."

[863]

Or Luke 3:3-6—*Make ready the way of the Lord.*

Reader: The Gospel of the Lord.
R/. Praise to you, Lord Jesus Christ.

[868]

The leader says the prayer of blessing with hands joined.

Let us pray.
All-powerful God,
Creator of heaven and earth,
in the rich depths of your wisdom
you have empowered us to produce great and
    beautiful works.
Grant, we pray, that those who use this car
may travel safely, with care for the safety of others.
Whether they travel for business or pleasure,
let them always find Christ to be the companion of
    their journey,
who lives and reigns forever and ever.
R/. Amen.

[871]

The leader concludes the rite by saying:

May the Lord be the guide on our journeys,
so that we may travel in peace and reach eternal life.
R/. Amen.

—*From* Book of Blessings

Blessing of a Boat

[878]
Boats are an important means of transportation and are essential to the livelihood of fishermen. It is customary that God's blessing be sought for the protection of those who sail them.

❧

[881]
When the household has gathered, all make the sign of the cross.

[883]
The leader greets those present in the following words:

Let us praise and glorify God the Father and the Lord Jesus Christ, now and forever.
R/. Amen.

[884]
In the following or similar words, the minister prepares those present for the blessing.

Today we gather to bless this boat and those who will use it for work or pleasure. The Lord calmed the Sea of Galilee and brought his disciples to safety. We commend those who sail this craft into his care.

[885]
One of those present or the leader reads a text of sacred Scripture.

Listen to the words of the holy Gospel according
to Matthew: 8:23–27

> As Jesus got into a boat, his disciples followed
> him. Suddenly a violent storm came up on
> the sea, so that the boat was being swamped
> by waves; but he was asleep. They came and
> woke him, saying, "Lord, save us! We are
> perishing!" He said to them, "Why are you
> terrified, O you of little faith?" Then he got
> up, rebuked the winds and the sea, and there
> was great calm. The men were amazed and
> said, "What sort of man is this, whom even the
> winds and the sea obey?"

[886]

Or Mark 6:45–51a—*Jesus walks on the water.*

Reader: The Gospel of the Lord.
R/. Praise to you, Lord Jesus Christ.

[889]

The litany is then said.

Leader: At the command of the Son of God the sea was
calmed and the nets were filled to overflowing. Let us call
upon Christ with faith:
R/. Guide us safely, Lord.

In the face of wind and rain, we pray: **R/.**

In the stillness and calm of the sea, we pray: **R/.**

In our respect for the world's natural resources, we pray: **R/.**

After the litany the leader invites all present to say the
Lord's Prayer.

The leader says the prayer of blessing with hands joined.

God of boundless love,
at the beginning of creation
your Spirit hovered over the deep.
You called forth every creature,
and the seas teemed with life.

Through your Son, Jesus Christ,
you have given us the rich harvest of salvation.

Bless this boat, its equipment, and all who will use it.
Protect them from the dangers, wind and rain,
and all the perils of the deep.
May Christ, who calmed the storm
and filled the nets of his disciples,
bring us all to the harbor of light and peace.

Grant this through Christ our Lord.
R/. Amen.

The leader concludes the rite by signing himself or herself
with the sign of the cross and saying:

May the saving power of our Lord guide and protect us, now
and forever.
R/. Amen.

—From Book of Blessings

PRAYERS FOR WEATHER

Prayer for Protection During a Storm

Loving God, maker of heaven and earth,
protect us in your love and mercy.
Send the Spirit of Jesus to be with us,
to still our fears and give us confidence.

In the stormy waters,
Jesus reassured his disciples by his presence,
calmed the storm, and strengthened their faith.
Guard us from harm during this storm
and renew our faith to serve you faithfully.
Give us the courage to face all difficulties
and the wisdom to see the ways
your Spirit binds us together
in mutual assistance.

With confidence we make our prayer
through Jesus Christ our Lord.
R/. Amen.

Prayer for Rain

God our Creator,
maker of all things and protector of your people,
in your love look upon us in our time of need
and give us your help.

Open the heavens for us and send us the rain
we need for our lives and crops.
As our hearts long for you,
so we seek rain to refresh the earth;
as we long for life,
so let the earth produce its harvest in abundance.
May we rejoice in the good things of the earth
and raise our eyes to you, the source of all blessings.

Hear our cry for mercy and answer our prayer,
through Jesus Christ our Lord.
R/. Amen.

Prayer for Dry Weather

Almighty God,
look with mercy on us
and swiftly come to our help.
Give us the dry weather we need,
and deliver us from *(poor crops, the danger of floods, etc.)*.
Grant us the good things of the earth
and your spiritual blessings in abundance.

Teach us to be generous to others
and grateful to you for your goodness.

With confidence we make our prayer
though Jesus Christ our Lord.
R/. Amen.

PRAYERS AND BLESSINGS FOR OTHER NEEDS OR CIRCUMSTANCES

Prayer for Special Occasions of Life

Lord God,
from the abundance of your mercy
enrich your servants and safeguard them.
Strengthened by your blessing,
may they always be thankful to you
and bless you with unending joy.
We ask this through Christ our Lord.
R/. Amen.

Blessing in Times of Joy and Thanksgiving

[1966]

In the desire that the grace of the eucharistic celebration should reach deeply into their daily lives, Christians strive to remain in an attitude of thanksgiving. The gifts of God are a constant reminder to thank him at all times in return, and especially when he has granted some special favor to the faithful. On such occasions they should gather to praise him together and to bless him.

[1969]

All make the sign of the cross.

[1971]

The leader greets those present in the following words:

Give praise to God, who is rich in mercy and who has favored us in wonderful ways. Blessed be God now and forever.
R/. Amen.

[1972]

In the following or similar words, the leader prepares those present for the blessing.

St. Paul teaches us to give thanks to God always through Christ, in whom he has given us everything.

[1973]

One of those present or the leader reads a text of sacred Scripture.

Listen to the words of the Letter of St. Paul to the Philippians:

4:4–7

> Rejoice in the Lord always. I shall say it again: rejoice! Your kindness should be known to all. The Lord is near. Have no anxiety at all, but in everything, by prayer and petition, with thanksgiving, make your requests known to God. Then the peace of God that surpasses all understanding will guard your hearts and minds in Christ Jesus.

[1974]

Or Colossians 3:15–17—*Give thanks to God the Father through him*; 1 Thessalonians 5:12–24—*Render constant thanks; such is God's will for you.*

Reader: The Word of the Lord.
R/. Thanks be to God.

[1979]

The leader says the prayer of blessing with hands joined.

Almighty Father,
you are lavish in bestowing all your gifts,
and we give you thanks for the favors you have given us.
In your goodness you have favored us
and kept us safe in the past.
We ask that you continue to protect us
and to shelter us in the shadow of your wings.

We ask this through Christ our Lord.
R/. Amen.

[1982]

The leader concludes the rite by signing himself or herself
with the sign of the cross and saying:

May God the Father, with the Son and the Holy Spirit,
who has shown us such great mercy,
be praised and blessed forever and ever.
R/. Amen.

[1983]

The prayer may conclude with a song.

—*From Book of Blessings*

Prayer in Times of Suffering and Need

When a member of a household is passing through a time of anguish or great need, this prayer may be appropriate. This prayer includes optional prayers at the end for specific needs.

All make the sign of the cross. The leader begins:

God comforts us in all our afflictions.
Blessed be God forever.
R/. Blessed be God forever.

Then the Scripture is read:

Listen to the words of the Book of Job: 7:3-7, 11

> So I have been assigned months of misery,
>   and troubled nights have been told off for me.
>
> If in bed I say, "When shall I arise?"
>   Then the night drags on;
>   I am filled with restlessness until the dawn.
> My flesh is clothed with worms and scabs;
>   my skin cracks and festers;
> My days are swifter than a weaver's shuttle;
>   they come to an end without hope.
> Remember that my life is like the wind;
>   I shall not see happiness again.
>
> My own utterance I will not restrain;
>   I will speak in the anguish of my spirit;
>   I will complain in the bitterness of my soul.

Reader: The Word of the Lord.
R/. Thanks be to God.

> After a time of silence, all join in prayers of intercession and in the Lord's Prayer. Then the leader prays:

God of all mercies, God of all consolation,
comfort us in our afflictions
that we in turn might comfort those who are in trouble
with the same consolation we have received.

Grant this through Christ our Lord.
R/. Amen.

> All make the sign of the cross as the leader concludes:

Let us bless the Lord.
R/. Thanks be to God.

> The prayer may conclude with "Amazing Grace" or another appropriate song.

PRAYERS IN TIMES OF FAMILY STRIFE

A

God of compassion and grace,
in your steadfast love accompany N. and N.
As you ever work to restore and renew your people,
overcome bitterness with your joy,
hatred with your love, brokenness with your life;
and give us hope
through the death and Resurrection of your Son,
Jesus Christ our Lord.
R/. Amen.

B

O God, you have bound us together in a common life.
Help us in the midst of our struggles
to confront one another without hatred or bitterness,
and to work together with mutual forbearance and respect.
We ask this through Jesus Christ our Lord.
R/. Amen.

PRAYER IN TIME OF FINANCIAL DIFFICULTIES

God of mercy and compassion,
you promise to give us all that we need.
As we face this time of financial struggle,
help us to trust in your providence
and keep our hearts fixed on the treasures of heaven.

We ask this through Christ our Lord.
R/. Amen.

PRAYER IN TIME OF NEIGHBORHOOD OR RACIAL STRIFE

O God, the Lord of all,
your Son commanded us to love our enemies
and to pray for them.
Lead us from prejudice to truth;
deliver us from hatred, cruelty, and revenge;
and enable us to stand before you,
reconciled through your Son, Jesus Christ our Lord.
R/. Amen.

Prayer in Times of Penance and Reconciliation

On Fridays and during the season of Lent, the whole Church is called to do penance: to turn away from evil and to seek reconciliation with God and one another in prayer and in deeds. The following prayer may be appropriate when the household needs to express sorrow over past deeds and to make peace. Works of kindness and of justice (the spiritual and corporal works of mercy) should accompany such prayer.

All make the sign of the cross. The leader begins:

Let us come with confidence before the throne of grace
    to receive God's mercy,
and we shall find pardon and strength in our time of need.
Blessed be God forever.
R/. Blessed be God forever.

Then the Scripture is read. Any appropriate Bible reading may be selected. The following examples should not limit the choice.

A
Listen to the words of the Prophet Isaiah: 1:2, 15–18

    Hear, O heavens, and listen, O earth,
        for the LORD speaks:

    When you spread out your hands,
        I close my eyes to you;
    Though you pray the more,
        I will not listen.
    Your hands are full of blood!

Wash yourselves clean!
Put away your misdeeds from before my eyes;
cease doing evil; learn to do good.
Make justice your aim: redress the wronged,
hear the orphan's plea, defend the widow.

Come now, let us set things right, says the Lord:
Though your sins be like scarlet,
they may become white as snow;
Though they be crimson red,
they may become white as wool.

Or:

B
Listen to the words of the First Letter of St. John: 1:6; 2:1–2

If we say, "We have fellowship with [God],"
while we continue to walk in darkness, we lie
and do not act in truth.
My children, I am writing this to you so
that you may not commit sin. But if anyone
does sin, we have an Advocate with the Father,
Jesus Christ the righteous one. He is expiation
for our sins, and not for our sins only but for
those of the whole world.

Reader: The Word of the Lord.
R/. Thanks be to God.

After a time of silence, all kneel. The leader may begin:

We may now speak of the wrong we have done and the good we have not done. Let us ask forgiveness of one another, of others, and of God.

After this, all may join in the *Confiteor* (page 8, in Part I: Basic Prayers) or the Act of Contrition (pages 8 or 21). There may then be prayers of intercession. All stand and join hands for the Lord's Prayer. The leader then prays:

Loving God, our source of life,
you know our weakness.
May we reach out with joy to grasp your hand
and walk more readily in your ways.
We ask this through Christ our Lord.
R/. Amen.

All make the sign of the cross as the leader concludes:

May God, who frees us from sin,
bless us and keep us always in peace.
R/. Amen.

The prayer may conclude with the exchange of peace and with an appropriate song such as "Amazing Grace."

Prayer in Times of Seeking God's Will

When important decisions are to be made, the following psalm may be a part of the table prayer or may be used at another time. "Come, Holy Spirit" (the Pentecost Sequence, in Part III: Days and Seasons) is also appropriate.

PSALM 27:7–9, 13–14

Hear, O LORD, the sound of my call;
    have pity on me, and answer me.
Of you my heart speaks; you my glance seeks;
    your presence, O LORD, I seek.
Hide not your face from me;
    do not in anger repel your servant.
You are my helper: cast me not off;
    forsake me not, O God my savior.

I believe that I shall see the bounty of the LORD
    in the land of the living.
Wait for the LORD with courage;
    be stouthearted, and wait for the LORD.

Prayers After a Community or Natural Disaster

Suffering loss of life or severe property damage through flood, earthquake, windstorm, snowstorm, widespread fire, or terrorism, a family or community may turn to God for help, consolation and strength.

Those gathered make the sign of the cross.

Leader: Blessed be the name of the Lord.
R/. Who hears the cries of those in distress.

The leader introduces the prayer in these or similar words:

We gather in our sorrow to bring our pain and our concerns to the Lord and to ask that he give us strength and courage to face the days ahead.

Then the Scripture is read:

Listen to the words of the Book of Revelation: 21:1–5a

> I, John, saw a new heaven and a new earth. The former heaven and the former earth had passed away, and the sea was no more. I also saw the holy city, a new Jerusalem, coming down out of heaven from God, prepared as a bride adorned for her husband. I heard a

loud voice from the throne saying, "Behold, God's dwelling is with the human race. He will dwell with them and they will be his people and God himself will always be with them as their God. He will wipe every tear from their eyes, and there shall be no more death or mourning, wailing or pain, for the old order has passed away."

The One who sat on the throne said, "Behold, I make all things new."

(The family's Bible may be used for an alternate reading such as Romans 8:31b–39.)

Reader: The Word of the Lord.
R/. Thanks be to God.

After a time of silence, all join in prayers of intercession and in the Lord's Prayer. Then the leader prays:

God our Father,
you set the earth on its foundation
and all elements of nature obey your command.
Help us in our time of trouble;
calm the (*flood, earthquake, widespread fire, or other disaster*)
that threatens us
and turn our fear of your power
into praise of your goodness.

If people have died:

Have mercy on those who have died
and welcome them into your Kingdom of peace and joy.
In your compassion look upon us
and give us tears to mourn their loss.

Let us always feel the presence of your love.
We ask this through Jesus Christ our Lord.
R/. Amen.

All make the sign of the cross as the leader concludes:

Guide us in the days that lie ahead
and give us strength to rebuild our lives.
Protect us and help us to live for you.
R/. Amen.

Blessing of a Victim of Crime or Oppression

[430]

The personal experience of crime, political oppression, or social oppression can be traumatic and not easily forgotten. A victim often needs the assistance of others, and no less that of God, in dealing with this experience.

[431]

This blessing is intended to assist the victim and help him or her come to a state of tranquility and peace.

[433]

When the household has gathered, all make the sign of the cross.

[435]

The leader greets those present in the following words.

May the Lord grant us peace, now and forever.
R/. Amen.

[436]

In the following or similar words, the leader prepares those present for the blessing.

Throughout history God has manifested his love and care for those who have suffered from violence, hatred, and oppression. We commend N. to the healing mercy of God, who binds up all our wounds and enfolds us in his gentle care.

One of those present or the leader reads a text of sacred
Scripture.

Listen to the words of the holy Gospel
according to Matthew: 10:28–33

> Jesus said to his disciples: "Do not be afraid
> of those who kill the body but cannot kill
> the soul; rather, be afraid of the one who can
> destroy both soul and body in Gehenna. Are
> not two sparrows sold for a small coin? Yet not
> one of them falls to the ground without your
> Father's knowledge. Even all the hairs of your
> head are counted. So do not be afraid; you are
> worth more than many sparrows. Everyone
> who acknowledges me before others I will
> acknowledge before my heavenly Father. But
> whoever denies me before others, I will deny
> before my heavenly Father."

Or Lamentations 3:49–59—*When I called, you came to
my aid.*

Reader: The Gospel of the Lord.
R/. Praise to you, Lord Jesus Christ.

The intercessions are then said.

Leader: Let us pray to the Lord God, the defender of the weak and powerless, who delivered our ancestors from harm.
R/. Deliver us from evil, O Lord.

For N., that he/she may be freed from pain and fear, we pray to the Lord. **R/.**

For all who are victims of crime or oppression, we pray to the Lord. **R/.**

For an end to all acts of violence and hatred, we pray to the Lord. **R/.**

For those who harm others, that they may change their lives and turn to God, we pray to the Lord. **R/.**

After the intercessions the leader invites all present to say the Lord's Prayer.

The leader says the prayer of blessing with hands joined.

Lord God,
your own Son was delivered into the hands of the wicked,
yet he prayed for his persecutors
and overcame hatred with the Blood of the Cross.
Relieve the suffering of N.;
grant him/her peace of mind
and a renewed faith in your protection and care.

(continued)

Protect us all from the violence of others,
keep us safe from the weapons of hate,
and restore to us tranquility and peace.

We ask this through Christ our Lord.
R/. Amen.

[445]

The leader concludes the rite by signing himself or herself
with the sign of the cross and saying:

May God bless us with his mercy,
strengthen us with his love,
and enable us to walk in charity and peace.
R/. Amen.

—*From Book of Blessings*

Blessing to Be Adapted for Various Circumstances

[1984]

This blessing may be adapted to various circumstances not explicitly provided for elsewhere in this book.

[1985]

It is not meant to be used in inappropriate or frivolous ways.

[1987]

All make the sign of the cross.

[1989]

The leader greets those present in the following words:

Let us bless and praise the Lord, the fountain of all
   goodness. Blessed be God now and forever.
R/. Amen.

[1990]

In the following or similar words, the leader prepares
those present for the blessing.

All that God has created and sustains, all the events he
guides, and all human works that are good and have a good
purpose, prompt those who believe to praise and bless the
Lord with hearts and voices. He is the source and origin of
every blessing. By this celebration, we proclaim our belief

that all things work together for the good of those who fear and love God. We are sure that in all things, we must seek the help of God, so that in complete reliance on his will we may, in Christ, do everything for his glory.

[1991]

One of those present or the leader reads a text of sacred Scripture.

[1993]

Listen to the words of the First Letter of St. Paul to Timothy: 4:4–5

> Everything created by God is good, and
> nothing is to be rejected when received with
> thanksgiving, for it is made holy by the
> invocation of God in prayer.

[1991, 1994]

Or Colossians 1:9–14—*Multiplying good works of every sort*; Deuteronomy 33:1, 13–16—*This is the blessing of Moses.*

Reader: The Word of the Lord.
R/. Thanks be to God.

[1997]

After a time of silence, all join in prayers of intercession and in the Lord's Prayer.

[1999]

Then the leader speaks the blessing, chosen from appropriate prayers elsewhere in this book.

—From Book of Blessings

PRAYERS OF INTERCESSION

Prayer for All Needs

We beg you, Lord,
to help and defend us.

Deliver the oppressed.
Pity the insignificant.
Raise the fallen.
Show yourself to the needy.
Heal the sick.
Bring back those of your people who have gone astray.
Feed the hungry.
Lift up the weak.
Take off the prisoners' chains.

May every nation come to know
that you alone are God,
that Jesus is your Child,
that we are your people, the sheep that you pasture.
R/. Amen.

—Clement of Rome

Evening Intercessions

In peace, let us pray to the Lord.
R/. Lord, have mercy.

For an evening that is perfect, holy, peaceful, and without sin, let us pray to the Lord. **R/.**

For an angel of peace, a faithful guide, and guardian of our souls and bodies, let us pray to the Lord. **R/.**

For the pardon and forgiveness of our sins and offenses, let us pray to the Lord. **R/.**

For the holy Church of God, that God may give it peace and unity and protect and prosper it throughout the whole world, let us pray to the Lord. **R/.**

For this nation, its government, and all who serve and protect us, let us pray to the Lord. **R/.**

For this city/town/village of N. and for every city and land and for all those living in them, let us pray to the Lord. **R/.**

For seasonable weather, bountiful harvests, and peaceful times, let us pray to the Lord. **R/.**

For the safety of travelers, the recovery of the sick, the deliverance of the oppressed, and the release of captives, let us pray to the Lord. **R/.**

For all that is good and profitable to our souls and for the peace of the world, let us pray to the Lord. **R/.**

For a peaceful and Christian end to our lives without shame or pain, and for a good defense before the awesome judgment seat of Christ, let us pray to the Lord. **R/.**

Help, save, pity, and defend us, O God, by your grace.

Pause for silent prayer and/or additional petitions.

Rejoicing in the communion of the Blessed Virgin Mary and of all the saints, let us commend ourselves and one another to the living God through Christ our Lord.
R/. To you, O Lord.

—*Ancient Byzantine Litany*

Other Intercessions
R/. Lord, have mercy.

For the peace of the world, that a spirit of respect and forbearance may grow among nations and peoples, let us pray to the Lord. **R/.**

For the holy Church of God, that it may be filled with truth and love and be found without fault at the day of your coming, let us pray to the Lord. **R/.**

For those in positions of public trust, (especially N.,) that they may serve justice and promote the dignity and freedom of all people, let us pray to the Lord. **R/.**

For a blessing upon the labors of all, and for the right use of the riches of creation, let us pray to the Lord. **R/.**

For the poor, the persecuted, the sick, and all who suffer; for refugees, prisoners, and all who are in danger, that they may be relieved and protected, let us pray to the Lord. **R/.**

For this household: for those who are present, and for those who are absent, that we may be delivered from hardness of heart and show forth your glory in all that we do, let us pray to the Lord. **R/.**

For our enemies and those who wish us harm, and for all whom we have injured or offended, let us pray to the Lord. **R/.**

For all who have died in the faith of Christ, that with all the saints, they may have rest in that place where there is no pain or grief, but life eternal, let us pray to the Lord. **R/.**

—*Ancient Byzantine Litany*

Shorter Intercessions

Let us pray to God who cares for all, and with earnest humility say:
R/. Have mercy on your people, Lord.

Guard the Church. **R/.**

Watch over N., our pope. **R/.**

Protect and bless N., our bishop. **R/.**

Save your people. **R/.**

Preserve peace among the nations. **R/.**

Bring an end to strife and hatred. **R/.**

Guide the rulers of nations. **R/.**

Guide parents in the fulfillment of their responsibilities. **R/.**

Nourish children by your loving care. **R/.**

Support and give solace to the aged. **R/.**

Be a helper to the poor. **R/.**

Comfort those who are troubled. **R/.**

Grant deliverance to captives. **R/.**

Bring exiles back to their homeland. **R/.**

Grant health to the sick. **R/.**

Be present to those who are dying. **R/.**

Admit those who have died into the company of the saints. **R/.**

PART VI
PRAYERS FOR THE CHURCH AND THE WORLD

PRAYERS FOR THE CHURCH AND THE WORLD

*A*s baptized Christians, it is our right and duty to pray for the needs of the Church and the world. As members of Christ's Body, we share in the joys and struggles of others, especially those who are poor and vulnerable. In faith and trust, the prayers in this section lay before God the hopes and concerns of a broken world awaiting redemption.

For Christian Unity

Prayer for Christian Unity

Lord Jesus Christ,
you call us together in faith and love.
Breathe again the new life of your Holy Spirit among us
that we may hear your holy Word,
pray in your name,
seek unity among Christians,
and live more fully the faith we profess.
All glory and honor be yours
with the Father, and the Holy Spirit, forever and ever.
Amen.

For the Church in Need

Prayer for the Church in Need

God of power and of mercy,
you gave courage to the martyrs who died for their faith.
In many places in the world, our brothers and sisters
    in Christ
continue to suffer for their belief in you and in your Son.
Strengthen all those who suffer religious persecution.
May we work for the day
when all your children may worship you in freedom and in joy.
Amen.

FOR A CULTURE OF LIFE

A Prayer for Life

Father and maker of all,
you adorn all creation
with splendor and beauty,
and fashion human lives
in your image and likeness.
Awaken in every heart
reverence for the work of your hands,
and renew among your people
a readiness to nurture and sustain
your precious gift of life.

Grant this through our Lord
Jesus Christ, your Son,
who lives and reigns with you in
the unity of the Holy Spirit,
God, forever and ever.
Amen.

Evangelium Vitae Prayer

O Mary,
bright dawn of the world,
Mother of the living,
to you do we entrust the *cause of life*:
look down, O Mother, upon the vast numbers
of babies not allowed to be born,
of the poor whose lives are made difficult,
of men and women who are victims of brutal violence,
of the elderly and the sick killed by indifference
or out of misguided mercy.

Grant that all who believe in your Son
may *proclaim the Gospel of life*
with honesty and love to the people of our time.

Obtain for them the grace to *accept that Gospel*
as a gift ever new,
the joy *of celebrating* it with gratitude
throughout their lives
and the courage to *bear witness to it*
resolutely, in order to build,
together with all people of good will,
the civilization of truth and love,
to the praise and glory of God, the Creator and lover of life.

—*Pope John Paul II, Jubilee of Families*

Prayer for Victims of Abortion

Lord God,
ever caring and gentle,
we commit to your love these little ones,
quickened to life for so short a time.
Enfold them in your love.

We pray for all responsible for the death of these children.
Give them the gift of true repentance,
and comfort them with a full portion of your mercy.

Heavenly Father,
transform our selfishness and sin
and make us turn to your love.
Help us to embrace the Gospel of life
to repudiate sin, selfishness, and death,
and to live only as your children.

We ask this through Christ our Lord.
Amen.

For Evangelization and Missions

Prayer to Mary, Star of Evangelization

O Blessed Virgin Mary,
we ask you, who prayed to strengthen the faith of the
    first disciples,
to obtain for the Church in the United States an outpouring
    of the Holy Spirit,
to guide us in a new evangelization.
Help us teach the faith in such a way that the members of
    the Church today
will truly be Christ's disciples of this new millennium,
drawing people throughout the world to the saving message
    and power of Christ.
We ask this through Jesus Christ, your Son and our
    Lord. Amen.
Mary, Star of Evangelization, pray for us.

Go and Make Disciples: Prayer for Evangelization

Lord God,
set our hearts ablaze with a desire to live our faith fully and
    share it freely with others.
May we be eager to share our faith and transform our
    nation and,
with missionary dedication, the whole world.

Open our hearts to see the need for the Gospel in each life,
in our nation and on our planet.
We ask Mary, the one through whom Jesus entered our world,
to guide us as we present Jesus to those who live in our land.
May her prayers help us to share in her courage
     and faithfulness.
May they lead us to imitate her discipleship,
her turning to Jesus,
her love for God and for all.
May the compassion that Mary has always reflected be
     present in our hearts.

Like the disciples walking that Easter morning to Emmaus,
may all Catholics feel the presence of Jesus burn
     in their hearts.
As those two disciples felt the presence of Jesus
     in their journey,
we ask that our evangelization will help believers feel anew
     the presence of Jesus
and that it will help others discover his gracious presence.

We pray that the fire of Jesus enkindled in us by God's
     Spirit may lead
more and more people in our land to become disciples,
formed in the image of Christ our Savior.
Amen.

Prayer for Missions

God of mercy and compassion,
you who have called us your children,
we remember our brothers and sisters around the world
who need our help, our love and, most especially,
    our prayers.
Send your loving Spirit upon us
to help us be better missionaries
so that the Good News of your Son
will spread to the ends of the earth.
We ask this through Christ our Lord.
Amen.

FOR LEADERS IN
THE CHURCH AND
COMMUNITY

Prayer for the Clergy and Laity of the Church

Let us pray
for N., our bishop;
for all bishops, priests, and deacons;
for all who have a special ministry in the Church, and for all
    God's people.

Almighty and eternal God,
your Spirit guides the Church and makes it holy.
Listen to our prayers
and help each of us

in his or her own vocation
to do your work more faithfully.
We ask this through Christ our Lord.
Amen.

Prayer for Civic Leaders

God our Father,
you guide everything in wisdom and love.
Accept the prayers we offer for our nation.
In your goodness,
watch over those in authority,
so that people everywhere may enjoy
freedom, security, and peace.
We ask this through our Lord Jesus Christ.
Amen.

BEFORE AND AFTER
AN ELECTION

Prayer Before an Election

Lord God,
as the election approaches,
we seek to better understand the issues and concerns that
    confront our city/state/country,
and how the Gospel compels us to respond as faithful
    citizens in our community.

(continued)

We ask for eyes that are free from blindness
so that we might see each other as brothers and sisters,
one and equal in dignity,
especially those who are victims of abuse and violence,
    deceit and poverty.
We ask for ears that will hear the cries of children unborn
    and those abandoned,
men and women oppressed because of race or creed,
    religion or gender.
We ask for minds and hearts that are open to hearing the
    voice of leaders who will bring us closer to
    your Kingdom.

We pray for discernment
so that we may choose leaders who hear your Word,
live your love,
and keep in the ways of your truth
as they follow in the steps of Jesus and his Apostles
and guide us to your Kingdom of justice and peace.

We ask this in the name of your Son Jesus Christ and
    through the power of the Holy Spirit. Amen.

Prayer After an Election

God of all nations,
Father of the human family,
we give you thanks for the freedom we exercise
and the many blessings of democracy we enjoy
in these United States of America.

We ask for your protection and guidance
for all who devote themselves to the common good,
working for justice and peace at home and around the world.

We lift up all our duly elected leaders and public servants,
those who will serve us as president, as legislators and judges,
those in the military and law enforcement.

Heal us from our differences and unite us, O Lord,
with a common purpose,
dedication, and commitment to achieve liberty and justice
in the years ahead for all people,
and especially those who are most vulnerable in our midst.
Amen.

FOR MIGRANTS AND REFUGEES

Called to One Table: A Prayer for Migrants and Refugees

Dear Jesus, you came into this world as a migrant	We welcome you, Jesus
There was no room for your family at the inn	We welcome you, Jesus
Along with the angels in heaven	We welcome you, Jesus
Along with the shepherds who wandered the hills	We welcome you, Jesus
Along with the Magi who traveled from the East	We welcome you, Jesus

(continued)

Your family became refugees fleeing from Herod	We welcome you, Jesus
In Egypt you were an alien	We welcome you, Jesus
In your public life you did not have a place to rest	We welcome you, Jesus
Dear Jesus, we see you today	We welcome you, Jesus
In refugees fleeing war and violence	We welcome you, Jesus
In immigrants seeking a better life	We welcome you, Jesus
In migrant workers who enrich our land with their labor	We welcome you, Jesus
In seafarers and other people on the move	We welcome you, Jesus

Let us pray. Dear Jesus, you are the refuge of people on the move. We ask you to grant immigrants, refugees, and other migrants peace, protection, and comfort. Help us to recognize that whenever we welcome the stranger in your name, we welcome you. Teach us to recognize your presence in every human being. Bring us together as one family, at the banquet table of your love, with you who live and reign with the Father, and the Holy Spirit, now and forever. R/. Amen.

Welcoming the Stranger: Prayer for Hospitality

Loving God, your Son Jesus said
your Kingdom is like a banquet:
a festive gathering for all people
of every race and color—
a table at which the lonely find company,

the hungry savor rich foods and fine wine,
and strangers enjoy warm family ties.
Jesus calls us to build this Kingdom here on earth.

Teach us, Lord, the ways of hospitality.
Give us the spirit of joyful welcome and
the sensitivity to help people on the move
to feel they belong.

Grant that our tables at home may draw our
new neighbors from other lands
into a loving community
and that the eucharistic tables in
our parishes may prefigure that banquet
in heaven where all are one with you,
Father, Son, and Holy Spirit,
one God, forever and ever.
Amen.

FOR PEACE

Prayer for Peace: To Mary, the Light of Hope

Immaculate Heart of Mary,
help us to conquer the menace of evil,
which so easily takes root in the hearts of the people of today,
and whose immeasurable effects
already weigh down upon our modern world
and seem to block the paths toward the future.

(continued)

From famine and war, deliver us.

From nuclear war, from incalculable self-destruction, from every kind of war, deliver us.

From sins against human life from its very beginning, deliver us.

From hatred and from the demeaning of the dignity of the children of God, deliver us.

From every kind of injustice in the life of society, both national and international, deliver us.

From readiness to trample on the commandments of God, deliver us.

From attempts to stifle in human hearts the very truth of God, deliver us.

From the loss of awareness of good and evil, deliver us.

From sins against the Holy Spirit, deliver us.

Accept, O Mother of Christ,
this cry laden with the sufferings of all individual
     human beings,
laden with the sufferings of whole societies.
Help us with the power of the Holy Spirit to conquer all sin:
individual sin and the "sin of the world,"
sin in all its manifestations.
Let there be revealed once more in the history of the world
the infinite saving power of the redemption:
the power of merciful love.

May it put a stop to evil.
May it transform consciences.
May your Immaculate Heart reveal for all the light of hope.
Amen.

—Pope John Paul II

PEACE CANTICLES OF ISAIAH

Isaiah 2:2–5

In days to come,
The mountain of the LORD's house
  shall be established as the highest mountain
  and raised above the hills.
All nations shall stream toward it;
  many peoples shall come and say:
"Come, let us climb the LORD's mountain,
  to the house of the God of Jacob,
That he may instruct us in his ways,
  and we may walk in his paths."
For from Zion shall go forth instruction,
  and the word of the LORD from Jerusalem.
He shall judge between the nations,
  and impose terms on many peoples.
They shall beat their swords into plowshares
  and their spears into pruning hooks;
One nation shall not raise the sword against another,
  nor shall they train for war again.
O house of Jacob, come,
  let us walk in the light of the LORD!

Isaiah 11:1–10

But a shoot shall sprout from the stump of Jesse,
  and from his roots a bud shall blossom.
The Spirit of the LORD shall rest upon him:
  a Spirit of wisdom and of understanding,

(continued)

A Spirit of counsel and of strength,
    a Spirit of knowledge and of fear of the Lord,
    and his delight shall be the fear of the Lord.
Not by appearance shall he judge,
    nor by hearsay shall he decide,
But he shall judge the poor with justice,
    and decide aright for the land's afflicted.
He shall strike the ruthless with the rod of his mouth,
    and with the breath of his lips he shall slay the wicked.
Justice shall be the band around his waist,
    and faithfulness a belt upon his hips.

Then the wolf shall be a guest of the lamb,
    and the leopard shall lie down with the kid;
The calf and the young lion shall browse together,
    with a little child to guide them.
The cow and the bear shall be neighbors,
    together their young shall rest;
    the lion shall eat hay like the ox.
The baby shall play by the cobra's den,
    and the child lay his hand on the adder's lair.
There shall be no harm or ruin on all my holy mountain;
    for the earth shall be filled with knowledge of the Lord,
    as water covers the sea.

    On that day,
The root of Jesse,
    set up as a signal for the nations,
The Gentiles shall seek out,
    for his dwelling shall be glorious.

FOR PERSONS
WITH DISABILITIES

Prayer to Be a Witness

Loving God,
you teach us that the power of the Holy Spirit
means more than any human limitation or weakness.
Through our surrender to your will,
may we bear witness to the truth
that the source of our human dignity
is not the outward condition of the body,
but our likeness to the Creator.
We ask this through Christ our Lord.
Amen.

Prayer for Openness

Living and true God,
You created all that is good and holy.
Be close to us, your servants,
who gather here today.
Be our constant help and protection.
Enable us to reach out lovingly to all your children,
to show understanding and awareness,
comfort and consolation,
justice and equality,
so that together we may participate fully in parish
    life and worship.
We ask this through Jesus Christ, your Son, our Lord,
who lives and reigns with you and the Holy Spirit,
one God, forever and ever.
Amen.

Blessing of Assistive Aids for Those with Disabilities

Creator God,
you give us all good things.
You know our needs and fulfill our desires.
You protect us when we are fragile
and give us courage for each new day.
You give us strength when we are weak
and humility when we are boastful.

Bless this new (*name of aid: e.g., cane, hearing aid, ramp,
    shower rail*)
and he/she who will use it.

May it open up a world of possibilities.
May it bring friends and family to gatherings,
so that we may share the divine love that is in our midst.

May we never take for granted any of your gifts,
especially the gift of each other.
We ask this through Christ our Lord.
Amen.

FOR SOCIAL JUSTICE

Prayer for Social Justice

Lord God,
you are the source of all good things.
You show mercy and bring justice to your afflicted people.

Help us to recognize your Son in
    the victim of disaster, famine, or conflict struggling
       to survive,
    the displaced migrant or persecuted refugee unable to
       return home,
    the newcomer to our land seeking legal help and
       material support,
    the villager in need of resources to improve
       living conditions,
    the citizen seeking a place of peace and reconciliation in
       a war-torn country,
    the person suffering from HIV/AIDS and other
       deadly diseases.

May we, to whom much has been given,
respond with generosity and compassion
to our suffering brothers and sisters worldwide.

Grant us the grace and courage
to speak out against injustice everywhere.

(continued)

Open our hearts and minds to work for an end
to the root causes of global poverty.

Help us to build lasting peace in our relationships
with our neighbors, both here and abroad.

We ask all these things through Christ our Lord,
who hears the cry of the poor and oppressed.
Amen.

FOR STEWARDSHIP

Stewardship Prayer

Lord God,
you alone are the source of every good gift,
of the vast array of our universe,
and the mystery of each human life.
We praise you and we thank you for
your tender, faithful love.

Everything we are and everything we have is your gift.
After having created us,
you have given us into the keeping of
your Son, Jesus Christ.

Fill our minds with his truth and
our hearts with his love,
that in his spirit we may be bonded together
in a community of faith,
a parish family, a caring people.

In the name and Spirit of Jesus,
we commit ourselves to be good stewards of the gifts
    entrusted to us,
to share our time, our talent, and our material gifts
as an outward sign of the treasure we hold in Jesus.
Amen.

FOR VICTIMS OF ABUSE

Prayer for Healing

God of endless love,
ever caring, ever strong,
always present, always just:
you gave your only Son
to save us by the Blood of his Cross.

Gentle Jesus, shepherd of peace,
join to your own suffering
the pain of all who have been hurt
in body, mind, and spirit
by those who betrayed the trust placed in them.

Hear our cries as we agonize
over the harm done to our brothers and sisters.
Breathe wisdom into our prayers,
soothe restless hearts with hope,
steady shaken spirits with faith:
show us the way to justice and wholeness,
enlightened by truth and enfolded in your mercy.

(continued)

Holy Spirit, comforter of hearts,
heal your people's wounds
and transform our brokenness.
Grant us courage and wisdom, humility and grace,
so that we may act with justice
and find peace in you.
We ask this through Christ our Lord.
Amen.

FOR VOCATIONS

Prayer for Discerning Vocations

Loving Mother, Our Lady of Guadalupe,
you asked Juan Diego to help build a Church that would
   serve a new people in a new land.
You left your image upon his cloak as a visible sign of your
   love for us,
so that we may come to believe in your Son Jesus,
   the Christ.
Our Lady of Guadalupe and St. Juan Diego,
help us respond to God's call to build your Son's
   Church today.
Help us recognize our personal vocation to serve God as
   married or single persons or priests, brothers, or sisters
   as our way to help extend the Reign of God here
   on earth.

Help us to pay attention to the promptings of the Holy Spirit.
May all of us have the courage of Juan Diego to say "Yes" to
    our personal call!
May we always encourage one another to follow Jesus, no
    matter where that path takes us.
Amen.

Prayer for Vocations to the Priesthood and Religious Life

O Father, raise up among Christians
    abundant and holy vocations to the priesthood,
    who keep the faith alive
    and guard the blessed memory of your Son Jesus
    through the preaching of his Word
    and the administration of the sacraments,
    with which you continually renew your faithful.

Grant us holy ministers of your altar,
    who are careful and fervent guardians of the Eucharist,
    the Sacrament of the supreme gift of Christ
    for the redemption of the world.

Call ministers of your mercy,
    who, through the Sacrament of Reconciliation,
    spread the joy of your forgiveness.

Grant, O Father, that the Church may welcome with joy
    the numerous inspirations of the Spirit of your Son
    and, docile to his teachings,
    may she care for vocations to the ministerial priesthood
    and to the consecrated life.

(continued)

Sustain the bishops, priests, and deacons,
   consecrated men and women, and all the baptized in Christ,
   so that they may faithfully fulfill their mission
   at the service of the Gospel.

This we pray through Christ our Lord. Amen.
Mary, Queen of apostles, pray for us.

—Pope Benedict XVI, World Day of Prayer for Vocations

Prayer for All Vocations

Gracious God, source of all life,
we praise you for your abundant blessings.
You sow your seed freely and generously among us.
You nourish, protect, sustain, and strengthen us on our
   faith journey.
By our Baptism you call us by name and commission us to
   sow your Word.
We join our hearts and voices in prayer that you enrich your
   Church with people who embrace the call to holiness
   and service.
Bless each of us as we respond to your call.
May we encourage and support one another in discerning
   and living out our Christian vocation.
Help us foster a culture of vocation in which your seed will
   bear much fruit.
We offer this prayer in the name of Jesus, in the power of
   the Holy Spirit, with your blessing now and forever.
Amen.

PART VII
LITANIES

LITANIES

*L*itanies are a style of prayer that goes back thousands of years. Litanies include an invocation and a phrase that is repeated after each invocation. In these litanies, we call upon God and his holy ones to stand with us, to rejoice with us, to comfort us, and to hold us in mercy.

Litany of the Holy Name of Jesus

Lord, have mercy	Lord, have mercy
Christ, have mercy	Christ, have mercy
Lord, have mercy	Lord, have mercy
God our Father in heaven	have mercy on us
God the Son, Redeemer of the world	have mercy on us
God the Holy Spirit	have mercy on us
Holy Trinity, one God	have mercy on us
Jesus, Son of the living God	have mercy on us
Jesus, splendor of the Father	have mercy on us
Jesus, brightness of everlasting light	have mercy on us
Jesus, king of glory	have mercy on us
Jesus, dawn of justice	have mercy on us
Jesus, Son of the Virgin Mary	have mercy on us
Jesus, worthy of our love	have mercy on us
Jesus, worthy of our wonder	have mercy on us
Jesus, mighty God	have mercy on us
Jesus, father of the world to come	have mercy on us
Jesus, prince of peace	have mercy on us
Jesus, all-powerful	have mercy on us
Jesus, pattern of patience	have mercy on us
Jesus, model of obedience	have mercy on us
Jesus, gentle and humble of heart	have mercy on us
Jesus, lover of chastity	have mercy on us
Jesus, lover of us all	have mercy on us
Jesus, God of peace	have mercy on us
Jesus, author of life	have mercy on us
Jesus, model of goodness	have mercy on us
Jesus, seeker of souls	have mercy on us
Jesus, our God	have mercy on us
Jesus, our refuge	have mercy on us

Jesus, father of the poor	have mercy on us
Jesus, treasure of the faithful	have mercy on us
Jesus, Good Shepherd	have mercy on us
Jesus, the true light	have mercy on us
Jesus, eternal wisdom	have mercy on us
Jesus, infinite goodness	have mercy on us
Jesus, our way and our life	have mercy on us
Jesus, joy of angels	have mercy on us
Jesus, King of patriarchs	have mercy on us
Jesus, Teacher of apostles	have mercy on us
Jesus, Master of evangelists	have mercy on us
Jesus, courage of martyrs	have mercy on us
Jesus, light of confessors	have mercy on us
Jesus, purity of virgins	have mercy on us
Jesus, crown of all saints	have mercy on us
Lord, be merciful	Jesus, save your people
From all evil	Jesus, save your people
From every sin	Jesus, save your people
From the snares of the devil	Jesus, save your people
From your anger	Jesus, save your people
From the spirit of infidelity	Jesus, save your people
From everlasting death	Jesus, save your people
From neglect of your Holy Spirit	Jesus, save your people
By the mystery of your Incarnation	Jesus, save your people
By your birth	Jesus, save your people
By your childhood	Jesus, save your people
By your hidden life	Jesus, save your people
By your public ministry	Jesus, save your people
By your agony and crucifixion	Jesus, save your people
By your abandonment	Jesus, save your people
By your grief and sorrow	Jesus, save your people
By your death and burial	Jesus, save your people

By your rising to new life	Jesus, save your people
By your return in glory to the Father	Jesus, save your people
By your gift of the Holy Eucharist	Jesus, save your people
By your joy and glory	Jesus, save your people

| Christ, hear us | Christ, hear us |
| Lord Jesus, hear our prayer | Lord Jesus, hear our prayer |

Lamb of God, you take away the sins of the world	have mercy on us
Lamb of God, you take away the sins of the world	have mercy on us
Lamb of God, you take away the sins of the world	have mercy on us

Let us pray. Lord, may we who honor the holy name of Jesus enjoy his friendship in this life and be filled with eternal joy in the Kingdom where he lives and reigns forever and ever. Amen.

Litany of the Sacred Heart of Jesus

Lord, have mercy	Lord, have mercy
Christ, have mercy	Christ, have mercy
Lord, have mercy	Lord, have mercy

God our Father in heaven	have mercy on us
God the Son, Redeemer of the world	have mercy on us
God the Holy Spirit	have mercy on us
Holy Trinity, one God	have mercy on us

Heart of Jesus, Son of the eternal Father	have mercy on us
Heart of Jesus, formed by the Holy Spirit in the womb of the Virgin Mother	have mercy on us
Heart of Jesus, one with the eternal Word	have mercy on us
Heart of Jesus, infinite in majesty	have mercy on us
Heart of Jesus, holy temple of God	have mercy on us
Heart of Jesus, tabernacle of the Most High	have mercy on us
Heart of Jesus, house of God and gate of heaven	have mercy on us
Heart of Jesus, aflame with love for us	have mercy on us
Heart of Jesus, source of justice and love	have mercy on us
Heart of Jesus, full of goodness and love	have mercy on us
Heart of Jesus, wellspring of all virtue	have mercy on us
Heart of Jesus, worthy of all praise	have mercy on us
Heart of Jesus, King and center of all hearts	have mercy on us
Heart of Jesus, treasurehouse of wisdom and knowledge	have mercy on us
Heart of Jesus, in whom there dwells the fullness of God	have mercy on us

Heart of Jesus, in whom the Father is well pleased	have mercy on us
Heart of Jesus, from whose fullness we have all received	have mercy on us
Heart of Jesus, desire of the eternal hills	have mercy on us
Heart of Jesus, patient and full of mercy	have mercy on us
Heart of Jesus, generous to all who turn to you	have mercy on us
Heart of Jesus, fountain of life and holiness	have mercy on us
Heart of Jesus, atonement for our sins	have mercy on us
Heart of Jesus, overwhelmed with insults	have mercy on us
Heart of Jesus, broken for our sins	have mercy on us
Heart of Jesus, obedient even to death	have mercy on us
Heart of Jesus, pierced by a lance	have mercy on us
Heart of Jesus, source of all consolation	have mercy on us
Heart of Jesus, our life and resurrection	have mercy on us
Heart of Jesus, our peace and reconciliation	have mercy on us
Heart of Jesus, victim of our sins	have mercy on us
Heart of Jesus, salvation of all who trust in you	have mercy on us
Heart of Jesus, hope of all who die in you	have mercy on us
Heart of Jesus, delight of all the saints	have mercy on us

Lamb of God, you take away
the sins of the world

                    have mercy on us

Lamb of God, you take away
the sins of the world

                    have mercy on us

Lamb of God, you take away
the sins of the world

                    have mercy on us

Jesus, gentle and
humble of heart.

                    Touch our hearts and
                    make them like your own.

Let us pray. Father, we rejoice in the gifts of love we have
received from the heart of Jesus your Son. Open our hearts
to share his life and continue to bless us with his love. We
ask this in the name of Jesus the Lord. Amen.

Litany of the Most Precious Blood

Lord, have mercy   Lord, have mercy
Christ, have mercy   Christ, have mercy
Lord, have mercy   Lord, have mercy

God our Father in heaven   have mercy on us
God the Son, Redeemer of the world   have mercy on us
God the Holy Spirit   have mercy on us
Holy Trinity, one God   have mercy on us

Blood of Christ, only Son of the Father   save us
Blood of Christ, Incarnate Word   save us
Blood of Christ, of the new and eternal covenant   save us
Blood of Christ, that spilled to the ground   save us
Blood of Christ, that flowed at the scourging   save us
Blood of Christ, dripping from the thorns   save us
Blood of Christ, shed on the Cross   save us
Blood of Christ, the price of our redemption   save us
Blood of Christ, our only claim to pardon   save us
Blood of Christ, our blessing cup   save us
Blood of Christ, in which we are washed   save us
Blood of Christ, torrent of mercy   save us
Blood of Christ, that overcomes evil   save us
Blood of Christ, strength of the martyrs   save us
Blood of Christ, endurance of the saints   save us
Blood of Christ, that makes the barren fruitful   save us
Blood of Christ, protection of the threatened   save us

Blood of Christ, comfort of the weary   save us
Blood of Christ, solace of the mourner   save us
Blood of Christ, hope of the repentant   save us
Blood of Christ, consolation of the dying   save us
Blood of Christ, our peace and refreshment   save us
Blood of Christ, our pledge of life   save us
Blood of Christ, by which we pass to glory   save us
Blood of Christ, most worthy of honor   save us

Lamb of God, you take away
  the sins of the world   have mercy on us
Lamb of God, you take away
  the sins of the world   have mercy on us
Lamb of God, you take away
  the sins of the world   have mercy on us

Lord, you redeemed us by
your Blood.   You have made us a Kingdom
                         to serve our God.

Let us pray. Father, by the Blood of your Son you have set us free and saved us from death. Continue your work of love within us, that by constantly celebrating the mystery of our salvation we may reach the eternal life it promises. We ask this through Christ our Lord. Amen.

Litany of the Blessed Virgin Mary (Litany of Loreto)

Lord, have mercy	Lord, have mercy
Christ, have mercy	Christ, have mercy
Lord, have mercy	Lord, have mercy
God our Father in heaven	have mercy on us
God the Son, Redeemer of the world	have mercy on us
God the Holy Spirit	have mercy on us
Holy Trinity, one God	have mercy on us
Holy Mary	pray for us
Holy Mother of God	pray for us
Most honored of virgins	pray for us
Mother of Christ	pray for us
Mother of the Church	pray for us
Mother of divine grace	pray for us
Mother most pure	pray for us
Mother of chaste love	pray for us
Mother and Virgin	pray for us
Sinless Mother	pray for us
Dearest of mothers	pray for us
Model of motherhood	pray for us
Mother of good counsel	pray for us
Mother of our Creator	pray for us
Mother of our Savior	pray for us
Virgin most wise	pray for us
Virgin rightly praised	pray for us
Virgin rightly renowned	pray for us

Virgin most powerful	pray for us
Virgin gentle in mercy	pray for us
Faithful Virgin	pray for us
Mirror of justice	pray for us
Throne of wisdom	pray for us
Cause of our joy	pray for us
Shrine of the Spirit	pray for us
Glory of Israel	pray for us
Vessel of selfless devotion	pray for us
Mystical Rose	pray for us
Tower of David	pray for us
Tower of ivory	pray for us
House of gold	pray for us
Ark of the covenant	pray for us
Gate of heaven	pray for us
Morning Star	pray for us
Health of the sick	pray for us
Refuge of sinners	pray for us
Comfort of the troubled	pray for us
Help of Christians	pray for us
Queen of angels	pray for us
Queen of patriarchs and prophets	pray for us
Queen of apostles and martyrs	pray for us
Queen of confessors and virgins	pray for us
Queen of all saints	pray for us
Queen conceived without sin	pray for us
Queen assumed into heaven	pray for us
Queen of the rosary	pray for us
Queen of families	pray for us
Queen of peace	pray for us

Lamb of God, you take away
the sins of the world   have mercy on us
Lamb of God, you take away
the sins of the world   have mercy on us
Lamb of God, you take away
the sins of the world   have mercy on us

Pray for us, holy Mother of God. That we may become worthy of the promises of Christ.

Let us pray. Eternal God, let your people enjoy constant health in mind and body. Through the intercession of the Virgin Mary free us from the sorrows of this life and lead us to happiness in the life to come. Grant this through Christ our Lord. Amen.

Litany of St. Joseph

Lord, have mercy | Lord, have mercy
Christ, have mercy | Christ, have mercy
Lord, have mercy | Lord, have mercy

God our Father in heaven | have mercy on us
God the Son, Redeemer of the world | have mercy on us
God the Holy Spirit | have mercy on us
Holy Trinity, one God | have mercy on us

Holy Mary | pray for us
St. Joseph | pray for us
Noble son of the House of David | pray for us
Light of patriarchs | pray for us
Husband of the Mother of God | pray for us
Guardian of the Virgin | pray for us
Foster father of the Son of God | pray for us
Faithful guardian of Christ | pray for us
Head of the Holy Family | pray for us
Joseph, chaste and just | pray for us
Joseph, prudent and brave | pray for us
Joseph, obedient and loyal | pray for us
Pattern of patience | pray for us
Lover of poverty | pray for us
Model of workers | pray for us
Example to parents | pray for us
Guardian of virgins | pray for us
Pillar of family life | pray for us
Comfort of the troubled | pray for us
Hope of the sick | pray for us
Patron of the dying | pray for us
Terror of evil spirits | pray for us
Protector of the Church | pray for us

Lamb of God, you take away
the sins of the world   have mercy on us
Lamb of God, you take away
the sins of the world   have mercy on us
Lamb of God, you take away
the sins of the world   have mercy on us

God made him master of
his household.   And put him in charge of
                                         all that he owned.

Let us pray. Almighty God, in your infinite wisdom and love
you chose Joseph to be the husband of Mary, the mother of
your Son. As we enjoy his protection on earth may we have
the help of his prayers in heaven. We ask this through Christ
our Lord. Amen.

Litany of the Saints

Lord, have mercy	Lord, have mercy
Christ, have mercy	Christ, have mercy
Lord, have mercy	Lord, have mercy

Holy Mary, Mother of God	pray for us
St. Michael	pray for us
Holy angels of God	pray for us
St. John the Baptist	pray for us
St. Joseph	pray for us
St. Peter and St. Paul	pray for us
St. Andrew	pray for us
St. John	pray for us
St. Mary Magdalene	pray for us
St. Stephen	pray for us
St. Ignatius of Antioch	pray for us
St. Lawrence	pray for us
St. Perpetua and St. Felicity	pray for us
St. Agnes	pray for us
St. Gregory	pray for us
St. Augustine	pray for us
St. Athanasius	pray for us
St. Basil	pray for us
St. Martin	pray for us
St. Benedict	pray for us
St. Francis and St. Dominic	pray for us
St. Francis Xavier	pray for us
St. John Vianney	pray for us
St. Catherine	pray for us
St. Teresa of Jesus	pray for us
All holy men and women	pray for us

Lord, be merciful	Lord, deliver us, we pray
From all evil	Lord, deliver us, we pray
From every sin	Lord, deliver us, we pray
From everlasting death	Lord, deliver us, we pray
By your coming as man	Lord, deliver us, we pray
By your death and rising to new life	Lord, deliver us, we pray
By your gift of the Holy Spirit	Lord, deliver us, we pray
Be merciful to us sinners	Lord, we ask you, hear our prayer
Guide and protect your holy Church	Lord, we ask you, hear our prayer
Keep the pope and all the clergy in faithful service to your Church	Lord, we ask you, hear our prayer
Bring all peoples together in trust and peace	Lord, we ask you, hear our prayer
Strengthen us in your service	Lord, we ask you, hear our prayer
Jesus, Son of the living God	Lord, we ask you, hear our prayer
Christ, hear us	Christ, hear us
Christ, graciously hear us	Christ, graciously hear us

Let us pray. God of our ancestors who set their hearts on you, of those who fell asleep in peace, and of those who won the martyrs' violent crown: we are surrounded by these witnesses as by clouds of fragrant incense. In this age we would be counted in this communion of all the saints; keep us always in their good and blessed company. In their midst we make every prayer through Christ who is our Lord forever and ever. Amen.

Litany of the Holy Eucharist

Lord, have mercy

Christ, have mercy

Lord, have mercy

Lord, have mercy

Christ, have mercy

Lord, have mercy

Jesus, the Most High

have mercy on us

Jesus, the holy One

have mercy on us

Jesus, Word of God

have mercy on us

Jesus, only Son of the Father

have mercy on us

Jesus, Son of Mary

have mercy on us

Jesus, crucified for us

have mercy on us

Jesus, risen from the dead

have mercy on us

Jesus, reigning in glory

have mercy on us

Jesus, coming in glory

have mercy on us

Jesus, our Lord

have mercy on us

Jesus, our hope

have mercy on us

Jesus, our peace

have mercy on us

Jesus, our Savior

have mercy on us

Jesus, our salvation

have mercy on us

Jesus, our resurrection

have mercy on us

Jesus, Judge of all

have mercy on us

Jesus, Lord of the Church

have mercy on us

Jesus, Lord of creation

have mercy on us

Jesus, Lover of all

have mercy on us

Jesus, life of the world

have mercy on us

Jesus, freedom for the imprisoned

have mercy on us

Jesus, joy of the sorrowing

have mercy on us

Jesus, giver of the Spirit

have mercy on us

Jesus, giver of good gifts

have mercy on us

Jesus, source of new life

have mercy on us

Jesus, Lord of life

have mercy on us

Jesus, eternal high priest

have mercy on us

Jesus, priest and victim

have mercy on us

Jesus, true Shepherd	have mercy on us
Jesus, true light	have mercy on us
Jesus, bread of heaven	have mercy on us
Jesus, bread of life	have mercy on us
Jesus, bread of thanksgiving	have mercy on us
Jesus, life-giving bread	have mercy on us
Jesus, holy manna	have mercy on us
Jesus, new covenant	have mercy on us
Jesus, food for everlasting life	have mercy on us
Jesus, food for our journey	have mercy on us
Jesus, holy banquet	have mercy on us
Jesus, true Sacrifice	have mercy on us
Jesus, perfect Sacrifice	have mercy on us
Jesus, eternal Sacrifice	have mercy on us
Jesus, divine Victim	have mercy on us
Jesus, Mediator of the new covenant	have mercy on us
Jesus, mystery of the altar	have mercy on us
Jesus, mystery of faith	have mercy on us
Jesus, medicine of immortality	have mercy on us
Jesus, pledge of eternal glory	have mercy on us

Jesus, Lamb of God,
     you take away the sins
     of the world   have mercy on us
Jesus, Bearer of our sins,
     you take away the sins
     of the world   have mercy on us
Jesus, Redeemer of the world,
     you take away the sins
     of the world   have mercy on us

Christ, hear us	Christ, hear us
Christ, graciously hear us	Christ, graciously hear us
Lord Jesus, hear our prayer	Lord Jesus, hear our prayer

PART VIII
GOD'S WORD IN
TIMES OF NEED

GOD'S WORD IN
TIMES OF NEED

*I*n the Word of God, "the Church constantly finds her nourishment and her strength" (*Catechism of the Catholic Church*, no. 104). This section contains Scripture passages that you may wish to read prayerfully in various circumstances. While this listing is far from exhaustive, it may open to you the wealth of the Scriptures through which God speaks to us.

ANGER

Exodus 32:9–14

"I see how stiff-necked this people is," continued the LORD to Moses. "Let me alone, then, that my wrath may blaze up against them to consume them. Then I will make of you a great nation."

But Moses implored the LORD, his God, saying, "Why, O LORD, should your wrath blaze up against your own people, whom you brought out of the land of Egypt with such great power and with so strong a hand? Why should the Egyptians say, 'With evil intent he brought them out, that he might kill them in the mountains and exterminate them from the face of the earth'? Let your blazing wrath die down; relent in punishing your people. Remember your servants Abraham, Isaac and Israel, and how you swore to them by your own self, saying, 'I will make your descendants as numerous as the stars in the sky; and all this land that I promised, I will give your descendants as their perpetual heritage.'" So the LORD relented in the punishment he had threatened to inflict on his people.

Psalm 22

My God, my God, why have you forsaken me,
 far from my prayer, from the words of my cry?
O my God, I cry out by day, and you answer not;
 by night, and there is no relief for me.
Yet you are enthroned in the holy place,
 O glory of Israel!

In you our father trusted;
  they trusted, and you delivered them.
To you they cried, and they escaped;
  in you they trusted, and they were not put to shame.

But I am a worm, not a man;
  the scorn of men, despised by the people.
All who see me scoff at me;
  they mock me with parted lips, they wag their heads:
"He relied on the LORD; let him deliver him,
  let him rescue him, if he loves him."
You have been my guide since I was first formed,
  my security at my mother's breast.
To you I was committed at birth,
  from my mother's womb you are my God.

Be not far from me, for I am in distress;
  be near, for I have no one to help me.

Many bullocks surround me;
  the strong bulls of Bashan encircle me.
They open their mouths against me
  like ravening and roaring lions.
I am like water poured out;
  all my bones are racked.
My heart has become like wax
  melting away within my bosom.
My throat is dried up like baked clay,
  my tongue cleaves to my jaws;
  to the dust of death you have brought me down.

Indeed, many dogs surround me,
  a pack of evildoers closes in upon me;
They have pierced my hands and my feet;
  I can count all my bones.

(continued)

They look on and gloat over me;
    they divide my garments among them,
    and for my vesture they cast lots.

But you, O LORD, be not far from me;
    O my help, hasten to aid me.
Rescue my soul from the sword,
    my loneliness from the grip of the dog.
Save me from the lion's mouth;
    from the horns of the wild bulls, my wretched life.

Jonah 2:3–10

Out of my distress I called to the LORD,
    and he answered me;
From the midst of the nether world I cried for help,
    and you heard my voice.
For you cast me into the deep, into the heart of the sea,
    and the flood enveloped me;
All your breakers and your billows
    passed over me.
Then I said, "I am banished from your sight!
    yet would I again look upon your holy temple."
The waters swirled about me, threatening my life;
    the abyss enveloped me;
    seaweed clung about my head.
Down I went to the roots of the mountains;
    the bars of the nether world
    were closing behind me forever,
But you brought my life up from the pit,
    O LORD, my God.
When my soul fainted within me,
    I remembered the LORD;

My prayer reached you
    in your holy temple.
Those who worship vain idols
    forsake their source of mercy.
But I, with resounding praise,
    will sacrifice to you;
What I have vowed I will pay:
    deliverance is from the LORD.

Matthew 16:21–23

From that time on, Jesus began to show his disciples that
he must go to Jerusalem and suffer greatly from the elders,
the chief priests, and the scribes, and be killed and on the
third day be raised. Then Peter took him aside and began
to rebuke him, "God forbid, Lord! No such thing shall ever
happen to you." He turned and said to Peter, "Get behind
me, Satan! You are an obstacle to me. You are thinking not
as God does, but as human beings do."

John 2:13–17

Since the Passover of the Jews was near, Jesus went up to
Jerusalem. He found in the temple area those who sold
oxen, sheep, and doves, as well as the money-changers
seated there. He made a whip out of cords and drove them
all out of the temple area, with the sheep and oxen, and
spilled the coins of the money-changers and overturned their
tables, and to those who sold doves he said, "Take these out
of here, and stop making my Father's house a marketplace."
His disciples recalled the words of scripture, "Zeal for your
house will consume me."

Ephesians 4:26–27

Be angry but do not sin; do not let the sun set on your anger, and do not leave room for the devil.

FORGIVENESS

See also Psalm 51 in the Penitential Psalms in Part III: Days and Seasons.

Matthew 5:23–26

Therefore, if you bring your gift to the altar, and there recall that your brother has anything against you, leave your gift there at the altar, go first and be reconciled with your brother, and then come and offer your gift. Settle with your opponent quickly while on the way to court with him. Otherwise your opponent will hand you over to the judge, and the judge will hand you over to the guard, and you will be thrown into prison. Amen, I say to you, you will not be released until you have paid the last penny.

Luke 6:37–38

Stop judging and you will not be judged. Stop condemning and you will not be condemned. Forgive and you will be forgiven. Give and gifts will be given to you; a good measure, packed together, shaken down, and overflowing, will be poured into your lap. For the measure with which you measure will in return be measured out to you.

Luke 15:11–32 (Prodigal Son)

Then he said, "A man had two sons, and the younger son said to his father, 'Father, give me the share of your estate that should come to me.' So the father divided the property between them. After a few days, the younger son collected all his belongings and set off to a distant country where he squandered his inheritance on a life of dissipation. When he had freely spent everything, a severe famine struck that country, and he found himself in dire need. So he hired himself out to one of the local citizens who sent him to his farm to tend the swine. And he longed to eat his fill of the pods on which the swine fed, but nobody gave him any. Coming to his senses he thought, 'How many of my father's hired workers have more than enough food to eat, but here am I, dying from hunger. I shall get up and go to my father and I shall say to him, "Father, I have sinned against heaven and against you. I no longer deserve to be called your son; treat me as you would treat one of your hired workers."'
So he got up and went back to his father. While he was still a long way off, his father caught sight of him, and was filled with compassion. He ran to his son, embraced him and kissed him. His son said to him, 'Father, I have sinned against heaven and against you; I no longer deserve to be called your son.' But his father ordered his servants, 'Quickly bring the finest robe and put it on him; put a ring on his finger and sandals on his feet. Take the fattened calf and slaughter it. Then let us celebrate with a feast, because this son of mine was dead, and has come to life again; he was lost, and has been found.' Then the celebration began. Now the older son had been out in the field and, on his way back, as he neared the house, he heard the sound of music and dancing. He called one of the servants and asked what this might mean. The servant said to him, 'Your brother has returned and your father has slaughtered the fattened calf

because he has him back safe and sound.' He became angry, and when he refused to enter the house, his father came out and pleaded with him. He said to his father in reply, 'Look, all these years I served you and not once did I disobey your orders; yet you never gave me even a young goat to feast on with my friends. But when your son returns who swallowed up your property with prostitutes, for him you slaughter the fattened calf.' He said to him, 'My son, you are here with me always; everything I have is yours. But now we must celebrate and rejoice, because your brother was dead and has come to life again; he was lost and has been found.'"

2 Corinthians 5:18–20

And all this is from God, who has reconciled us to himself through Christ and given us the ministry of reconciliation, namely, God was reconciling the world to himself in Christ, not counting their trespasses against them and entrusting to us the message of reconciliation. So we are ambassadors for Christ, as if God were appealing through us. We implore you on behalf of Christ, be reconciled to God.

Colossians 3:12–13

Put on then, as God's chosen ones, holy and beloved, heartfelt compassion, kindness, humility, gentleness, and patience, bearing with one another and forgiving one another, if one has a grievance against another; as the Lord has forgiven you, so must you also do.

SICKNESS, DISABILITY, OR WEARINESS

Isaiah 53:4

Yet it was our infirmities that he bore,
    our sufferings that he endured,
While we thought of him as stricken,
    as one smitten by God and afflicted.

Mark 2:1–12

When Jesus returned to Capernaum after some days,
it became known that he was at home. Many gathered
together so that there was no longer room for them, not
even around the door, and he preached the word to them.
They came bringing to him a paralytic carried by four men.
Unable to get near Jesus because of the crowd, they opened
up the roof above him. After they had broken through, they
let down the mat on which the paralytic was lying. When
Jesus saw their faith, he said to the paralytic, "Child, your
sins are forgiven." Now some of the scribes were sitting
there asking themselves, "Why does this man speak that
way? He is blaspheming. Who but God alone can forgive
sins?" Jesus immediately knew in his mind what they were
thinking to themselves, so he said, "Why are you thinking
such things in your hearts? Which is easier, to say to the
paralytic, 'Your sins are forgiven,' or to say, 'Rise, pick up
your mat and walk'? But that you may know that the Son
of Man has authority to forgive sins on earth"—he said to

the paralytic, "I say to you, rise, pick up your mat, and go home." He rose, picked up his mat at once, and went away in the sight of everyone. They were all astounded and glorified God, saying, "We have never seen anything like this."

1 Corinthians 12:12–14, 26

As a body is one though it has many parts, and all the parts of the body, though many, are one body, so also Christ. For in one Spirit we were all baptized into one body, whether Jews or Greeks, slaves or free persons, and we were all given to drink of one Spirit.

Now the body is not a single part, but many. . . . If (one) part suffers, all the parts suffer with it; if one part is honored, all the parts share its joy.

Galatians 4:13–14

You know that it was because of a physical illness that I originally preached the gospel to you, and you did not show disdain or contempt because of the trial caused you by my physical condition, but rather you received me as an angel of God, as Christ Jesus.

James 5:13–16

Is anyone among you suffering? He should pray. Is anyone in good spirits? He should sing praise. Is anyone among you sick? He should summon the presbyters of the church, and they should pray over him and anoint (him) with oil in the name of the Lord, and the prayer of faith will save the sick person, and the Lord will raise him up. If he has committed any sins, he will be forgiven.

Therefore, confess your sins to one another and pray for one another, that you may be healed. The fervent prayer of a righteous person is very powerful.

DISCERNMENT AND DECISION MAKING

1 Samuel 3:1-10

During the time young Samuel was minister to the LORD under Eli, a revelation of the LORD was uncommon and vision infrequent. One day Eli was asleep in his usual place. His eyes had lately grown so weak that he could not see. The lamp of God was not yet extinguished, and Samuel was sleeping in the temple of the LORD where the ark of God was. The LORD called to Samuel, who answered, "Here I am." He ran to Eli and said, "Here I am. You called me." "I did not call you," Eli said. "Go back to sleep." So he went back to sleep. Again the LORD called Samuel, who rose and went to Eli. "Here I am," he said. "You called me." But he answered, "I did not call you, my son. Go back to sleep." At that time Samuel was not familiar with the LORD, because the LORD had not revealed anything to him as yet. The LORD called Samuel again, for the third time. Getting up and going to Eli, he said, "Here I am. You called me." Then Eli understood that the LORD was calling the youth. So he said to Samuel, "Go to sleep, and if you are called, reply, 'Speak, LORD, for your servant is listening.'" When Samuel went to sleep in his place, the LORD came and revealed his presence, calling out as before, "Samuel, Samuel!" Samuel answered, "Speak, for your servant is listening."

Psalm 139:23–24

Probe me, O God, and know my heart;
    try me, and know my thoughts;
See if my way is crooked,
    and lead me in the way of old.

Isaiah 6:5–8

Then I said, "Woe is me, I am doomed! For I am a man of unclean lips, living among a people of unclean lips; yet my eyes have seen the King, the LORD of hosts!" Then one of the seraphim flew to me, holding an ember which he had taken with tongs from the altar.

He touched my mouth with it. "See," he said, "now that this has touched your lips, your wickedness is removed, your sin purged."

Then I heard the voice of the Lord saying, "Whom shall I send? Who will go for us?" "Here I am," I said; "send me!"

Mark 10:17–21

As he was setting out on a journey, a man ran up, knelt down before him, and asked him, "Good teacher, what must I do to inherit eternal life?" Jesus answered him, "Why do you call me good? No one is good but God alone. You know the commandments: 'You shall not kill; you shall not commit adultery; you shall not steal; you shall not bear false witness; you shall not defraud; honor your father and your mother.'" He replied and said to him, "Teacher, all of these I have observed from my youth." Jesus, looking at him, loved him and said to him, "You are lacking in one thing. Go, sell what you have, and give to [the] poor and you will have treasure in heaven; then come, follow me."

Luke 1:38

Mary said, "Behold, I am the handmaid of the Lord. May it be done to me according to your word."

Luke 10:41–42

The Lord said to her in reply, "Martha, Martha, you are anxious and worried about many things. There is need of only one thing. Mary has chosen the better part and it will not be taken from her."

John 6:67–69

Jesus then said to the Twelve, "Do you also want to leave?" Simon Peter answered him, "Master, to whom shall we go? You have the words of eternal life. We have come to believe and are convinced that you are the Holy One of God."

Hope, Doubt, and Fear

Psalm 16:1–6

Keep me, O God, for in you I take refuge;
 I say to the LORD, "My LORD are you.
 Apart from you I have no good."
How wonderfully has he made me cherish
 they holy ones who are in his land!
They multiply their sorrows
 who court other gods.
Blood libations to them I will not pour out,
 nor will I take their names upon my lips.
O LORD, my allotted portion and my cup,
 you it is who hold fast my lot.
For me the measuring lines have fallen on pleasant sites;
 fair to me indeed is my inheritance.

Psalm 23

The LORD is my shepherd; I shall not want.
 In verdant pastures he gives me repose;
Beside restful waters he leads me;
 he refreshes my soul.
He guides me in right paths
 for his name's sake.
Even though I walk in the dark valley
 I fear no evil; for you are at my side
With your rod and your staff
 that give me courage.

You spread the table before me
    in the sight of my foes;
You anoint my head with oil;
    my cup overflows.
Only goodness and kindness follow me
    all the days of my life;
And I shall dwell in the house of the LORD
    for years to come.

Psalm 27

The LORD is my light and my salvation;
    whom should I fear?
The LORD is my life's refuge;
    of whom should I be afraid?
When evildoers come at me
    to devour my flesh,
My foes and my enemies
    themselves stumble and fall.
Though an army encamp against me,
    my heart will not fear;
Though war be waged upon me,
    even then will I trust.

One thing I ask of the LORD;
    this I seek:
To dwell in the house of the LORD
    all the days of my life,
That I may gaze on the loveliness of the LORD
    and contemplate his temple.
For he will hide me in his abode
    in the day of trouble;
He will conceal me in the shelter of his tent,
    he will set me high upon a rock.

(continued)

Even now my head is held high
　　above my enemies on every side.
And I will offer in his tent
　　sacrifices with shouts of gladness;
I will sing and chant praise to the Lord.

Hear, O Lord, the sound of my call;
　　have pity on me, and answer me.
Of you my heart speaks; you my glance seeks;
　　your presence, O Lord, I seek.
Hide not your face from me;
　　do not in anger repel your servant.
You are my helper: cast me not off;
　　forsake me not, O God my savior.
Though my father and mother forsake me,
　　yet will the Lord receive me.

Show me, O Lord, your way, and lead me on a level path,
　　because of my adversaries.
Give me not up to the wishes of my foes;
　　for false witnesses have risen up against me,
　　and such as breathe out violence.
I believe that I shall see the bounty of the Lord
　　in the land of the living.
Wait for the Lord with courage;
　　be stouthearted, and wait for the Lord.

Isaiah 41:10

Fear not, I am with you;
　　be not dismayed; I am your God.
I will strengthen you, and help you,
　　and uphold you with my right hand of justice.

Isaiah 43:1b–3a

Fear not, for I have redeemed you;
  I have called you by name: you are mine.
When you pass through the water, I will be with you;
  in the rivers you shall not drown.
When you walk through fire, you shall not be burned;
  the flames shall not consume you.
For I am the LORD, your God,
  the Holy One of Israel, your savior.

Jeremiah 1:2–8

The word of the LORD first came to him in the days of Josiah,
son of Amon, king of Judah, in the thirteenth year of his
reign, and continued through the reign of Jehoiakim, son
of Josiah, king of Judah, and until the downfall and exile
of Jerusalem in the fifth month of the eleventh year of
Zedekiah, son of Josiah, king of Judah.

The word of the LORD came to me thus:

Before I formed you in the womb I knew you,
  before you were born I dedicated you,
  a prophet to the nations I appointed you.
"Ah, Lord GOD!" I said,
  "I know not how to speak; I am too young."

But the LORD answered me,

Say not, "I am too young."
  To whomever I send you, you shall go;
  whatever I command you, you shall speak.
Have no fear before them, because I am with you to
  deliver you, says the LORD.

Jeremiah 29:11

For I know well the plans I have in mind for you, says the LORD, plans for your welfare, not for woe! plans to give you a future full of hope.

Matthew 10:28–31

And do not be afraid of those who kill the body but cannot kill the soul; rather, be afraid of the one who can destroy both soul and body in Gehenna. Are not two sparrows sold for a small coin? Yet not one of them falls to the ground without your Father's knowledge. Even all the hairs of your head are counted. So do not be afraid; you are worth more than many sparrows.

Romans 5:3–5

Not only that, but we even boast of our afflictions, knowing that affliction produces endurance, and endurance, proven character, and proven character, hope, and hope does not disappoint, because the love of God has been poured out into our hearts through the holy Spirit that has been given to us.

LOSS AND GRIEF

Psalm 91

You who dwell in the shelter of the Most High,
    who abide in the shadow of the Almighty,
Say to the LORD, "My refuge and my fortress,
    my God, in whom I trust."
For he will rescue you from the snare of the fowler,
    from the destroying pestilence.
With his pinions he will cover you,
    and under his wings you shall take refuge;
his faithfulness is a buckler and a shield.
You shall not fear the terror of the night
    nor the arrow that flies by day;
Not pestilence that roams in darkness
    nor the devastating plague at noon.
Though a thousand fall at your side,
    ten thousand at your right side,
    near you it shall not come.
Rather with your eyes shall you behold
    and see the requital of the wicked,
Because you have the LORD for your refuge;
    you have made the Most High your stronghold.
No evil shall befall you,
    nor shall affliction come near your tent,
For to his angels he has given command about you,
    that they guard you in all your ways.
Upon their hands they shall bear you up
    lest you dash your foot upon a stone.
You shall tread upon the asp and the viper,
    you shall trample down the lion and the dragon.

(continued)

Because he clings to me, I will deliver him;
   I will set him on high because he acknowledges my name.
He shall call upon me, and I will answer him;
   I will be with him in distress;
I will deliver him and glorify him;
   with length of days I will gratify him
   and will show him my salvation.

Wisdom 3:1–3

But the souls of the just are in the hand of God,
   and no torment shall touch them.
They seemed, in the view of the foolish, to be dead;
   and their passing away was thought an affliction
   and their going forth from us, utter destruction.
But they are in peace.

John 11:25–26

Jesus told her, "I am the resurrection and the life; whoever believes in me, even if he dies, will live, and everyone who lives and believes in me will never die. Do you believe this?"

John 14:2–6

"In my Father's house there are many dwelling places. If there were not, would I have told you that I am going to prepare a place for you? And if I go and prepare a place for you, I will come back again and take you to myself, so that where I am you also may be. Where [I] am going you know the way." Thomas said to him, "Master, we do not know where you are going; how can we know the way?" Jesus said to him, "I am the way and the truth and the life. No one comes to the Father except through me."

Romans 6:3–5, 9–11

Or are you unaware that we who were baptized into Christ Jesus were baptized into his death? We were indeed buried with him through Baptism into death, so that, just as Christ was raised from the dead by the glory of the Father, we too might live in newness of life.

For if we have grown into union with him through a death like his, we shall also be united with him in the resurrection. . . . We know that Christ, raised from the dead, dies no more; death no longer has power over him. As to his death, he died to sin once and for all; as to his life, he lives for God. Consequently, you too must think of yourselves as (being) dead to sin and living for God in Christ Jesus.

Revelation 21:4

He will wipe every tear from their eyes, and there shall be no more death or mourning, wailing or pain, [for] the old order has passed away.

Need and Loneliness

Psalm 88:14–19

But I, O Lord, cry out to you;
　　with my morning prayer I wait upon you.
Why, O Lord, do you reject me;
　　why hide from me your face?
I am afflicted and in agony from my youth;
　　I am dazed with the burden of your dread.
Your furies have swept over me;
　　your terrors have cut me off.
They encompass me like water all the day;
　　on all sides they close in upon me.
Companion and neighbor you have taken away from me;
　　my only friend is darkness.

Psalm 139:1–5

O Lord, you have probed me and you know me;
　　you know when I sit and when I stand;
　　you understand my thoughts from afar.
My journeys and my rest you scrutinize,
　　with all my ways you are familiar.
Even before a word is on my tongue,
　　behold, O Lord, you know the whole of it.
Behind me and before, you hem me in
　　and rest your hand upon me.

Psalm 145:15–18

The eyes of all look hopefully to you,
    and you give them their food in due season;
You open your hand
    and satisfy the desire of every living thing.

The Lord is just in all his ways
    and holy in all his works.
The Lord is near to all who call upon him,
    to all who call upon him in truth.

Matthew 7:7–11

Ask and it will be given to you; seek and you will find;
knock and the door will be opened to you. For everyone
who asks, receives; and the one who seeks, finds; and to
the one who knocks, the door will be opened. Which one of
you would hand his son a stone when he asks for a loaf of
bread, or a snake when he asks for a fish? If you then, who
are wicked, know how to give good gifts to your children,
how much more will your heavenly Father give good things
to those who ask him.

Matthew 28:20

And behold, I am with you always, until the end of the age.

Luke 8:22–25

One day he got into a boat with his disciples and said to
them, "Let us cross to the other side of the lake." So they
set sail, and while they were sailing he fell asleep. A squall

blew over the lake, and they were taking in water and were in danger. They came and woke him saying, "Master, master, we are perishing!" He awakened, rebuked the wind and the waves, and they subsided and there was a calm. Then he asked them, "Where is your faith?" But they were filled with awe and amazed and said to one another, "Who then is this, who commands even the winds and the sea, and they obey him?"

John 15:14–15

You are my friends if you do what I command you. I no longer call you slaves, because a slave does not know what his master is doing. I have called you friends, because I have told you everything I have heard from my Father.

LOVE

Song of Songs 8:6–7a

Set me as a seal on your heart,
    as a seal on your arm;
For stern as death is love,
    relentless as the nether world is devotion;
    its flames are a blazing fire.
Deep waters cannot quench love,
    nor floods sweep it away.

Matthew 22:35–40

And one of them (a scholar of the law) tested him by asking, "Teacher, which commandment in the law is the greatest?" He said to him, "You shall love the Lord, your God, with all your heart, with all your soul, and with all your mind. This is the greatest and the first commandment. The second is like it: You shall love your neighbor as yourself. The whole law and the prophets depend on these two commandments."

John 15:9–12

As the Father loves me, so I also love you. Remain in my love. If you keep my commandments, you will remain in my love, just as I have kept my Father's commandments and remain in his love.

I have told you this so that my joy may be in you and your joy may be complete. This is my commandment: love one another as I love you.

1 Corinthians 12:31–13:8a

Strive eagerly for the greatest spiritual gifts.

But I shall show you a still more excellent way.

If I speak in human and angelic tongues but do not have love, I am a resounding gong or a clashing cymbal. And if I have the gift of prophecy and comprehend all mysteries and all knowledge; if I have all faith so as to move mountains but do not have love, I am nothing. If I give away everything I own, and if I hand my body over so that I may boast but do not have love, I gain nothing. Love is patient, love is kind. It is not jealous, (love) is not pompous, it is not inflated, it is not rude, it does not seek its own interests, it is not quick-tempered, it does not brood over injury, it does not rejoice over wrongdoing but rejoices with the truth. It bears all things, believes all things, hopes all things, endures all things. Love never fails. If there are prophecies, they will be brought to nothing; if tongues, they will cease; if knowledge, it will be brought to nothing.

1 John 4:7–12

Beloved, let us love one another, because love is of God; everyone who loves is begotten by God and knows God. Whoever is without love does not know God, for God is love. In this way the love of God was revealed to us: God sent his only Son into the world so that we might have life through him. In this is love: not that we have loved God, but that he loved us and sent his Son as expiation for our sins. Beloved, if God so loved us, we also must love one another. No one has ever seen God. Yet, if we love one another, God remains in us, and his love is brought to perfection in us.

PRAISE, THANKSGIVING, AND CELEBRATION

Psalm 75:2

We give you thanks, O God, we give thanks
   and we invoke your name; we declare your
   wondrous deeds.

Psalm 100

Sing joyfully to the LORD, all you lands,
    serve the LORD with gladness;
    come before him with joyful song.
Know that the LORD is God;
    he made us, his we are;
    his people, the flock he tends.
Enter his gates with thanksgiving,
    his courts with praise;
Give thanks to him; bless his name, for he is good:
    the LORD, whose kindness endures forever,
    and his faithfulness, to all generations.

Psalm 118:1, 28–29

Give thanks to the LORD, for he is good,
    for his mercy endures forever.

You are my God, and I give thanks to you;
    O my God, I extol you.
Give thanks to the LORD, for he is good;
    for his kindness endures forever.

Psalm 150

Praise the LORD in his sanctuary,
    praise him in the firmament of his strength.
Praise him for his mighty deeds,
    praise him for his sovereign majesty.
Praise him with the blast of the trumpet,
    praise him with lyre and harp,
Praise him with timbrel and dance,
    praise him with strings and pipe.

(continued)

Praise him with sounding cymbals,
    praise him with clanging cymbals.
Let everything that has breath
    praise the LORD! Alleluia.

Philippians 1:3–6

I give thanks to my God at every remembrance of you,
praying always with joy in my every prayer for all of you,
because of your partnership for the gospel from the first day
until now. I am confident of this, that the one who began a
good work in you will continue to complete it until the day
of Christ Jesus.

Colossians 3:12–16

Put on then, as God's chosen ones, holy and beloved,
heartfelt compassion, kindness, humility, gentleness, and
patience, bearing with one another and forgiving one
another, if one has a grievance against another; as the Lord
has forgiven you, so must you also do. And over all these
put on love, that is, the bond of perfection. And let the peace
of Christ control your hearts, the peace into which you were
also called in one body. And be thankful. Let the word of
Christ dwell in you richly, as in all wisdom you teach and
admonish one another, singing psalms, hymns, and spiritual
songs with gratitude in your hearts to God.

QUIET

1 Kings 19:11–13

Then the LORD said, "Go outside and stand on the mountain before the LORD; the LORD will be passing by." A strong and heavy wind was rending the mountains and crushing rocks before the LORD—but the LORD was not in the wind. After the wind there was an earthquake—but the LORD was not in the earthquake. After the earthquake there was fire—but the LORD was not in the fire. After the fire there was a tiny whispering sound. When he heard this, Elijah hid his face in his cloak and went and stood at the entrance of the cave. A voice said to him, "Elijah, why are you here?"

Psalm 46:11

Desist! and confess that I am God,
    exalted among the nations, exalted upon the earth.

Psalm 62:2–3, 6–9

Only in God is my soul at rest;
    From him comes my salvation.
He only is my rock and my salvation,
    my stronghold; I shall not be disturbed at all.

Only in God be at rest, my soul,
    For from him comes my hope.
He only is my rock and my salvation,
    my stronghold; I shall not be disturbed.

(continued)

With God is my safety and my glory,
    he is the rock of my strength; my refuge is in God.
Trust in him at all times, O my people!
    Pour out your hearts before him;
    God is our refuge!

Psalm 131

O LORD, my heart is not proud,
    nor are my eyes haughty;
I busy not myself with great things,
    nor with things too sublime for me.
Nay rather, I have stilled and quieted
    my soul like a weaned child.
Like a weaned child on its mother's lap,
    [so is my soul within me.]
    O Israel, hope in the LORD,
    both now and forever.

STUDY

1 Kings 3:11–14

So God said to him: "Because you have asked for this—not
for a long life for yourself, nor for riches, nor for the life of
your enemies, but for understanding so that you may know
what is right—I do as you requested. I give you a heart so
wise and understanding that there has never been anyone
like you up to now, and after you there will come no one to

equal you. In addition, I give you what you have not asked for, such riches and glory that among kings there is not your like. And if you follow me by keeping my statutes and commandments, as your father David did, I will give you a long life."

Psalm 1

Happy the man who follows not
    the counsel of the wicked
Nor walks in the way of sinners,
    nor sits in the company of the insolent,
But delights in the law of the LORD
    and meditates on his law day and night.
He is like a tree
    planted near running water,
That yields its fruit in due season,
    and whose leaves never fade.
    [Whatever he does, prospers.]

Sirach 6:32–37

My son, if you wish, you can be taught;
    if you apply yourself, you will be shrewd.
If you are willing to listen, you will learn;
    if you give heed, you will be wise.
Frequent the company of the elders;
    whoever is wise, stay close to him.
Be eager to hear every godly discourse;
    let no wise saying escape you.
If you see a man of prudence, seek him out;
    let your feet wear away his doorstep!

(continued)

Reflect on the precepts of the LORD,
    let his commandments be your constant meditation;
Then he will enlighten your mind,
    and the wisdom you desire he will grant.

Mark 4:1–9

On another occasion he began to teach by the sea. A very large crowd gathered around him so that he got into a boat on the sea and sat down. And the whole crowd was beside the sea on land. And he taught them at length in parables, and in the course of his instruction he said to them, "Hear this! A sower went out to sow. And as he sowed, some seed fell on the path, and the birds came and ate it up. Other seed fell on rocky ground where it had little soil. It sprang up at once because the soil was not deep. And when the sun rose, it was scorched and it withered for lack of roots. Some seed fell among thorns, and the thorns grew up and choked it and it produced no grain. And some seed fell on rich soil and produced fruit. It came up and grew and yielded thirty, sixty, and a hundredfold." He added, "Whoever has ears to hear ought to hear."

TROUBLE, CRISIS, AND CONFLICT

See also Psalm 130 in the Penitential Psalms in Part III: Days and Seasons.

Psalm 141

O LORD, to you I call; hasten to me;
  hearken to my voice when I call upon you.
Let my prayer come like incense before you;
  the lifting up of my hands, like the evening sacrifice.

O LORD, set a watch before my mouth,
  a guard at the door of my lips.
Let not my heart incline to the evil
  of engaging in deeds of wickedness
With men who are evildoers;
  and let me not partake of their dainties.
Let the just man strike me; that is kindness;
  let him reprove me; it is oil for the head,
Which my head shall not refuse,
  but I will still pray under these afflictions.
Their judges were cast down over the crag,
  and they heard how pleasant were my words.
As when a plowman breaks furrows in the field,
  so their bones are strewn by the edge of the
  nether world.

(continued)

For toward you, O GOD, my Lord, my eyes are turned;
   in you I take refuge; strip me not of life.
Keep me from the trap they have set for me,
   and from the snares of evildoers.
Let all the wicked fall, each into his own net,
   while I escape.

John 14:1

Do not let your hearts be troubled. You have faith in God;
have faith also in me.

1 Peter 1:6b–9

In this you rejoice, although now for a little while you may
have to suffer through various trials, so that the genuineness
of your faith, more precious than gold that is perishable
even though tested by fire, may prove to be for praise,
glory, and honor at the revelation of Jesus Christ. Although
you have not seen him you love him; even though you do
not see him now yet believe in him, you rejoice with an
indescribable and glorious joy, as you attain the goal of
[your] faith, the salvation of your souls.

PART IX
STATIONS OF
THE CROSS

STATIONS OF
THE CROSS

*T*he Stations of the Cross grew from
the practice of pilgrims to the Holy
Land who literally followed the last steps of
Jesus as he went to the Cross to save us from
our sins and open the gates of eternal life.
To this day, the faithful use these Stations
to reflect on the Passion of Christ and to
increase their resolve to take up their cross
and follow him.

TRADITIONAL STATIONS OF THE CROSS

Traditional Stations

Before each station:

Leader: We adore you, O Christ, and we bless you.
R/. Because by your holy Cross you have redeemed the world.

After each station:

R/. Lord Jesus, help us walk in your steps.

OPENING PRAYER
Leader:
God of power and mercy,
in love you sent your Son
that we might be cleansed of sin
and live with you forever.
Bless us as we gather to reflect
on his suffering and death
that we may learn from his example
the way we should go.

We ask this through that same Christ our Lord.
R/. Amen.

FIRST STATION: JESUS IS CONDEMNED TO DEATH

The Words of Christ
"Watch out for yourselves. They will hand you over to the courts. You will be beaten in synagogues. You will be arraigned before governors and kings because of me, as a witness before them" (Mk 13:9).

Prayer
Leader:
Lord,
give us strength to stand as a witness
and praise your name
through all struggles and condemnation.
May we rejoice as we follow you
even to death
and share in the hope of your everlasting Kingdom.
R/. Amen.

SECOND STATION: JESUS TAKES UP HIS CROSS

The Words of Christ
"Whoever wishes to come after me must deny himself, take up his cross, and follow me" (Mt 16:24).

Prayer
Leader:
Lord,
grant us humility
as we stand before your Cross,
burdened by the weight of our sins.
May we faithfully follow you
for you are the way, the truth, and the life
that leads us everlasting freedom.
R/. Amen.

THIRD STATION: JESUS FALLS THE FIRST TIME

The Words of Christ
"Father, if you are willing, take this cup away from me; still, not my will but yours be done" (Lk 22:42).

Prayer
Leader:
Lord,
open our hearts
that we might graciously accept your will for us.
May we not be discouraged or distracted
by words and actions that seek to harm us
as we travel along your way to the Kingdom.
R/. Amen.

FOURTH STATION: JESUS MEETS HIS MOTHER

The Words of Christ
"Woman, behold, your son" (Jn 19:26).

Prayer
Leader:
Lord,
like your Blessed Mother,
may we be faithful
to your command to follow you
so that at the end of time
we may join the lowly in proclaiming your glory.
R/. Amen.

FIFTH STATION: SIMON OF CYRENE HELPS JESUS

The Words of Christ

"You know that the rulers of the Gentiles lord it over them, and the great ones make their authority over them felt. But it shall not be so among you. Rather, whoever wishes to be great among you shall be your servant" (Mt 20:25–26).

Prayer

Leader:
Lord,
you are the Creator and author of all things.
You show us the strength of the weak,
the greatness of the servant.
Give us prayerful hands and supple knees
that we might bend easily to your will
and serve those whom you love.
R/. Amen.

SIXTH STATION: VERONICA WIPES THE FACE OF JESUS

The Words of Christ

"Courage, daughter! Your faith has saved you" (Mt 9:22).

"You are the light of the world. . . . Your light must shine before others, that they may see your good deeds and glorify your heavenly Father" (Mt 5:14, 16).

Prayer

Leader:
Give us faith,
that we might pursue you with loving and dedicated hearts.
Give us courage,
that we may stand before others
and reflect your presence in the world.
R/. Amen.

SEVENTH STATION: JESUS FALLS A SECOND TIME

The Words of Christ

"Blessed are you when they insult you and persecute you and utter every kind of evil against you [falsely] because of me" (Mt 5:11).

Prayer

Leader:

Lord,
grant us the strength and courage
to rise again each time we fall
and to seek your mercy in compassion.
R/. Amen.

EIGHTH STATION: JESUS SPEAKS TO THE WOMEN OF JERUSALEM

The Words of Christ

"Daughters of Jerusalem, do not weep for me; weep instead for yourselves and for your children, for indeed, the days are coming when people will say, 'Blessed are the barren, the wombs that never bore and the breasts that never nursed.' At that time people will say to the mountains, 'Fall upon us!' and to the hills, 'Cover us!' for if these things are done when the wood is green what will happen when it is dry?" (Lk 23:28–31).

Prayer

Leader:

Lord,
turn our cries of mourning
for what we have lost
to songs of joy
for we have found you
who opened the gates to God's heavenly Kingdom.
R/. Amen.

NINTH STATION: JESUS FALLS THE THIRD TIME

The Words of Christ

"When they lead you away and hand you over, do not worry beforehand about what you are to say. But say whatever will be given to you at that hour. For it will not be you who are speaking but the holy Spirit" (Mk 13:11).

Prayer
Leader:
Lord,
put your name on our lips
that we may rely on you for help
to remain steadfast in times of struggle.
R/. Amen.

TENTH STATION: JESUS IS STRIPPED OF HIS CLOTHES

The Words of Christ

"Bless those who curse you, pray for those who mistreat you. To the person who strikes you on one cheek, offer the other one as well, and from the person who takes your cloak, do not withhold even your tunic" (Lk 6:28–29).

Prayer
Leader:
Lord,
may we be clothed only in your truth
as we walk among the faithless
and may we be freed from the desires that lead us away
    from you.
R/. Amen.

ELEVENTH STATION: JESUS IS NAILED TO THE CROSS

The Words of Christ
"Father, forgive them, they know not what they
do" (Lk 23:34).

Prayer
Leader:
Lord,
for our sake
you were nailed to a Cross
and given over as a Sacrifice for our sins.
In gratitude may we boldly embrace your Cross
and live in the love that you poured out to save us.
R/. Amen.

TWELFTH STATION: JESUS DIES ON THE CROSS

The Words of Christ
"Eloi, Eloi, lema sabachthani? . . . My God, my God, why
have you forsaken me?" (Mk 15:33–34, 37).

"Amen, I say to you, today you will be with me in
Paradise" (Lk 23:43).

Prayer
Leader:
Lord,
you did not forsake us
when we disobeyed your Word,
but sent your only Son
as a sign of your love for us.
May his Sacrifice on the Cross
lead us to love others
and seek the good of your Kingdom.
R/. Amen.

THIRTEENTH STATION: JESUS IS REMOVED FROM THE CROSS

The Words of Christ

"The hour has come for the Son of Man to be glorified. Amen, amen, I say to you, unless a grain of wheat falls to the ground and dies, it remains just a grain of wheat; but if it dies, it produces much fruit" (Jn 12:23–24).

Prayer

Leader:

Lord,

may our bodies always be one with the Body of Christ
broken and shared for others
so that all might live in the new life of your Resurrection.

R/. Amen.

FOURTEENTH STATION: JESUS IS PLACED IN THE TOMB

The Words of Christ

"This is my commandment: love one another as I love you. No one has greater love than this, to lay down one's life for one's friends" (Jn 15:12–13).

Prayer

Leader:

Lord,

your love for us exceeds all bounds.
Even death cannot separate us from your love.
May we share the love that knows no end
with all who seek you.

R/. Amen.

FIFTEENTH STATION: RESURRECTION OF JESUS

The Words of Christ

"All power in heaven and on earth has been given to me. Go, therefore, and make disciples of all nations, baptizing them in the name of the Father, and of the Son, and of the Holy Spirit, teaching them to observe all that I have commanded you. And behold, I am with you always, until the end of the age" (Mt 28:18–20).

Prayer
All:

> Blessed are the poor in spirit,
> > for theirs is the kingdom of heaven.
> Blessed are they who mourn,
> > for they will be comforted.
> Blessed are the meek,
> > for they will inherit the land.
> Blessed are they who hunger and thirst for righteousness,
> > for they will be satisfied.
> Blessed are the merciful,
> > for they will be shown mercy.
> Blessed are the clean of heart,
> > for they will see God.
> Blessed are the peacemakers,
> > for they will be called children of God.
> Blessed are they who are persecuted for the
> > sake of righteousness,
> > for theirs is the kingdom of heaven. (Mt 5:3–10)

CLOSING PRAYER

Leader:

Lord Jesus Christ,

your Passion and death is the Sacrifice that unites earth
and heaven

and reconciles all people to you.

May we who have faithfully reflected on these mysteries

follow in your steps and so come to share your
glory in heaven

where you live and reign with the Father and the Holy Spirit,
one God, forever and ever.

R/. Amen.

SCRIPTURE-BASED STATIONS OF THE CROSS

The following Stations of the Cross are an alternative to the traditional Stations. They reflect more deeply on the scriptural accounts of Christ's Passion. Similar Stations were used by Pope John Paul II at various times during his pontificate. (Note that these Stations differ from the traditional Stations arranged along the interior or exterior walls of many churches.)

Scriptural Stations

Before each station:

Leader: We adore you, O Christ, and we bless you.
R/. Because by your holy Cross you have redeemed the world.

After each station:

R/. Lord Jesus, help us walk in your steps.

OPENING PRAYER

Leader:
God of power and mercy,
in love you sent your Son
that we might be cleansed of sin
and live with you forever.

Bless us as we gather to reflect
on his suffering and death
that we may learn from his example
the way we should go.
We ask this through that same Christ our Lord.
R/. Amen.

FIRST STATION: JESUS IN THE GARDEN OF GETHSEMANE

Reader:
"Then Jesus came with them to a place called Gethsemane,
and he said to his disciples, 'Sit here while I go over there and
pray.' He took along Peter and the two sons of Zebedee, and
began to feel sorrow and distress. Then he said to them,
'My soul is sorrowful even to death. Remain here and keep
watch with me.' He advanced a little and fell prostrate in
prayer, saying, 'My Father, if it is possible, let this cup
pass from me; yet, not as I will, but as you will.' When he
returned to his disciples he found them asleep. He said to
Peter, 'So you could not keep watch with me for one hour?
Watch and pray that you may not undergo the test. The
spirit is willing, but the flesh is weak'" (Mt 25:36–41).

Leader:
Lord,
grant us your strength and wisdom,
that we may seek to follow your will in all things.

SECOND STATION: JESUS, BETRAYED BY JUDAS, IS ARRESTED

Reader:

"Then, while [Jesus] was still speaking, Judas, one of the Twelve, arrived, accompanied by a crowd with swords and clubs, who had come from the chief priests, the scribes, and the elders. His betrayer had arranged a signal with them, saying, 'the man I shall kiss is the one; arrest him and lead him away securely.' He came and immediately went over to him and said, 'Rabbi.' And he kissed him. At this they laid hands on him and arrested him" (Mk 14:43–46).

Leader:

Lord,
grant us the courage of our convictions,
that our lives may faithfully reflect the Good News you bring.

THIRD STATION: JESUS IS CONDEMNED BY THE SANHEDRIN

Reader:

"When day came the council of elders of the people met, both chief priests and scribes, and they brought him before their Sanhedrin. They said, 'If you are the Messiah, tell us,' but he replied to them, 'If I tell you, you will not believe, and if I question, you will not respond. But from this time on the Son of Man will be seated at the right hand of the power of God.' They all asked, 'Are you then the Son of God?' He replied to them, 'You say that I am.' Then they said, 'What further need have we for testimony? We have heard it from his own mouth'" (Lk 22:66–71).

Leader:
Lord,
grant us your sense of righteousness,
that we may never cease to work
to bring about the justice of the Kingdom that you promised.

FOURTH STATION: JESUS IS DENIED BY PETER

Reader:
"Now Peter was sitting outside in the courtyard. One of
the maids came over to him and said, 'You too were with
Jesus the Galilean.' But he denied it in front of everyone,
saying, 'I do not know what you are talking about!' As he
went out to the gate, another girl saw him and said to those
who were there, 'This man was with Jesus the Nazorean.'
Again he denied it with an oath, 'I do not know the man!'
A little later the bystanders came over and said to Peter,
'Surely you too are one of them; even your speech gives
you away.' At that he began to curse and to swear, 'I do not
know the man.' And immediately a cock crowed. Then Peter
remembered the word that Jesus had spoken: 'Before the
cock crows you will deny me three times.' He went out and
began to weep bitterly" (Mt 26:69–75).

Leader:
Lord,
grant us the gift of honesty,
that we may not fear to speak the truth even when difficult.

FIFTH STATION: JESUS IS JUDGED BY PILATE

Reader:

"The chief priests with the elders and the scribes, that is, the whole Sanhedrin, held a council. They bound Jesus, led him away, and handed him over to Pilate. Pilate questioned him, 'Are you the king of the Jews?' He said to him in reply, 'You say so.' The chief priests accused him of many things. Again Pilate questioned him, 'Have you no answer? See how many things they accuse you of.' Jesus gave him no further answer, so that Pilate was amazed. . . . Pilate, wishing to satisfy the crowd, released Barrabas . . . [and] handed [Jesus] over to be crucified" (Mk 15:1–5, 15).

Leader:

Lord,
grant us discernment,
that we may see as you see, not as the world sees.

SIXTH STATION: JESUS IS SCOURGED AND CROWNED WITH THORNS

Reader:

"Then Pilate took Jesus and had him scourged. And the soldiers wove a crown out of thorns and placed it on his head, and clothed him in a purple cloak, and they came to him and said, 'Hail, King of the Jews!' And they struck him repeatedly" (Jn 19:1–3).

Leader:

Lord,
grant us patience in times of suffering,
that we may offer our lives as a sacrifice of praise.

SEVENTH STATION: JESUS BEARS THE CROSS

Reader:

"When the chief priests and the guards saw [Jesus] they cried out, 'Crucify him, crucify him!' Pilate said to them, 'Take him yourselves and crucify him. I find no guilt in him.' . . . They cried out, 'Take him away, take him away! Crucify him!' Pilate said to them, 'Shall I crucify your king?' The chief priests answered, 'We have no king but Caesar.' Then he handed him over to them to be crucified. So they took Jesus, and carrying the cross himself he went out to what is called the Place of the Skull, in Hebrew, *Golgotha*" (Jn 19:6, 15–17).

Leader:
Lord,
grant us strength of purpose,
that we may faithfully bear our crosses each day.

EIGHTH STATION: JESUS IS HELPED BY SIMON THE CYRENIAN TO CARRY THE CROSS

Reader:

"They pressed into service a passer-by, Simon, a Cyrenian, who was coming in from the country, the father of Alexander and Rufus, to carry his cross" (Mk 15:21).

Leader:
Lord,
grant us willing spirits,
that we may be your instruments on earth.

NINTH STATION: JESUS MEETS THE WOMEN OF JERUSALEM

Reader:
"A large crowd of people followed Jesus, including many women who mourned and lamented him. Jesus turned to them and said, 'Daughters of Jerusalem, do not weep for me; weep instead for yourselves and for your children, for indeed, the days are coming when people will say, "Blessed are the barren, the wombs that never bore and the breasts that never nursed." At that time, people will say to the mountains, "Fall upon us!" and to the hills, "Cover us!" for if these things are done when the wood is green what will happen when it is dry?'" (Lk 23:27–31).

Leader:
Lord,
grant us gentle spirits,
that we may comfort those who mourn.

TENTH STATION: JESUS IS CRUCIFIED

Reader:
"When they came to the place called the Skull, they crucified him and the criminals there, one on his right, the other on his left. [Then Jesus said, 'Father, forgive them, they know not what they do']" (Lk 23:33–34).

Leader:
Lord,
grant us merciful hearts,
that we may bring your reconciliation and forgiveness to all.

ELEVENTH STATION: JESUS PROMISES HIS KINGDOM TO THE GOOD THIEF

Reader:

"Now one of the criminals hanging there reviled Jesus, saying, 'Are you not the Messiah? Save yourself and us.' The other, however, rebuking him, said in reply, 'Have you no fear of God, for you are subject to the same condemnation? And indeed, we have been condemned justly, for the sentence we received corresponds to our crimes, but this man has done nothing criminal.' Then he said, 'Jesus, remember me when you come into your kingdom.' He replied to him, 'Amen, I say to you, today you will be with me in Paradise'" (Lk 23:39–43).

Leader:

Lord,
grant us perseverance,
that we may never stop seeking you.

TWELFTH STATION: JESUS SPEAKS TO HIS MOTHER AND THE DISCIPLE

Reader:

"Standing by the cross of Jesus were his mother and his mother's sister, Mary the wife of Clopas, and Mary of Magdala. When Jesus saw his mother and the disciple there whom he loved, he said to his mother, 'Woman, behold, your son.' Then he said to the disciple, 'Behold, your mother.' And from that hour the disciple took her into his home" (Jn 19:25–27).

Leader:

Lord,
grant us constancy,
that we may be willing to stand by those in need.

THIRTEENTH STATION: JESUS DIES ON THE CROSS

Reader:

"It was now about noon and darkness came over the whole land until three in the afternoon because of an eclipse of the sun. Then the veil of the temple was torn down the middle. Jesus cried out in a loud voice, 'Father, into your hands I commend my spirit'; and when he had said this he breathed his last" (Lk 23:44–46).

Leader:

Lord,
grant us trust in you,
that when our time on earth is ended
our spirits may come to you without delay.

FOURTEENTH STATION: JESUS IS
PLACED IN THE TOMB

Reader:

"When it was evening, there came a rich man from Arimathea named Joseph, who was himself a disciple of Jesus. He went to Pilate and asked for the body of Jesus; then Pilate ordered it to be handed over. Taking the body, Joseph wrapped it [in] clean linen and laid it in his new tomb that he had hewn in the rock. Then he rolled a huge stone across the entrance to the tomb and departed" (Mt 27:57–60).

Leader:

Lord,
grant us your compassion,
that we may always provide for those in need.

CLOSING PRAYER

Leader:
Lord Jesus Christ,
your Passion and death is the Sacrifice that unites
    earth and heaven
and reconciles all people to you.
May we who have faithfully reflected on these mysteries
follow in your steps and so come to share your
    glory in heaven
where you live and reign with the Father and
    the Holy Spirit,
one God, forever and ever.
R/. Amen.

PART X
CALENDAR OF
THE SAINTS

CALENDAR OF
THE SAINTS

Throughout the year, in addition to her celebration of the mysteries of Christ, the Church recalls the witness of the saints, holy men and women who have gone before us as examples of faithful living. They have come into the Kingdom of God, where they praise God and intercede on our behalf.

These days are assigned different designations, depending on their importance. Days of greatest significance are called solemnities. Then come feasts, memorials, and optional memorials.

While blessings for some saints and seasons are found in Part III: Days and Seasons, you may wish to celebrate the saints for whom members of your family are named, special patrons, or other saints whose holiness you wish to imitate.

CALENDAR

Days without designations are optional memorials.

January

1   Blessed Virgin Mary, Mother of God, Solemnity
2   Sts. Basil the Great and Gregory Nazianzen, bishops
        and doctors of the Church, Memorial
3   The Most Holy Name of Jesus
4   St. Elizabeth Ann Seton, religious, Memorial
5   St. John Neumann, bishop, Memorial
6   Blessed André Bessette, religious
7   St. Raymond of Peñafort, priest
13   St. Hilary, bishop and doctor of the Church
17   St. Anthony, abbot, Memorial
20   St. Fabian, pope and martyr, OR St. Sebastian, martyr
21   St. Agnes, virgin and martyr, Memorial
22   St. Vincent, deacon and martyr
24   St. Francis de Sales, bishop and doctor
        of the Church, Memorial
25   The Conversion of St. Paul, Apostle, Feast
26   Sts. Timothy and Titus, bishops, Memorial
27   St. Angela Merici, virgin
28   St. Thomas Aquinas, priest and doctor
        of the Church, Memorial
31   St. John Bosco, priest, Memorial

February

2	The Presentation of the Lord, Feast
3	St. Blase, bishop and martyr, OR St. Ansgar, bishop
5	St. Agatha, virgin and martyr, Memorial
6	St. Paul Miki, priest and martyr, and his companions, martyrs, Memorial
8	St. Jerome Emiliani, priest, OR St. Josephine Bakhita, virgin
10	St. Scholastica, virgin, Memorial
11	Our Lady of Lourdes
14	Sts. Cyril and Methodius, bishops, Memorial
17	Seven Founders of the Order of Servites, religious
21	St. Peter Damian, bishop and doctor of the Church
22	The Chair of St. Peter, Apostle, Feast
23	St. Polycarp, bishop and martyr, Memorial

March

3	St. Katharine Drexel, virgin
4	St. Casimir
7	Sts. Perpetua and Felicity, martyrs, Memorial
8	St. John of God, religious
9	St. Frances of Rome, religious
17	St. Patrick, bishop
18	St. Cyril of Jerusalem, bishop and doctor of the Church
19	St. Joseph, husband of the Blessed Virgin Mary, Solemnity
23	St. Toribio de Mogrovejo, bishop
25	The Annunciation of the Lord, Solemnity

April

2   St. Francis of Paola, hermit
4   St. Isidore [of Seville], bishop and doctor of
        the Church
5   St. Vincent Ferrer, priest
7   St. John Baptist de la Salle, priest, Memorial
11   St. Stanislaus, bishop, martyr, Memorial
13   St. Martin I, pope and martyr
21   St. Anselm, bishop and doctor of the Church
23   St. George, martyr, OR St. Adalbert, bishop and martyr
24   St. Fidelis of Sigmaringen, priest and martyr
25   St. Mark, evangelist, Feast
26   St. Peter Chanel, priest and martyr, OR
        St. Louis Mary de Montfort, priest
29   St. Catherine of Siena, virgin and
        doctor of the Church, Memorial
30   St. Pius V, pope, religious

May

1   St. Joseph the Worker
2   St. Athanasius, bishop and doctor
        of the Church, Memorial
3   Sts. Philip and James, Apostles, Feast
10   Blessed Damien Joseph de Veuster of Moloka'i, priest
12   Sts. Nereus and Achilleus, martyrs, OR
        St. Pancras, martyr
13   Our Lady of Fatima
14   St. Matthias, Apostle, Feast
15   St. Isidore [the Farmer]
18   St. John I, pope, martyr
20   St. Bernardine of Siena, priest
21   St. Christopher Magallanes, priest and martyr,
        and his companions, martyrs

22	St. Rita of Cascia, religious
25	St. Bede the Venerable, priest and doctor of the Church, OR St. Gregory VII, pope, religious, OR St. Mary Magdalene de' Pazzi, virgin
26	St. Philip Neri, priest, Memorial
27	St. Augustine of Canterbury, bishop
31	Visitation of the Blessed Virgin Mary, Feast

Saturday following the Second Sunday after Pentecost:
The Immaculate Heart of the Blessed Virgin Mary, Memorial

June

1	St. Justin, martyr, Memorial
2	Sts. Marcellinus and Peter, martyrs
3	St. Charles Lwanga and companions, martyrs, Memorial
5	St. Boniface, bishop and martyr, Memorial
6	St. Norbert, bishop
9	St. Ephrem, deacon and doctor of the Church
11	St. Barnabas, Apostle, Memorial
13	St. Anthony of Padua, priest and doctor of the Church, Memorial
19	St. Romuald, abbot
21	St. Aloysius Gonzaga, religious, Memorial
22	St. Paulinus of Nola, bishop, OR St. John Fisher, bishop and martyr, and St. Thomas More, martyr
24	The Nativity of St. John the Baptist, Solemnity
27	St. Cyril of Alexandria, bishop and doctor of the Church
28	St. Irenaeus, bishop and martyr, Memorial
29	Sts. Peter and Paul, Apostles, Solemnity
30	The First Holy Martyrs of the Holy Roman Church

July

1	Blessed Junipero Serra, priest
3	St. Thomas, Apostle, Feast
4	St. Elizabeth of Portugal
5	St. Anthony Mary Zaccaria, priest
6	St. Maria Goretti, virgin and martyr
9	St. Augustine Zhao Rong, priest and martyr, and his companions, martyrs
11	St. Benedict, abbot, Memorial
13	St. Henry
14	Blessed Kateri Tekakwitha, virgin
15	St. Bonaventure, bishop and doctor of the Church, Memorial
16	Our Lady of Mount Carmel
18	St. Camillus de Lellis, priest
20	St. Apollinaris, bishop and martyr
21	St. Lawrence of Brindisi, priest and doctor of the Church
22	St. Mary Magdalene, Memorial
23	St. Bridget of Sweden, religious
24	St. Sharbel Makhluf, priest
25	St. James, Apostle, Feast
26	Sts. Joachim and Anne, parents of the Blessed Virgin Mary, Memorial
29	St. Martha, Memorial
30	St. Peter Chrysologus, bishop and doctor of the Church
31	St. Ignatius of Loyola, priest, Memorial

August

1   St. Alphonsus Liguori, bishop and doctor
       of the Church, Memorial

2   St. Eusebius of Vercelli, bishop, OR
       St. Peter Julian Eymard, priest

4   St. John Mary Vianney, priest, Memorial

5   Dedication of the Basilica of St. Mary Major in Rome

6   The Transfiguration of the Lord, Feast

7   St. Sixtus II, pope and martyr, and his companions,
       martyrs, OR St. Cajetan, priest

8   St. Dominic, priest, Memorial

9   St. Teresa Benedicta of the Cross, virgin and martyr

10   St. Lawrence, deacon and martyr, Feast

11   St. Clare, virgin, Memorial

13   St. Pontian, pope and martyr, and St. Hippolytus,
       priest and martyr

14   St. Maximilian Mary Kolbe, priest and
       martyr, Memorial

15   The Assumption of the
       Blessed Virgin Mary, Solemnity

16   St. Stephen of Hungary

18   St. Jane Frances de Chantal, religious

19   St. John Eudes, priest

20   St. Bernard, abbot and doctor
       of the Church, Memorial

21   St. Pius X, pope, Memorial

22   The Queenship of the Blessed Virgin Mary, Memorial

23   St. Rose of Lima, virgin

24   St. Bartholomew, Apostle, Feast

25   St. Louis of France, OR St. Joseph Calasanz, priest

27   St. Monica, Memorial

28   St. Augustine, bishop and doctor
       of the Church, Memorial

29   The Martyrdom of St. John the Baptist, Memorial

September

October

1	St. Thérèse of the Child Jesus, virgin and doctor of the Church, Memorial
2	The Guardian Angels, Memorial
4	St. Francis of Assisi, religious, Memorial
6	St. Bruno, priest, OR Blessed Marie-Rose Durocher, virgin
7	Our Lady of the Rosary, Memorial
9	St. Denis, bishop and martyr, and his companions, martyrs, OR St. John Leonardi, priest
14	St. Callistus I, pope and martyr
15	St. Teresa of Jesus, virgin and doctor of the Church, Memorial
16	St. Hedwig, religious, OR St. Margaret Mary Alacoque, virgin
17	St. Ignatius of Antioch, bishop and martyr, Memorial
18	St. Luke, evangelist, Feast
19	Sts. John de Brébeuf and Isaac Jogues, priests and martyrs, and their companions, martyrs, Memorial
20	St. Paul of the Cross, priest
23	St. John of Capistrano, priest
24	St. Anthony Mary Claret, bishop
28	Sts. Simon and Jude, Apostles, Feast

November

1	All Saints, Solemnity
2	The Commemoration of All the Faithful Departed (All Souls)
3	St. Martin de Porres, religious
4	St. Charles Borromeo, bishop, Memorial
9	The Dedication of the Lateran Basilica in Rome, Feast
10	St. Leo the Great, pope and doctor of the Church, Memorial
11	St. Martin of Tours, bishop, Memorial
12	St. Josaphat, bishop and martyr, Memorial
13	St. Frances Xavier Cabrini, virgin, Memorial
15	St. Albert the Great, bishop and doctor of the Church
16	St. Margaret of Scotland OR St. Gertrude, virgin
17	St. Elizabeth of Hungary, religious, Memorial
18	Dedication of the Basilica of Sts. Peter and Paul, Apostles, OR St. Rose Philippine Duchesne, virgin
21	The Presentation of the Virgin Mary, Memorial
22	St. Cecilia, virgin and martyr, Memorial
23	St. Clement I, pope and martyr, OR St. Columban, abbot, OR Blessed Miguel Agustín Pro, priest and martyr
24	St. Andrew Dung-Lac, priest and martyr, and his companions, martyrs, Memorial
25	St. Catherine of Alexandria, virgin and martyr
30	St. Andrew, Apostle, Feast

December

3	St. Francis Xavier, priest, Memorial
4	St. John of Damascus, priest, religious, doctor of the Church
6	St. Nicholas, bishop
7	St. Ambrose, bishop and doctor of the Church, Memorial
8	The Immaculate Conception of the Blessed Virgin Mary, Solemnity
9	St. Juan Diego, hermit
11	St. Damasus I, pope
12	Our Lady of Guadalupe, Feast
13	St. Lucy, virgin and martyr, Memorial
14	St. John of the Cross, priest and doctor of the Church, Memorial
21	St. Peter Canisius, priest and doctor of the Church
23	St. John of Kanty, priest
25	The Nativity of the Lord, Solemnity
26	St. Stephen, first martyr, Feast
27	St. John, Apostle and evangelist, Feast
28	The Holy Innocents, martyrs, Feast
29	St. Thomas Becket, bishop and martyr
31	St. Sylvester I, pope

Acknowledgments

Scripture texts used in this work are taken from the *New American Bible*, copyright © 1991, 1986, and 1970 by the Confraternity of Christian Doctrine, Washington, DC 20017, and are used by permission of the copyright owner. All rights reserved.

Excerpts from the English translation of *Lectionary for Mass* © 1969, 1981, 1997, International Committee on English in the Liturgy, Inc. (ICEL); excerpts from the English translation of *Rite of Baptism for Children* © 1969, ICEL; excerpts from the English translation of *Rite of Holy Week* © 1972, ICEL; excerpts from the English translation of *The Liturgy of the Hours* © 1973, 1974, 1975, ICEL; excerpts from the English translation of *The Roman Missal* © 1973, ICEL; excerpts from the English translation of *Holy Communion and Worship of the Eucharist Outside Mass* © 1974, ICEL; excerpts from the English translation of *Rite of Penance* © 1974, ICEL; excerpts from the English translation of *The Roman Calendar* © 1975, ICEL; excerpts from the English translation of *A Book of Prayers* © 1982, ICEL; the English translation of "General Norms for the Liturgical Year and Calendar" from *Documents on the Liturgy, 1963–1979: Conciliar, Papal, and Curial Texts* © 1982, ICEL; excerpts from the English translation of *Pastoral Care of the Sick: Rites of Anointing and Viaticum* © 1982, ICEL; excerpts from the English translation of *Order of Christian Funerals* © 1985, ICEL; excerpts from the English translation of *Opening Prayers for Experimental Use at Mass* © 1986, ICEL; excerpts from the English translation of *Book of Blessings* © 1988, ICEL. All rights reserved.

Excerpts from the *Manual of Indulgences* © 2006 Libreria Editrice Vaticana (LEV), Vatican City; excerpts adapted from *Pastores Dabo Vobis* © 1992 LEV; Prayer of Pope John Paul II at the Western Wall of the Temple in Jerusalem © 2000 LEV; adaptation of a speech by Pope Benedict XVI at Auschwitz © 2006 LEV; *Evangelium Vitae* Prayer by the Pontifical Council for the Family © 2000 LEV; Prayer for Peace: To Mary, the Light of Hope © 1996 LEV; excerpt from *Resources for the Week of Prayer for Christian Unity* by the Pontifical Council for Promoting Christian Unity © 2006 LEV; Pope Benedict XVI, Prayer for the World Day of Vocations © 2006 LEV. Used with permission.

Excerpts from *Blessings and Prayers for Home and Family*, © Concacan Inc., 2004. Used and adapted by permission of the Canadian Conference of Catholic Bishops.

English translations of *Te Deum, Magnificat, Nunc Dimittis, Benedictus*, Doxology, and *Sanctus* by the International Consultation on English texts.

"*Phos Hilaron*": Ancient Greek Hymn for Evening, Evening Intercessions, and Other Intercessions by Dr. William Storey. Used with permission.

"Prayers in Times of Family Strife" and "Prayer in Time of Neighborhood or Racial Strife" from *Lutheran Book of Occasional Service*, Augsburg Fortress Press. Used with permission.

Prayer "After an Election" by Cardinal Adam Maida, Archbishop of Detroit. Used with permission.

Prayers for "Labor Day" and for "Strength" from *The Book of Common Prayer* (1979) of the Episcopal Church, USA.

Psalms in the *Liturgy of the Hours* Copyright © 1963, The Grail, England. GIA Publications, Inc., exclusive North American agent, 7404 S. Mason Ave., Chicago, IL 60638, *www.giamusic.com*, (800) 442–1358 All rights reserved. Used with permission.

Prayer for "Missions" from *Lenten Prayer Service*, 2007, Holy Childhood Association. Used with permission.

"Prayer for Discerning Vocations" from the National Coalition for Church Vocations. © NRVC. Used with permission. *www.nccv-vocations.org*.

"Prayer for All Vocations" from the National Coalition for Church Vocations. © NCCV. Used with permission. *www.nccv-vocations.org*.

"Canticle of St. Francis (Canticle of the Sun)" from *Francis of Assisi: The Early Documents*, edited by Armstrong, Short, and Hellman. Used with permission of New City Press.

Adoro Te Devote and "Novena in Honor of St. Jude Thaddeus" from *Manual of Prayers*, Third Edition, by Pontifical North American College. Used with permission.

"The Chaplet of the Divine Mercy" from *Diary of St. Maria Faustina Kowalska: Divine Mercy in My Soul*, © 1987 Congregation of Marians of the Immaculate Conception, Stockbridge, MA 01263, *www.marian.org*. Used with permission.

"Blessing of the Father" by Steven Redmond. Used with permission.

"Stewardship Prayer" from *Building Up the Kingdom Today: A Guide to Parish Stewardship*, Diocese of Charleston, *www.catholic-doc.org*. Used with permission.

SCRIPTURAL INDEX

The numbers following each citation refer to the page numbers in the text. An asterisk (*) indicates that the passage is only referenced, not quoted.

OLD TESTAMENT

Genesis

1	326*
1:1	143, 155
1:11–12	143
1:14–19	85
1:20–25	155
1:29–31a	143
9:1–7	147*
12:1–9	285*
12:2	xiii*

Exodus

32:9–14	410
34:6	58

Deuteronomy

6:4–7	253
6:4–9	289
16:1–8	126*
30:15–20	94*
33:1	354*
33:13–16	354*

1 Samuel

3:1–10	150*, 419

1 Kings

3:11–14	438
19:11–13	437

Tobit

4:7	59
8:5–7	251

Judith

9:11	59

Job

7:3–7	339
7:11	339
19:23–27	267*
28:1–28	325*
38	326*
39	326*

Psalms

1	439
6	98
8	326*
16	150*, 252
16:1–6	422
22	117*, 410
23	204*, 267*, 294, 422
23:4	266
25	267*
25:1	266
27	423
27:7–9	345
27:13–14	345
31:5a	266

Index of First Lines and Common Titles

The International Bestseller!
Over Eight Million Copies in Print Worldwide

Four centuries in the making, this is the complete summary of what Catholics throughout the world believe in common. This book, what Blessed John Paul II called "a special gift," is a positive, coherent, and contemporary map for our spiritual journey toward transformation.

CATECHISM OF THE CATHOLIC CHURCH
pages: 864 | ISBN: 978-0-385-47967-7 | $8.99 US/$9.99 CAN

Also available in hardcover and Spanish editions:

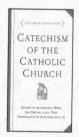

**CATECHISM OF THE
CATHOLIC CHURCH**

Pages: 848

ISBN: 978-0-385-50819-3
$14.95 US/$22.95 CAN

**CATECISMO DE
LA IGLESIA CATOLICA**

Pages: 880

ISBN: 978-0-385-47984-4
$8.99 US/$12.99 CAN